Witchland

Witchland

A Tale of Witch Hunting and War in Seventeenth-Century Britain

MARION GIBSON

SIMON & SCHUSTER

London · New York · Amsterdam/Antwerp · Sydney/Melbourne · Toronto · New Delhi

First published in Great Britain by Simon & Schuster UK Ltd, 2026

1 3 5 7 9 10 8 6 4 2

Simon & Schuster UK Ltd, 7th Floor
199 Bishopsgate, London EC2M 3TY

www.simonandschuster.co.uk
www.simonandschuster.com.au
www.simonandschuster.co.in

Simon & Schuster Australia, Sydney
Simon & Schuster India, New Delhi

The authorised representative in the EEA is Simon & Schuster Netherlands BV, Herculesplein 96, 3584 AA Utrecht, Netherlands. info@simonandschuster.nl

A CIP catalogue record for this book
is available from the British Library

Hardback ISBN: 978-1-3985-4514-4
eBook ISBN: 978-1-3985-4516-8

Typeset in Sabon by M Rules
Printed and Bound in the UK using 100% Renewable Electricity
at CPI Group (UK) Ltd

Contents

PART 4
FEAR AND FRENZY: EAST ANGLIA AND THE ENGLISH MIDLANDS

PART 5
FIGHTING BACK: CORNWALL AND TYNESIDE

Beloved, what makes all this opposition and strange censorious dealings that are between the people of God?

PAUL HOBSON, *A Treatise Containing Three Things*, 1653

PART 1

Welcome to the Witch Hunt

INTRODUCTION

The Rediscovery of Witches

Meggs was a stupid witch. So says the witchfinder Matthew Hopkins, in his 1647 book *The Discovery of Witches*. Meggs, Hopkins tells us, was a Norfolk baker who deliberately sought out the witchfinder because he *wanted* to be stripped and searched for demonic marks: moles or growths that would supposedly prove he was guilty of witchcraft. Meggs, confident in his own knowledge that he wasn't a witch and that therefore nothing would be found, voluntarily presented himself for screening. Surprisingly, Hopkins informs us that such zeal wasn't uncommon. In his experience, several people like Meggs had

> come ten or twelve miles to be searched of their own accord, and hanged for their labour, (as one Meggs a Baker did, who lived within seven miles of Norwich, and was hanged at Norwich Assizes for witchcraft).

Meggs's tragic story merits just a single sentence in Hopkins's book: a few words stuffed in between two brackets, the baker's fate tacked on as a casual afterthought. There is even an air of amusement in Hopkins's report that the reward for all Meggs's 'labour', his trouble and anxiety in presenting himself for searching, was execution. The witchfinder presents Meggs as an idiot and a criminal, justly caught and killed as a result of his own folly. This single sentence tells us lots about Hopkins – it sizzles with cruelty, arrogance, vanity and the love of power – but almost nothing about Meggs.

Stories like this one are why I wrote this book. Why should Meggs be forgotten, or remembered at best as the butt of a joke, while Hopkins is a name many readers will know? Even if you don't know his name, maybe you've heard of the title he gave himself: Witchfinder General. Look up Hopkins online and you'll find plenty about him and other witchfinders, but much less about the people they killed. However, there are places where more information about these individuals lurks, details that can give them back their rounded human identity, some respect and dignity. In Norfolk Record Office, Norwich, there are several documents telling us more about Meggs. The first is a tiny piece of paper, just a few inches long. It's an indictment, the formal charge brought against a witchcraft suspect in court. This indictment refers to 'Henr. Maggs', adding a forename and changing the spelling of his surname from the one in Hopkins's book. 'Henr' is a contraction of 'Henricus', the Latinised version of Henry. Henry Maggs's indictment further tells us that he was 'de Hempnall', of or from Hempnall, a village about nine miles south of Norwich, and it states that he was a baker – confirming that this man is indeed the person belittled by Hopkins.

On 10 August 1645, the indictment asserts, Henry Maggs used 'witchcraft & sorcery' to attack a sow belonging to William Dunnett, also from Hempnall, causing the animal to die ten days later. No other charges are recorded against Henry, but when he was found guilty of this offence, the court clerk wrote 'cul' (*culpabilis*, or guilty) on the indictment. Following this, Henry would have been sentenced for his crime, which, if it was a first offence, should have earned him a year's imprisonment under the 1604 Witchcraft Act – not execution. But it's likely that, in addition to this indictment, other charges were made against Henry. These may have included the keeping and feeding of demonic spirits. That was a specific offence under the 1604 Witchcraft Act and a common charge made by the witchfinders of the 1640s, related to the claim that suspects had marks or teats on their bodies made by demons so the creatures could suck their host witch's blood. If Henry was indeed searched for such bodily marks – as Matthew Hopkins says – and convicted on a now lost charge of interacting with demonic spirits, or if he had previously been convicted of witchcraft at a trial whose records are now missing, his punishment would have been death. Since Hopkins says Henry was searched and demonic marks were found, the witchfinder's report that he was hanged at the end of the 1645 Assizes – the court trial for serious crimes like witchcraft – is sadly all too likely. On the back of Henry's indictment are written the names of two witnesses against him, the men whose accusations brought him to his fate: Robert Chettleborough and Robert Whittred. These same two men also accused a poor woman from Hempnall, Alice Cooke, whose indictment survives as well.

So, what else can we find out about Henry Maggs and his neighbours in Hempnall? Some of the village's parish records from the 1600s still survive, and there we find Henry, his wife Anne and two children: Henry junior, born in 1614 and baptised on 10 May, and Sarah, born in 1616 and baptised on 15 October. Tragically, little Henry died in 1615, and his mother Anne in 1640 – she was buried on 12 May of that year. After that, Henry senior was a widower, who apparently did not remarry. But we know he had a family, some of whom probably remained to mourn him after his execution. In 1632, he was wealthy enough to pay three shillings and eightpence in parish taxes, money that went to needy neighbours like Alice Cooke. In 1635, Henry was actually a churchwarden, suggesting he was loved, respected and had a place in his community. However, his younger neighbours – Robert and Susanna Whittred, Robert and Margaret Chettleborough and William and Margaret Dunnett, all of whom had children born in the 1630s – came to dislike him. The Dunnetts were bakers like Henry, so perhaps it was a professional rivalry that prompted William Dunnett to accuse Henry of killing his sow. Robert Chettleborough, whose family leased many acres of land in Hempnall, was a churchwarden alongside Henry in 1635, as well as sometimes managing property transactions for Hempnall manor along with his co-accuser Robert Whittred. Did they fall out with Henry Maggs over religion, land or some more personal disagreement? Much of his story will remain unknown to us, but now Henry Maggs is no longer alone in history, reduced to the punchline of a vile joke.

The records of Henry's life help us see him as a real human being: a husband and father, a churchgoer who stood by the font in May 1614 and October 1616 as his children were christened. We can imagine him, proud and nervous in his best clothes, awkwardly holding his babies as the vicar Thomas Porter named them. Then we can see him as a sadder, older man who buried his wife some thirty years after their wedding. In 1635, Henry was perceived as a respectable church official, showing worshippers to their seats, passing round the collection plate at the end of religious services, counting the pennies donated by the congregation and doling them out to his neighbours in need. Henry signed the church's accounts in that year, confirming that its finances were transparent, by making a mark under his name, which shows us that he could not write. Although he was illiterate, he was clearly seen as a capable, honest, decent neighbour, serving God at the heart of his community. In their eyes at this time, he was the opposite of a witch. Yet, just ten years later, that's exactly what some people thought he was. This shows how the witch hunt of the 1640s, the one involving Matthew Hopkins and his witch-finding friends, turned everything upside down: even previously secure citizens, people just like you or me, might be accused of Satanic crimes.

You can visit the place where Henry lived and worked as a churchwarden, to get a sense of how safe he must have felt in his world. St Margaret's church looks much the same as it would have when Henry last left it in the summer of 1645. It stands at the centre of Hempnall, overlooking whitewashed, brown-tiled Tudor cottages. Henry's home was just over the churchyard wall to the north, a cottage in the area called 'the Cookshop'. A view of the church's square tower would have filled his windows: it dominates the village, its crenellated walls speckled with flint, gothic windows sparkling in the sun. The graveyard between Henry's house and his church is embanked above the lane leading towards Norwich, the road Henry took to his trial. His son, little Henry, and wife, Anne Maggs, are buried there under the neat green grass and ivied trees – Henry himself would have been buried in Norwich in unconsecrated ground, near the site of his execution. The church's interior is plain – white stone columns, clear glass windows, dusty red tiles. A Jacobean Communion table lurks under a lace cloth beside the altar. Communion tables replaced older church furnishings in many of the more radical parish churches of the sixteenth and seventeenth centuries. Religious reformers of the time, people who wanted Protestantism to be even more fundamentalist than when their new church broke away from Catholicism in the 1530s, thought an ordinary table was a simpler, purer location for Communion than a stone altar. Such older church features felt too traditional to them: Catholic, and maybe even a bit pagan. Hempnall's plain Communion table, and the simplicity of the church's open, bright interior, suggest that although by the 1640s the village's vicar was the traditionalist William Barwick, Henry Maggs likely lived among a puritanical congregation made up mainly of reformers. Perhaps it was these people who accused him of witchcraft and set him on his bitter, futile quest to prove he was not an agent of the devil but just an ordinary elderly man.

Back outside in the sunshine, there's one last echo of Henry as we leave Hempnall. Just south of the church, under a bridge on the main road called The Street, runs a brook that once served as a mill leat. Henry would have baked with flour from that mill.[1] Now that we know a bit more about him, we can almost see him: hauling sacks of grain in the summer sun and winter frost, kneading loaves and crimping pie tops, dusting the flour from his hands. He's not the stupid witch 'Meggs', but Henry Maggs, churchwarden, father, husband and baker, someone we can recognise as a person like us.

This book tells the story of 'witches' like Henry Maggs and the people who surrounded them: their families, neighbours, fellow suspects and also their friends, the people who tried to defend them. Over a decade and across much of Britain, we will trace the spread of the witch-hunting panic that claimed Henry Maggs's life along with many others.

We begin in the early 1640s, in a country on the brink of civil war. The witch-hunting inferno started in Essex in 1645 and moved north across East Anglia, into the Midlands and north, but it came from sparks lit across middle England and in Scotland too. The witchfinders that drove this hunt were motivated by ideas about witchcraft that originated in previous decades, however – an era that began with the passing of the Witchcraft Acts in 1563.

In these, witches were defined as people who collaborated with the devil, often causing harm to their neighbours and working evil magic. Initially, only their most harmful activities were punishable by imprisonment or death, but in 1604 another Witchcraft Act imposed the death penalty for most types of witchcraft activity – including performing love spells, finding lost items by divination and any kind of contact with supposed spirits, good or bad – meaning that the people caught up in the witch hunt of the 1640s during the British civil wars were very likely to be executed if they were found guilty. Even apparently benign magic – any indication that the accused had recited charms, met a magical animal, heard spirit voices or promised magical healing – would likely lead to condemnation.

In England, convicted witches were hanged, while in Scotland they were strangled and their bodies burned at the stake. Between 1640 and 1650, many hundreds of people were executed as witches in Britain. But the witch hunt also had repercussions even further afield, some 3,000 miles away in America, where colonists soon began their own large-scale witch trials. Indeed, without the frenetic British witch hunt of the 1640s to show the way, the infamous Salem witch trials of 1692 may never have taken place.

Yet, until recently, with the digitisation and cataloguing of many previously unknown historical records, we knew little about most of the hunt's victims. This book tries to redress the triple historical injustice of the witch hunt, in which suspects were, firstly, convicted of an impossible crime; secondly, then forgotten by their communities; and thirdly, have subsequently been overlooked by history. There are many valuable histories – local, national and international – that tell the story of those who persecuted them: the professional witchfinders, the judges and magistrates, the godly gentlemen and churchmen who pursued Satan's agents on their estates and in their parishes. These people were important drivers of events, of course, but it is time to hear more about the accused people and their lives, especially who they were before someone labelled them 'witch'. What is left of their world and the lives they led within it? Can we grant them some empathy, a moment of our attention and respect, as we learn what we can of their circumstances and how they dealt with them? Such a rediscovery of their history is timely, because in our own world we can see only too clearly the resurgence of political and religious hatreds, misogyny, nationalistic prejudice and persecution. Valuing historical victims of injustice is part of understanding the rise of such trends, and – hopefully – of resisting them.

It's important to explore localised histories for their own sake, too: giving the witch trial's stories back to the places that made them, community by community, revealing the challenges that faced each town or village and its people, well before the witch-obsessed disruptors showed up to make everything worse. Local history is the foundation of national and global history. When we can recover a story from the past that's linked to places we know, it's likely we'll feel that history personally. Perhaps it's possible to own that history in a unique way, facing and acting on its lessons because it's very obviously ours. Many of us will even be the descendants of accused witches and witch hunters, in our home communities and from elsewhere, whether we know it or not. A compassionate exploration of our shared witch histories should make us think about what happened to those people and why – and whether the same things or something like them could, under the right circumstances, happen to us or people we know today. This book is a journey through some of the places where the British witch hunt of the 1640s happened, following the accused people singly or in groups to learn everything we can about them and their communities, the accusers and questioners, the defenders and mourners. Welcome, then, to Witchland.

CHAPTER 1

The Troubles of Seventeenth-Century Britain: Religion, War, Witchcraft

Although we can see many connections between our own lives and those of Henry Maggs and his fellow villagers, seventeenth-century Britain was very different from today. Look around you now and strip away the trappings of the present. No electricity, no phones, no bright screens flashing information, no cackling TV in the corner of the room. Quiet, isn't it? No planes, trains, cars; no distant noise of rush hour. No plastic, no fridge, no supermarket. No water you'd consider clean, no antibiotics, no anaesthetics. Keep going until you stand in a world that's hard, but not impossible, to imagine. Deep black nights, candlelit. Evenings filled with gossip, mending clothes and tools. Waking in the dark to a day of physical labour. Want some cheese? Make it. Want some candles, socks, a snare, a salve? Make them too. Organic food, skies full of birds, farmland webbed with hedgerows. Hunger, plague, influenza: waves of death that scoured the villages every few years, tearing away a third of your neighbours, the children next door, the love of your life. Compulsory worship with frightening dogma, which could lead you equally plausibly to heaven or hell. Tight, familial church communities, huddled in isolated villages and small towns; people held in place; a striking lack of privacy and liberty. Sin, suspicion, fear.

Poorer folk and women were especially firmly regulated by religion in this seventeenth-century world – people like Alice Cooke of Hempnall. That will matter in the story of the witch hunt. Without religion and its laws, there would have been no such thing as a 'witch', and these two social groups – the poor and the female – were disproportionately targeted by accusations of witchcraft. Yet the word 'witch' described an unreality: a person in league with the devil, using magic and evil spirits to hurt their neighbours, turning away from God to worship Satan. The creation of that unreal enemy depended on a complex belief structure regulating church congregations, especially their least conforming and most vulnerable members. The self-assured neighbours of these people would often target them at their lowest ebb to try to force compliance, frequently involving the confession of sin. Unmarried mothers were questioned about their 'fornication' and the paternity of their babies during their labour, their pain believed to prompt honesty. That was in part to force the fathers to pay child maintenance, thus saving taxpayers' money, but also supposedly to save the souls of both parents. It sounds bad enough in the abstract, doesn't it? But it's even worse when you realise that this was the reality for specific women: people like Susan Thrower of Kettleborough in Suffolk. In 1644, Susan was questioned during labour by her midwife, who then informed magistrates that Susan had named Cuthbert Dale as her child's father, in her 'extremity of pain'. The court ordered him to pay up and ordained that if he defaulted, he would be fined twenty pounds (about £2,300 in today's money) or imprisoned. Meanwhile, Susan was sent to the house of correction for a year with her baby, a prison-like facility where unmarried mothers were 'punished and set on work', as the magistrates smugly recorded.[1] This, the perfectly decent people of Kettleborough reasoned, was a natural and godly rebuke for Susan and Cuthbert's sin.

Poorer women were extremely vulnerable if they were judged to have sinned like this. They could be jailed, denied church charity and excluded from the congregation to which they'd belonged. Worst off were those displaced from the parish of their birth, driven out by conflict or condemnation. They would be hounded from any other parish, because they might claim 'relief' – welfare payments funded by parish taxes. Pregnant women and mothers were especially unwelcome. Sometimes they abandoned their children, as was the case with the baby 'found in the street' in Great Yarmouth, Norfolk, in 1639 and christened Charity before her death. Some poor families trudged from one village to another, falling victim to violence, hunger and cold. 'Samuel Wharton, son of Robert Wharton (a beggarman)', 'Mary Wharton, daughter of Robert (a beggarman)' and 'Robert Wharton (a beggarman)' were all buried in Manningtree in Essex on 3, 8 and 28 September 1624. 'A travelling child of thirteen years of age was found dead in a drift of snow', recorded Lawford's parish clerk, also in Essex, in February 1658. In Newcastle upon Tyne in February 1650, 'a poor boy' died outside the fine houses by the Tyne bridge, likely of cold and hunger.[2] In this world, it was easy to become an outcast, begging, falling out with neighbours who refused to help – a clash that was often a precondition for an accusation of witchcraft.

These unfortunate souls were supposed to stay in their birthplace, hoping church charity would sustain them. That fixity supposedly gave them a controllable identity under an all-seeing God, one that luckier folk imagined made society 'safe'. But that was always an illusion. And during the civil wars between King and Parliament that raged across Britain in the 1640s, such ideal stasis was impossible to preserve. After war broke out over religious and political differences in 1642, people had to flee when their villages became war zones, while other places were filled with desperate refugees. People left their parishes to fight in the wars, or to run away from the wars; many fled because of religious or political change, or disruption to trade or food supply, or simply relocated to take up new opportunities. The wars caused massive destruction of religious and civic buildings, mills and mines, housing, crops, herds and transport infrastructure, damaging prosperity and forcing some people to move or starve. Castles and stately homes were blown up, towns put under siege and their walls razed, churches stripped. Besieged towns such as Newcastle upon Tyne, Gloucester and Colchester were ravaged from both inside and out; houses, chapels, almshouses and barns around the towns were pulled down or burned by defenders to provide a clear field of fire, while the towns themselves were also bombarded by attackers. Some people lost everything, without compensation, and became homeless, throwing themselves on the charity of any parish where they ended up. The resulting climate of instability and fear meant church communities were constantly on guard against strangers without and enemies within.[3]

This perception of threat, intertwined with a harsh interpretation of religious morality, dominated seventeenth-century life, with the optimistic, protective and compassionate aspects of Christianity often overpowered by fear and a desire to judge. The impulse to hate, rather than love, thy neighbour – especially one who practised a different version of the same faith – was also depressingly strong. The British civil wars were, in part, fought because people wanted to create their own religious paths, but unfortunately that freedom did not generally lead to a kinder Christianity. While some newly prominent groups (such as those who later became known as Quakers) emphasised love, fellowship and justice, some members of other sects (like the Presbyterians) created new fears, new sins, new tests and new punishments. Perhaps this new mood – a narrower, harsher definition of religious truth – was what made Henry Maggs look like a witch in the eyes of his neighbours. It was a mood that had been brewing since the Reformation movement took hold in Britain around a hundred years earlier. The Reformation saw Protestantism become the favoured religion across England and Wales, replacing the Catholicism that had preceded it. King Henry VIII (reigned 1509–1547) declared himself head of the Church of England and Wales in 1534 and the Church of Ireland in 1536, and he and his successors gradually moved these churches away from Catholicism. The Church of Scotland, meanwhile, turned Protestant in the 1560s. Many English, Welsh and Scottish people and most Irish people remained Catholic and thus opposed to the official religion, but the state churches were marching steadily away from them and towards fundamentalist revolution.

Yet, for some British people, this march towards godly reform was not fast or ambitious enough. These fundamentalists saw even the new Protestant establishment as too ritualistic and wealthy, reminiscent (they thought) of the Catholicism that had shaped national religion until the mid-sixteenth century. So they formed their own breakaway sects, separating from the state church. The most disruptive innovators, and the originators of some of the harshest repressions, including the witch hunts, were the extreme Protestant sectarians often labelled 'puritans' by their enemies (they themselves preferred the names 'reformers' or 'the godly'). This overarching label encompassed Anabaptists, Baptists, Brownists, Levellers, Antinomians, Presbyterians, Ranters and many of the highly individual prophets and seers of 1640s Britain.

Beyond wanting reform of existing religious options, these various sects differed greatly from each other. And members of these new churches were mostly not the black-dressed, hypocritical, sour-faced, monocultural figures favoured by popular narrative, but often included colourful figures who were sometimes surprisingly modern in their desires. Some allowed women preachers and deaconesses, some worshipped in fields or barns instead of church buildings, which they saw as tainted by traditional design and doctrine. Some even stood up against witch hunting. But others promoted it.

Unfortunately, each of these fundamentalist groups believed they had a monopoly on truth. It was all too easy to see competitor churches and anomalous people as heretical, even demonic. What if even the slightest error in doctrine or practice allowed the devil to mislead and damn well-meaning Christians? And what if, having been shown the error of their ways, the unorthodox individuals refused to change? Then it became permissible to attack them, firstly with harsh words but then resorting to physical repression.[4] At the sectarian level, Baptists ridiculed Quakers, Presbyterians oppressed Anabaptists. And at the personal level, many people suffered painfully for their beliefs. In September 1644, Suffolk housewife Thomasine Stott was arrested for refusing to go to her state church. She admitted she was an Anabaptist, who had recently been rebaptised as an adult. She thought this adult rite better represented her informed commitment to her faith: Christ had not commanded his followers to baptise children, so baptism ought to be a later choice. For this argument Thomasine was jailed – stuffed into a damp, stinking, deadly stone cell crawling with rats and lice – to force her to change her beliefs.[5]

You won't need to know about all these sects to follow the story of the witch hunt, so don't worry. But the overall picture of religious infighting in 1640s Britain is essential to understanding how some people, especially poorer folk and especially women, found themselves on the wrong side of powerful, pious opponents. And, of course, such self-righteousness and entitled aggression created the perfect atmosphere in which to hunt witches: the ultimate, devil-loving heretics. It seems no accident that the largest single witch trial of the 1640s, involving about 140 suspects, was held in Bury St Edmunds, in Suffolk – where, overlooking the courtroom, hulks an enormous ruin: the former Catholic abbey. When it was closed down in 1539, its treasures, books and relics were seized and its lands and buildings sold off, some to local nobles and gentry, some to the town authorities of Bury. The building itself was then torn apart by builders scavenging stone, lead, glass and timber. By the time of the witch trial, the sacred building stood stripped of its roofing and outer masonry – a fleshless skeleton; its giant west window glassless, miming a stone scream. The glee with which the abbey was dismantled reflected centuries of tension between the town authorities and the monks. Once Protestants took over in national government, the town seemed to have won – but it was a hollow victory, because it ripped apart the social structures and economy that had held Bury and much of its county, Suffolk, together.

Then, in 1608, a fire began in a malthouse in Bury to the east of the ruined abbey complex. It burned for three days, destroying almost half the town. Warehouses full of fish, salt, sugar and spices, stores of corn and hay, as well as horses and cattle that could not be rescued, were burned. All that was left of over two hundred homes, public buildings and shops were 'heaps of stones and pieces of timber'. Previously wealthy families were reduced to begging; the cost of rebuilding was estimated at a hundred thousand pounds (about £22 million today). The scars would have been evident for decades – the backdrop to the events of the 1640s.

And in the seventeenth century, such events were explained as God's punishment. A printed news pamphlet labelled the blaze 'an imposition of calamity laid upon [the townspeople] by the hand and power of God for their secret sins and offences'. Such 'strange events' were 'prognostications of worse to come', it continued, unless Suffolk's citizenry sought 'to win grace and favour at God's hands by amendment of our lives'. When the civil wars began and witches were thought to be stalking the land, it was easy for people to assume that killing these enemies, these witches, would redeem their community – it offered a comforting semblance of power and control in an uncertain, religiously unstable situation.[6]

~

Alongside this fractured religious landscape, some of the challenges faced by the communities that were drawn into the witch hunt of the 1640s were specifically wartime ones, caused or exacerbated by the civil wars. This book's stories begin in the early years of the wars, in 1643, and end with the conclusion to the main period of fighting, which came to a shaky halt in the early 1650s. You won't need to know much about the civil wars to read the stories of the witchcraft trials, but here's what's important. The wars – plural, because at least four different national groups were involved and there were multiple outbreaks of fighting – began in earnest in 1642. Like the religious infighting of the time, they had their roots in the Reformation. By the early 1640s, it was clear that Henry VIII's royal takeover of religion had fatefully entangled the monarch's power in sectarian strife, and many people had come to feel hatred and contempt for their royal family. Since the monarch led both the church and state, all the kingdoms' ills could be traced back to him, leading to political meltdown.

Throughout the early 1600s there were disagreements between successive British kings – James VI and I (reigned 1603–1625) and his son Charles I (reigned 1625–1649) – and religious radicals. There was a localised war between English and Scottish armies when Charles I tried to impose religious policy north of the border. There was a Catholic revolt in Ireland. There were bitter disputes between the king and the English Parliament over tax-raising powers, his desire for alliances with Catholic countries, his Catholic queen, and the rights of Members of Parliament to determine religious policy. Members of the English Parliament's lower debating chamber, the House of Commons, wanted more power, and they wanted the bishops in the upper chamber, the House of Lords, to have less. Charles resisted, arguing that, as head of the church, such decisions were his, but the reformers didn't agree. Relations between the king and his peoples finally broke down in January 1642, when, after a failed attempt to arrest Members of Parliament in the Commons, the king realised he was under personal threat from radical, bishop-hating rioters and fled his capital city, London. The civil wars had begun.

Communities across Britain armed themselves, choosing sides: either King or Parliament. By the summer, the king had lost control of his capital, of government on a national and local scale, and of much of 'his' army and navy. He went on the run, moving between various English cities. Fighting began as noblemen and officers on both sides tried to take over territories that supported their opponents. The first large battle between Parliamentarians and Royalists was on 23 October 1642, in Warwickshire in the English Midlands, with a second battle three weeks later near London. By September 1643 – when this book begins – the war had dislocated everything. Courts no longer held their regular sessions; cities were besieged; trade between Royalist areas and Parliamentarian London had been cut off; the transport of key localised commodities like coal, metal, cloth and fish had ceased; banking was in crisis; refugees streamed from one town to another; ordinary life was unsafe. What the outcome of the fighting would be was unclear. Then, in autumn 1643, Parliamentarians began to win a series of decisive victories. A year later, Scottish forces had joined the English Parliamentarians, capturing northern English towns like Newcastle, while Royalists fought back in the southwest from their shrinking stronghold in Cornwall. By 1646, Parliament had won the first civil war and the king was under arrest.

Unfortunately, as they neared victory, the winning side – the Parliamentarians – began to quarrel among themselves, often about religion. There were two main factions: Presbyterians and Congregationalists (sometimes called Independents). Presbyterians rejected control of the church by bishops but sometimes accepted royal authority, especially after 1646, when they hoped to strike a deal with the king, establishing them as the state's chosen sect. Within local churches, they preferred the leadership of presbyteries, councils of parishioners, which were linked together by common policies across Britain. Congregationalists wanted none of this, demanding complete independence of thought, separation of church and state and freedom for members of each congregation to make localised decisions. The English Parliamentarian army was broadly Congregationalist and republican, while the Presbyterians had the support of the Scottish army. It was a complex, shifting pattern of loyalties, but in 1648 it prompted the Scots to invade England to try to impose Presbyterian church government and restore the king to his throne. They lost this second civil war and Parliament decided that the threat from Royalists and Presbyterians combined was now too strong to allow the king to remain alive. He was executed on 30 January 1649. Charles I's son, Charles II, was accepted as King of Scotland, causing further fighting between English and Scottish forces, as well as more fighting in Ireland, which lasted until 1651. Parliament was once again victorious, and Charles II spent the next nine years in exile before a deal was signed restoring him as king of all the British Isles.[7]

~

If you'd lived in the 1640s, you'd certainly have felt some emotions that are familiar today. One was the sense that everything was falling apart. There was too much change too fast, much of it for the worse. Ancient institutions were bent to new purposes. Everything became politicised. One example was the nightly watch, whose officers – known as Watchmen – patrolled the streets of larger towns and cities during the hours of darkness. In the 1640s, the Watch became more like a militia than the reassuring figures they had been in the past, with their half-hourly cries singing out the time, weather and security state: 'past three o'clock, fine and frosty, and all's well'. Like policemen, the Watch had looked out for and dealt with everyday trouble: fires, floods, burglars. But during times of war, both night watches and day watches were organised by communities in case of what they referred to as 'alarums' – sneak attacks or outbreaks of fighting. Wartime watchers worked in a twenty-four-hour, seven-days-a-week team staffed by (often unwilling) 'volunteers' who could be fined or summoned to court if they failed to show up. Many of the watchers now carried firearms, as well as or instead of the simple stick that city Watchmen normally held. Wartime watches might look out for other kinds of threat alongside military attacks, too. In 1643, the people of Newmarket in Suffolk set up a 'watch and ward' to stop people arriving in their town from plague-wracked Cambridge. Travellers were to be challenged from a safe distance and warded off.[8]

This mood of increased judicial wariness and surveillance fed into the witch hunt. Some witchfinders that we'll meet in the book, such as the Scotsmen Hew Kennedie and James Sandilands, and the southerners Matthew Hopkins and John Stearne, experimented with different types of watching as part of their efforts to detect criminality among their suspects. Each of them felt that keeping accused people under observation around the clock was vital and that everything they did ought to be documented. Witches, they thought, might be visited by demons or animal familiars or start confessing under such observational pressure. Some witchfinders forced suspects to remain still while they were being watched – standing up and balanced, for example, on a stool. Others insisted on continual motion, walking accused people up and down in an enclosed space or cell. Both types of bodily control meant that sleep was impossible for the subject of the surveillance, so wakefulness became part of the act of watching. Of course, witch watchers had to stay awake too, but they worked in shifts to allow each other to rest. Some witchfinders stripped their suspects, like the professional witch prickers who worked across Scotland and parts of England, to give complete assurance that nothing was being hidden. Stripping witches was an old practice, but it added to the sense of siege and universal surveillance experienced by the accused people and everyone else in wartime Britain.

What witch examiners were looking for was physical evidence of demonic contact. The best proof was the kind of mark that poor Henry Maggs had himself searched for at Norwich in summer 1645 – a mole, wart, growth or other skin abnormality. Such marks were thought by witch hunters to provide a teat where a demonic animal familiar might suck blood from a witch, as payment for doing magical harm on the witch's behalf. The blood also symbolised the pact or covenant supposedly made between witch and demon, during which – tacitly or explicitly – the witch promised to turn away from God, worship the devil and hand over their soul to Satan at the time of their death. Searching for marks was extremely invasive, with searchers probing every bodily orifice. A pile, prolapse or mouth ulcer would do just as well as a wart to indicate guilt. Male searchers inspected male suspects, while accused women were stripped by respectable matrons and midwives who were expected to know what was and was not normal for female anatomy. The process was frightening and demeaning and helped to break down resistance to confession, as every inch of flesh was prodded. Some searchers sought numb spots that did not bleed, identifying these by pricking the suspect's flesh. Such a spot could indicate previous demonic suckling, they thought, just like a teat.

As well as searching and surveillance, documentation was also important to witchfinders. The world, so broken and slipping daily into deeper chaos, needed to be captured, controlled, fixed and held to account with ink and paper. The main guide would be God's word (the Bible), of course, but the words of godly people and the actions those words recorded would also play a role in national reform. There was no point in gathering evidence of people's sin, crime and anti-Christian activity if it could not be presented to the relevant authorities as a dossier of evidence, hopefully resulting in a trial. The process could become quite bureaucratic, echoing the increased level of state interference in ordinary people's lives during the civil wars. More people were literate in the seventeenth century than ever before, so they noted down charges, confessions, additional pieces of information about suspects and stories gathered from witnesses. The wars were very destructive of archives in some places, with one parish register noting simply that its information is 'very defective, many persons not being registered ... all things in this nation being in confusion'.[9] Yet in many witchcraft cases a surprising variety of information survives about accusers and suspects, including pre-trial paperwork, court documents, handwritten accounts, printed newspaper-style booklets and signed statements. In others, hardly anything remains. Many trials must have been completely erased from the historical record so that we'll never know they happened.

~

Around eight hundred thousand people probably died because of the civil wars – from battle injuries, massacres, disease and famine linked to the fighting – although figures are very inexact. It was a horrific time for survivors, too. Throughout the story of the witch hunt we'll meet a crowd of terrified and impoverished people: welfare claimants adrift in a system under strain, parents alarmed for sick children and wary of their neighbours, pastors desperate to retain control of feuding parishioners, conscripted soldiers, overburdened administrators, refugees fleeing battle, tradespeople threatened by ruin, farmers, fishers, shopkeepers and servants trying to carry on their normal lives. In this book, we'll follow the trail of historical evidence to watch the hunt grow from scattered sparks in middle England and Scotland to a conflagration, spreading from Essex north through Suffolk, Norfolk and the northern counties. Eastern, middle and northern England were worst affected, while Scotland experienced a major witch hunt of its own. Wales and Ireland were least affected, and western England also appears to have been less interested in witch hunting. Even so, by the end of the hunt at least two hundred people would have been executed for an impossible crime, likely more. This is their story, recovered from fractured archives, pieced together to highlight ten different communities, each with its accused witch or witches, across Witchland.

While we can't explore the lives of all the 'witches' of the 1640s hunt – that would take a far fatter tome than this – I hope you'll be intrigued and appalled by the sheer scale of the persecution, more than a little concerned by the conspiracy theories and prejudice that fuelled it, and perhaps you'll want to find out more about people who were or are being subjected to witch trials in the history of your own community, wherever you live.

During the hunt of the 1640s, communities lost their moral compass and turned in on themselves, with neighbours polarised by mutual fear. Vulnerable people like Henry Maggs and Alice Cooke were stigmatised as outsiders and persecuted in self-righteous rage. Fanatics pursued their enemies with libellous caricature, and fake news flourished. Otherwise thoughtful citizens imagined their justice system perfect, their leaders infallible, their ministers holier than most, their lawgivers cleverer, their common sense intuitive. They were mistaken. The witch hunt that resulted is a story of well-meaning mass murder. Although the dead are dead, we can set right some of the wrongs done by remembering them and learning what we can about the witch-hunting phenomenon.

So the story of Witchland should prompt questions in anyone tempted to trust comfortable myths. And we should not shy away from the bigger question too: what do you think you or I would have done when the witchfinders came to our town? As we find ourselves once again facing the challenges of polarised, war-torn and persecutory times, can we learn from the mistakes made by our forebears in the era of the witch hunt? How concerned should we be about modern 'witch hunts', attacks by powerful people on those who are vulnerable? One of the chapters of this book focuses on a 'witch' from the 1640s who shares my name – a sobering discovery. Could I have been accused of witchcraft if I'd lived in the 1640s? Could you?

PART 2

Forebodings: Southern England and Lowland Scotland

CHAPTER 2

Murder on the Battlefield

The Nameless Water-Witch of Newbury, Berkshire, 1643

Before the Battle of Newbury, Berkshire, began on 20 September 1643, some hungry soldiers serving in the Earl of Essex's Parliamentarian army left their camp to gather what food they could from hedgerows and orchards – nuts, apples, plums and blackberries. As they foraged across the flood plain of a river, one of the soldiers climbed a tree to pick fruit and get a better view of any other possible supplies. It was from that vantage point that he saw an astonishing sight: a woman was apparently walking on water on the river nearby! Awestruck and rattled, he beckoned his comrades to come and see. The men debated what to do. Together they crept towards the riverbank, then surrounded and ambushed the woman. On closer inspection, they found that she was floating on a plank. However, this seemed to them no less miraculous than levitating on the water itself. How could she 'stand upon the board', they marvelled, 'turning and winding it which way she pleased, making it pastime [like a game] to her'? Primed by their initial belief that she was walking on water, they decided her command of this unusual boat must be a supernatural feat. The woman must be a witch. So the soldiers seized her and hauled her away to be questioned by their unit's commander, the Earl of Essex himself. Later their story was written up by a pro-Parliamentarian journalist and published as the sensational story of the detection of a witch caught in the very act of working magic.

Under questioning, the woman remained mute, or so we're told. Imagine her terror. Perhaps she'd been cutting reeds in the shallows, digging for roots or gathering wild food, just like the soldiers who'd arrested her. They'd come from nowhere: a gang of men with frightened, angry faces, all grabbing hands and pointing fingers. Now she was face to face with an armed military officer who was barking questions at her about miracles, God and devils. He would likely have demanded to know how she was able to walk on water. It would, no doubt, have reminded him of Christ's miracle at the Sea of Galilee – surely the woman must have had help from Satan to replicate such a feat! How long, he might have followed up, had she been a witch? Leading questions were common in witch interrogations, and he might have asked *when*, and not *if*, she had made a pact with the devil. Under this barrage of interrogation, how could the woman explain? 'It was just a plank boat, it was just in the calm water, I was only . . .' she might have stuttered. If so, no one was listening. The officer, like his men, was convinced the woman was a witch. He would have heard the circulating rumours that witches were being deployed by the Royalist forces to prey on their Parliamentarian enemies and turn the course of the coming battle. And so he decided that his men would 'make a shot at her' with their guns. Was it some sort of trial of her supernatural status, or a summary judgement that she was indeed a witch and should be executed by firing squad? We can't be sure.

The troops backed the woman against a wall or bank, and

two of them aimed and fired at her. At this point, her story takes a fantastical turn. The woman 'caught their bullets in her hands and chew'd them', reported the news pamphlet that published her story. Its author added that, as she champed on their ammunition, she laughed at the soldiers. That stung. Apparently nothing could hurt the 'witch' or dent her confidence. The gunmen tried to shoot her at point-blank range, but their musket balls bounced off her body. Moving in close, they stabbed at her with a sword, but no wound appeared. At last, one of the soldiers recalled that drawing blood on a witch's head – ideally her forehead or somewhere above her nose – was supposedly a means of stripping away her magic. He announced, therefore, that he would shoot her in the temple. The woman at last spoke. She was in despair, the pamphlet tells us: 'is it come to pass that I must die indeed?' she lamented. 'Why then his excellency the Earl of Essex shall be fortunate and win the field'. Having spoken her prophecy of Parliamentarian victory in the Battle of Newbury and admitted that she'd been trying to prevent it, the woman was shot in the head – and this time she died.[1] Or so the story goes.

Some aspects of this story must be fantasy or fake news, of course. Unless the woman really was a witch, she can't have caught bullets in her hands or hardened her body against lead and steel. Her dying prophecy is also suspiciously convenient for a writer who supported the Parliamentary cause, offering reassuring confirmation from the spirit world that Roundhead commanders, and especially the mighty Earl of Essex, would win the Battle of Newbury and, beyond that, the wider civil war. In fact, the battle was more balanced in its outcome than a simple Parliamentarian victory. Royalist forces commanded by their general, Prince Rupert, had hoped to trap Essex's army in the marshy area of Newbury Wash and defeat them. That would prevent the Parliamentarians from retreating towards their eastern English heartland. But the Royalist strategy failed, mostly because Prince Rupert's men ran out of gunpowder. The relieved Parliamentarians were able to retreat, hurrying back to London, but not exactly victorious. The witch's prophecy was therefore largely incorrect. The 1643 Battle of Newbury was a turning point – because in London the Earl of Essex's troops regrouped and began the long campaign which ultimately won the war – but it was not a Parliamentarian win.

Other details of the story of the 'Witch of Newbury' are more convincing, though. Any paddle boarder will show you how to float on a 'plank' and punt along, and the remains of prehistoric log boats are common on the slow rivers of southeast England – although if you were a Parliamentarian soldier from Devonshire or Derbyshire or Durham, you might not know that. The Kennet, which borders the Newbury battlefield to the north, is just such a smooth, calmly flowing river, winding through marshland spiky with reeds and yellow iris. Even today, with a canal, road and railway line having constrained its course, quieter stretches would need to be navigated by shallow, flat-bottomed craft. We also know that in 1643 some of the Parliamentarian forces decided to camp at Hamstead, right next to this river, before the battle. They reasoned that the marsh, with its multiple river channels and ditches, would protect their tents and baggage from attack. These seven hundred men were in a regiment directly under the command of the Earl of Essex. Brigades sub-commanded by his officers – the Cornish baronet John Robartes of Lanhydrock and the Norfolk gentleman Philip Skippon – were further south, but the Hamstead men were Essex's own, just as the Newbury witch story suggests. Indeed, a second Parliamentarian news booklet that repeated the story of the Newbury woman's killing suggested that she'd in fact approached the military camp 'to speak with Essex' himself.[2]

This last detail might be instrumental to the outcome of the story of the 'Witch of Newbury'. The Earl of Essex, Robert Devereux, had a vexed personal history with witchcraft. As a thirteen-year-old, he'd been forcibly married to Frances Howard, a teenaged granddaughter of the Duke of Norfolk. It was a marriage uniting two dynasties rather than a love match, and the young couple lived apart after their wedding. Unfortunately, during that time Frances fell in love with someone else. She began an affair with Robert Carr, a favoured courtier of King James VI and I, and tried to have her marriage to Essex annulled so that she could marry her lover. Since it appeared her marriage had not been consummated, the divorce or annulment was agreed in 1613. But Frances had to undergo a virginity test – which she passed, though rumour suggested she paid another girl to take it – and her young husband was subjected to public ridicule as an impotent cuckold. Three years after the split, Frances was accused of employing witches and poisoners to commit murder, supposedly killing a fellow courtier whose supporters denounced her. The Earl of Essex was at last able to explain the collapse of his marriage in terms that his sniggering critics could understand: his ex-wife had been working with witches! He hadn't been impotent or undesirable, just cursed and deceived by feminine craft. Although Frances and her second husband were convicted, they were reprieved. But the supposed poisoner – Anne Turner, who was accused of having practised witchcraft on their behalf, working with astrologers and magicians – was executed, with Essex's approval.[3]

Although he had a close connection with one of the accused – his ex-wife – the Earl had been a juror at the murder trial. There he probably sat fuming as he heard evidence of poisoning, spells and charms. By the end, he must have believed he knew all about witches. Perhaps, thirty years later, he really did interrogate the unlucky woman accused on the Newbury battlefield – after all, he led the unit said to have captured her. If so, his past experiences no doubt influenced his decision to judge her guilty, just as he'd judged his former wife's co-conspirators. Unlike them, however, the Newbury woman did not receive a conventional trial ending in an execution by hanging (as was normal in England, where witchcraft was considered a felony, a serious crime like arson or murder, which should be punished in the same way), but was hastily killed by gunfire. The military authorities did not want a lengthy engagement with her, since their campaign was already going badly.

Essex's forces were exhausted by a long retreating march from the West Country, chased by their enemies. They'd had new grey wool coats in August but were nevertheless soaked by continual rain throughout September. They hadn't slept in proper beds for days. Plague was spreading, and they were hungry. That the soldiers who spotted the 'witch' floating nearby were out foraging for food sounds entirely plausible. Their atrocity is horribly familiar, too. In modern terms, it's a war crime: the murder of a civilian by soldiers awaiting battle – even if several newspaper accounts from the time suggested that the soldiers considered her a Royalist saboteur, an enemy combatant. But there is at least one other example of soldiers attacking a perfectly ordinary civilian because they thought she was a witch. This was at Warminster, Wiltshire, where the suspect Anne Warberton's home was stormed, her child killed by falling debris and she was bitten and scratched by her accusers.[4]

The Newbury soldiers would have heard the report of Anne Warberton, and other stories like this, and some would have been convinced their enemies were using witchcraft as a weapon against them. Witches were one of the most common bogeymen they heard about in propaganda and sermons, along with Catholics, devils and the king's advisors. Some Royalist soldiers were thought to be witches themselves, and the leading Royalist commander Prince Rupert was even said to have a familiar spirit in the form of a dog, a creature named Boy. Boy did exist, although of course he was not a demon. Instead, he took the amusingly unthreatening form of a white poodle. He wasn't a lapdog, however – a small animal shaved in an intricate decorative pattern like many modern poodles. He was a large, shaggy dog about half a metre tall, bred for game sports, his rear clipped and the fur over his head and breast left long. Poodles (or 'pudels', their original German name) were 'water dogs', meaning they were expected to jump into lakes or rivers to retrieve wildfowl shot by hunters. The long curly portion of their coats acted as a barrier against the water as they dived in and kept them warm as they swam. They were expensive dogs, mostly owned by gentlemen or nobles, and because they had a mane of curls over their head and shoulders, people thought they looked rather like long-haired Royalist courtiers.

In part because of this visual similarity, Boy was seen as a kind of avatar for his curly-maned owner, Prince Rupert, a link between dog and human that was only strengthened by the fact that both had German origins. Rupert was the son of King Charles I's sister Elizabeth, who had married a German prince. Rupert had left Germany and come to England in 1641 to offer support to his uncle as Britain descended into civil war, and he had an impressive reputation as a general. He'd been fighting military battles since the age of fourteen and was regarded as an experienced tactician and personally fearless. He was also sometimes reckless, however, and perhaps it was his disregard for consequences that led him to take Boy to the Battle of Marston Moor in Yorkshire, northern England, in 1644. Boy was killed there, after escaping from Rupert's tent and running to join him in the thick of the fighting. The dog had been adopted as a mascot by Royalist troops, and they were horrified. Meanwhile, there was nasty rejoicing among Parliamentarian propagandists. They'd heard Boy was a shapeshifter, could catch bullets in his mouth and, like his owner Prince Rupert, was protected by demonic powers: 'weapon-proof' and 'shot free' so that he could not be harmed by swords or bullets. The soldiers who caught the 'Witch of Newbury' would have known these stories about Boy, and so it wasn't surprising that they imagined their witchcraft suspect to be weapon-proof and shot-free too.

Such myths about invulnerable, bullet-repellent enemies seem to have originated with Parliamentarians, but they were fostered by Royalists (who actually thought them ridiculous – perhaps they spread such superstitious stories to mess with the minds of their opponents or to mock them). Rumours about Boy the dog's ability to catch bullets in mid-air were circulating by 1643; several satirical pamphlets disseminated them widely and elaborated on them inventively. One writer claimed to have observed Boy and concluded that he was not 'a downright devil (as is supposed) or a spirit sent to nourish division in church or state', but instead was 'some Lapland lady' who had transformed herself into a dog. Lapland was the Arctic territory of the indigenous Sami people, who were thought to have dangerous abilities in spellcasting and divination; there had been extensive witch trials there in the 1620s and the place was a byword for magic. So a magical Lapland lady, the satirist joked, was now masquerading as the dog Boy. S/he was a shapeshifter who, as well as deflecting musket balls, could speak human languages, make themself invisible and utter prophecies. Boy had even made sure all the Royalists killed in the war so far were her/his enemies, those who'd kicked or sworn at her/him, and apparently s/he had also magically swayed the minds of the king's counsellors to make stupid decisions. In short, s/he was not an ordinary familiar spirit, but 'a witch, a sorceress'.[5]

Unfortunately, this amusing legend took on a life of its own and, like so many conspiracy theories created by a mixture of joke, exaggeration and paranoia, led to real harm. Boy was cut or shot down in battle, and apparently the witchcraft suspect at Newbury was killed in a similar way. By 1644, a propagandist was intuitively linking the two in a comic elegy for the dog, announcing that Boy had been 'whelp'd of a malignant water-witch' who could 'command the ebb or tide'. He was born as a devil-dog, soon 'excell'd his mother in her witchery', and so his chief mourners would be 'the witch, Pope and devil'. The elegy was a crazy mix of genuine political anxiety and silly slapstick. A real woman straying into that mix of fake news and wartime terror might well have fallen victim to it, especially in the pre-fight tension that characterised the Battle of Newbury. There, on the morning of 20 September, looking out across Newbury Wash, Parliamentarian troops knew Rupert was waiting with Boy, planning to annihilate them, to kill or capture the Earl of Essex, his men Robartes and Skippon, and end the war. If Rupert won, Britain would be forced back to the old world of kings and bishops, royal flirtation with Catholicism, soaring taxes to pay for silks and lace, fornicating actors and drunken lords, music and mistresses, yes sir and no ma'am. No thanks, thought the soaked, starving troops as they foraged for free food. If Rupert is a witch himself, he must have armies of sorceresses in his wake, flinging spells at us. This woman must be one of them; let's kill her before she kills us.

Of course, there's always the possibility that the story of the 'Witch of Newbury' is completely untrue, a lie created because it summed up so perfectly the fears of pious Parliamentarians.[6] In Holborn Library, London, is a forgery that shows how easy it is for fake news like that to become fake history. The forged document is a vellum-bound book called the 'Woodehouse Journal'. It appears to be Victorian and was bought by the library in the 1960s, purporting to be the scrapbook of an eighteenth-century London magistrate, William Woodehouse. 'His' book includes two tales about witches. One derives from the real seventeenth-century news pamphlet, *A most certain, strange and true discovery of a witch, being taken by some of the Parliament forces, as she was standing on a small plank board and sailing on it over the river of Newbury*, which preserved the longest version of the story of the 'Witch of Newbury', the one you've just read. The forger of the Woodehouse Journal pasted into his faux-antiquarian book a title page supposedly cut from this pamphlet. Then he copied out much of the pamphlet's text in ink. Like the real news pamphlet, his title page features an illustration in which our Newbury woman, barefoot, stands on a slab of wood in the middle of a river, her dress streaming behind her as she lunges forward. She holds a walking stick or punting pole and her free hand waves in the air for balance. Beside her hover two black birds, and in the background stands a tiny church.

But far from being an accurate account of what happened at Newbury in 1643, the forged pamphlet's title is 'A most certain, strange and true discovery of a witch, being taken by some of the Parliament forces, as she was standing on a small plank board and sailing on it over the river *of Pancrasse*'. St Pancras is in London, just a mile from Holborn Library, so its church must be the one in the pamphlet's illustration. And when you look closely at the Holborn version of the pamphlet's title page, you can see it's wholly fake: not actually printed but drawn in ink. Nevertheless, a nineteenth-century collector paid handsomely for this fake pamphlet. He was probably Rufus Decimus Stephen Waugh, a carpet dealer and antiquarian born at St Pancras.[7] The forgery was attractive to him because it seemed to be about his birthplace. But it was also desirable because it's about that most fascinating of subjects: witchcraft. Some 'certain, strange and true' witchcraft stories are so good they have to be invented. In this case, the fact that two sources (pamphlet and news book) tell more or less the same tale makes it likely to be true – more or less.

~

There was a long history among pious Protestant reformists of imagining themselves to be in direct military combat with the devil and his agents, which helped create not just the conditions for the assault on the 'Witch of Newbury', but for the whole witch hunt of the 1640s. As far back as the 1530s, Protestant preachers had been attracted to the Bible's more warlike passages, especially this one:

> Put on the whole armour of God, that ye may be able to stand against the wiles of the devil. For we wrestle not against flesh and blood, but against principalities, against powers, against the rulers of the darkness of this world, against spiritual wickedness in high places. Wherefore take unto you the whole armour of God, that ye may be able to withstand in the evil day, and having done all, to stand. Stand therefore, having your loins girt about with truth, and having on the breastplate of righteousness; And your feet shod with the preparation of the gospel of peace; Above all, taking the shield of faith, wherewith ye shall be able to quench all the fiery darts of the wicked. And take the helmet of salvation, and the sword of the Spirit, which is the word of God.[8]

Preaching in 1536 to the court of King Henry VIII, the reformist cleric Hugh Latimer expanded on this text, urging his congregation:

> Be ye therefore armed at all points with the armour of God, that ye may stand strongly against the assaults of the devil ... We may not sit, that is, not rest in sin, or lie along in sluggishness of sin; but continually fight against our enemy, and under our great Captain and Sovereign Lord Jesus Christ, and in his quarrel, armed with the armour of God, that we may be strong ... Let us fight manfully, and not cease ... We must therefore fight continually, and with this sword; and thus armed, and we shall receive the reward of victory.[9]

After over a hundred years of this reformist rhetoric, Parliamentarian forces of the 1640s often considered themselves to be an army of God. These tired, traumatised men expected to encounter Satan's forces directly arrayed against them in battle, and it's entirely plausible that at Newbury they murdered an innocent bystander because they believed she was an enemy combatant, a Royalist witch. The fact that we don't have a name for this woman doesn't mean she didn't exist: to fit into the role of an agent of the devil, she didn't need to be named.

Her namelessness creates a problem for historians, however – one that will keep recurring in this book and one that makes this chapter shorter than all the ones that follow, simply because there's a huge gap in this story. For a complete history of all the 1640s witch trials, we ideally need names, dates, places and events to be specified in historical records, but very often they are not. If a person suspected of witchcraft was tried by a regular court going about its business in an orderly, established way, there was every chance their name would be recorded, as well as details of their hometown, occupation or status, the date and place of their supposed crime, and the verdict of the court on the charges made against them. But the civil wars disrupted all of that. Around the courts, Britain changed day by day as sectarian infighting or rioting broke out unexpectedly, or formal battles sent streams of wounded men and refugees tramping across the land. In these circumstances, people like the 'Witch of Newbury' got caught by events far beyond their control. The normal schedule of criminal courts across England – the Assize courts that considered allegations of serious offences or 'felonies' – broke down in many places. Felony cases that would once have been heard by expert judges were handed over to soldiers, landowners, ministers: people who could be assembled quickly in wartime to make decisions. Some of these men would have had previous experience of courtroom work: local magistrates, bailiffs or stewards, for example, used to running borough, market, port or manor courts in their towns and villages, or county-wide Sessions of the Peace, which were quarterly courts hearing evidence of mostly non-felony offences. But some would have had very little idea of how to dispense justice.

Court systems varied too, and each had its own standards of evidence and procedures designed to establish the truth. In England and Wales, suspected witches were tried – or supposed to be tried – in Assize courts, where a grand jury of twenty-four men would examine each charge to see if it should go to trial, and if it did, the case would be heard by a petty jury of twelve men and a judge. But with the court system in confusion, witchcraft cases often ended up being judged in other ways: at borough courts in towns or quarterly sessions of local magistrates, in church courts and non-standard versions of Assizes. In Scotland, things were even more fragmented, with the king's Privy Council able to grant to any self-appointed local group the right to hold a witch trial. That could include church or kirk ministers, the church councils known as presbyteries, local lords and gentlemen – anyone the Council thought fit. By 1643, many of these already diverse legal systems were disrupted by war, meaning justice was done in a variety of new, even less predictable forms. Often, of course, that led in practice to injustice.

Records of what took place were in similar disarray, and many records of the 1640s witch trials were never created at all or were soon lost. Court records that had been added to year after year for a century or more in comfortable routine suddenly broke down into apologetic notes or blank pages, usually around 1642 or 1643. The same was true of parish registers, town meeting books and business records. Sometimes people unaccustomed to record-keeping took over and either generated no records at all or lost whatever they had noted down. If they held a witch trial, they didn't deposit their trial documentation in the usual places: the shire hall or the town's locked chest. Sometimes they departed from the usual format of documentation, forgetting or confusing details of accusations, places and names. Even where the courts tried to keep a record of what they'd done, witch trial authorities could be frustrated. Some people shed their identities during wartime, designedly or not. There were a surprising number of people known only by vague descriptions such as 'Mary that came from Norwich', 'the son of widow Dynes' or dubious nicknames like 'John Smith, timber leg'. In many communities, it was only recently that people had stopped being labelled in the medieval way: known primarily by their given, Christian name with an additional word or two that referred to their trade or place of origin. Some people were still known, as they would have been in Tudor times, as 'Mother Jones' or 'Father Hurrell' because of their age – 'mother' or 'father' being a term of respect for senior citizens.

In some places, local naming customs further obscured identities. Scottish women kept their maiden name when they married – a modern-seeming gesture of independence but one that makes it hard to trace their life history. If such a woman's husband is not mentioned in a document, then it's impossible to work out who she was married to. Conversely, in England, married women's Christian names were often omitted from records, if they were mentioned at all; a baptismal record could read simply 'John son of John Weaver', as if the child's mother did not exist. One Newcastle parish register failed to record the names of almost every bride for four years in the early seventeenth century, noting only their husbands' names next to a series of blank spaces. Then there were those who had several surnames: women who had been married more than once, children of blended families, people who shared a home. It was common to see names like Hart alias White or Clarke alias Bedingfield. Spellings varied over time, too: Bellchamber became Belconger, Fossett became Fassett, Rees became Rice.[10]

So, despite attempts to pin down and record the events of seventeenth-century witch trials, problems of clarity and truth have always dogged writers who have attempted to tell their stories. Even after they'd established suspects' identities and decided on naming conventions, seventeenth-century people who investigated witchcraft cases and recorded their outcomes were faced with insoluble problems. Which types of evidence should be accepted as truthful? An accusation with name, date, place and the presence of witnesses to confirm it in court? Confession under pressure? Confession freely offered? Was any or some of that enough? How should a magistrate or his scribe record evidence when so much of it was one person's word against another's, rambling responses to leading questions or hearsay? How to describe the workings of magic or the illusions of the devil, when there was theological uncertainty about such matters? And so on. Their difficulties have created even more of a problem for historians, who – in addition to their concerns about seventeenth-century interrogations and recording practices – don't accept that witchcraft is a reality. If a crime is impossible, then how should we interpret whatever records of its trial remain?

The Newbury woman was barely tried at all and instead was subjected to summary judgement by an informally convened military court. Because of this, no record of her remains beyond the self-evidently unreliable news pamphlets about her case. Her name is lost, and with that, any chance of reconstructing her life. While many of the witch trials we will go on to investigate left better records, in many ways the case of the 'Witch of Newbury' established a precedent for all those future trials. Even where a name was assigned to a witchcraft suspect, their individuality was still stripped from them. Witches were imagined as a generic enemy within, a spy or soldier of the devil, an enemy of God making sneak attacks on otherwise secure and respectable communities.

They were dehumanised because their behaviour was thought to be inhuman: subtle, secretive, deceitful, evasive, resistant. That meant they had to be trapped by cunning tricks of interrogation, punished in extreme ways – illegal ones if need be. Putting unusual pressure on suspects, ignoring their established rights and overriding objections to cruel treatment – objections based on common sense or decency – became acceptable. That willingness to bend the rules in questioning and judging witches, combined with the crumbling of the courts, opened the door to the witchfinders of the 1640s. It turned ordinary pre-trial questioning and courtroom trials into a free-for-all of amateur experimentation, something that looked a lot less like justice and a lot more like extrajudicial murder. Into this chaos were thrown ordinary people like you or me.

CHAPTER 3

Torture in the Church

Marion Gibson, Agnes Bishop and Margaret Thomsone of Mid Calder, West Lothian, 1643–44

Once upon a time, there was a woman called Marion Gibson. But this Marion Gibson wasn't me. She lived nearly four hundred years ago, and in 1644 she was accused of witchcraft. I was told about her story in a church in Linlithgow, West Lothian, Scotland, near where Marion once lived. The tiny church of St Peter's looks as if it belongs in a fairy tale: narrower than a tennis court, with a dinky conical-roofed tower, three storeys of Byzantine arches and a pillar-box red wooden door. Inside is a cool, white space which on this summer evening was packed with chatting readers. They were here for a talk about my book *Witchcraft: A History in Thirteen Trials*, and at the end of the question-and-answer session three women approached me, one of them carrying a photocopied document in a plastic sleeve. The women were from the Calder Witch Hunt Project, which was researching and publicising the stories of local women accused of witchcraft in the 1640s. When they handed the document to me, I could hardly believe my eyes:

here was a copy of the record of Marion Gibson, witch! I had to know more.

Scotland had its own troubled history with witchcraft. Marion Gibson lived in West Lothian, also then known as Linlithgowshire, and nearby East Lothian had experienced sensational witch trials in the 1590s, with some suspects being questioned by the Scottish king himself: James VI and I, father of the present king, Charles I. But that had been more than fifty years earlier, and although she must have heard stories of witchcraft, Marion likely remembered nothing of that turbulent time. Her troubles only began in April 1643, about a year before her witch trial.[1] It was then that a young minister eagerly took up his first post in her home parish, Mid Calder. Hew Kennedie was just twenty-two and had landed a plum opportunity. Known as Mid Calder to distinguish it from its neighbouring townships, his parish was rural but reasonably close to Edinburgh, allowing him access to the power and influence that was focused there. He was to live just fourteen miles west of the national capital, a day's ride. Soon after he arrived in his new parish, he met Marion among his other parishioners in church.

By 1643, the Calder area had three churches, or kirks as they were called in local Scottish speech. There was East Calder; the Kirk of Calder, which was the old Mid Calder church, dating back in its foundation to at least the twelfth century; and now some local people were building themselves a new church at West Calder. Hew would be responsible for this new church too, working with a group of elders – church officials picked from the congregation as worthy, godly men. The elders were chosen by the community to lead them spiritually, alongside the minister, as a presbytery or inner group of pious parishioners and also as a local court or 'kirk session'. There were usually a dozen or so elders per church community, but at Mid Calder there were just eight, led by William Sandilands of Hilderston and the castle-like Calder

House. As well as being a senior elder, William was guardian to the young landowner Lord Torphichen, an estate management position known as Tutor of Torphichen. Complementing the minister, chief elder and presbytery's religious governance of Mid Calder parish, there was also a local baillie – a type of magistrate, holding powers that linked church and state in the governance of place, society and behaviour. This position was currently occupied by James Sandilands, a relative of Tutor William, who lived at Muirhousedykes, seven miles from Mid Calder. These men would be Hew Kennedie's co-workers as he settled into his new job.

As their dominance over the Mid Calder church community shows, the Sandilands were a powerful family. They'd controlled the Calder area for centuries, as magnates who moved among the ranks of royal councillors and ambassadors, and they were still on the way up in Scottish society. They had a silver mine on their land at Hilderston, and one branch of their family had been ennobled: it was to this young Lord Torphichen that William Sandilands was Tutor. In the medieval wars between England and Scotland, the Sandilands family had strongly supported the Scottish kings and the Catholic earls of Douglas and Angus. But now most of them were fervent Protestant reformers, and since the 1560s, Scotland's state church had been Protestant – militantly so, offering officials like the Sandilands plenty of scope for social intervention and power plays. Their lands were still contested, however, because their country was in a state of near-permanent conflict between rival factions and – by the 1640s – the scene of ongoing international war with English armies. The Sandilands family were broadly aligned with English Parliamentarians during the civil wars but by no means simply politicians fighting a religiously focused culture war: instead, they lived in a remilitarising, destabilising society facing multiple military threats as civil war factions split and coalesced. It had become common once again for the area's noblemen to take part in battles as their ancestors once had. So men like William and James Sandilands lived in a state of military readiness. They were expected to respond to any local violence with violence of their own.[2]

This did not mean, though, that they weren't also sincere Christians. Then as now, devout religiosity is not incompatible with waging war and persecuting sectarian opponents. As part of their rule over the Calder area, William and James Sandilands had come to believe they had a duty to identify and harass enemies of their kirk. They were particularly interested in women who used healing spells, often known as 'charmers'. To us, such people might seem harmless, even an asset to their community if they used herbs with some small effect, or offered comforting rituals, as many of them did. To those who trusted in their skill, they provided divination, medical and midwifery services: finding stolen goods, blessing expectant mothers, easing coughs, sprains and labour pains, brewing love magic and lifting curses. Usually they claimed to do good with the aid of fairies or ghosts, benevolent spirits whom they could call on to boost their supernatural power, alongside prayers to God and appropriate rites to ensure luck, health or prosperity. But the Sandilands did not agree that God was the ultimate source of such charmers' power. Instead, they thought these women, and men who also practised such folk magic, might well be calling on demons to help them in their charms. What they were doing was thus an affront to God, and even when they appeared to pray to him, they could really be practising witchcraft and petitioning Satan. Mid Calder's new minister, Hew Kennedie, shared the Sandilands' concern: together they determined to act against these magical agents.[3]

There were precedents across Scotland, and in Mid Calder itself, for investigating the behaviour of charmers. In 1618, a practitioner from Dedridge, a mile west from Mid Calder's Kirk of Calder church, was questioned as part of a slander trial. She was Agnes Bishop – the wife of David Jack or Joch since 1609, but retaining her maiden name, as was the Scottish custom – and she had fallen out with one of her neighbours, James Aikman. It is hard to pinpoint the origin of the quarrel, but it appears that Agnes had been calling some of her neighbours, including James, names, and one of those names was 'witch'. So, initially, it was James who was accused of witchcraft by Agnes – slanderously, he said – even though Agnes was in fact a known charmer. Perhaps James was also a charmer himself: such rival operators sometimes quarrelled over who was curing whom. They often argued, too, about whether the patient being treated by one charmer had in fact been cursed by another one, a charmer gone rogue who was using their magic to do harm. Perhaps Agnes and James were fighting over something like this.

Whatever the precise circumstance was, it is not documented, but suspicions of evil magic were flying around in Mid Calder in 1618 and they spread wide. The quarrel between Agnes Bishop and James Aikman became so heated it was referred to the kirk session, Mid Calder's church court. The session dealt with reports of unneighbourly conduct, and its members – the elders who worked with Hew Kennedie – were, literally, the community's morality police. They were expected to uphold approved Christian behaviour, punish and reform sinners, and restore harmony among the congregation where it had broken down. Agnes and James's argument was exactly the sort of dispute the elders regularly settled. Agnes, the kirk session was told, had not only called people 'witch' during her practice as a charmer, but had also accused them of theft, and James had retaliated by complaining about her to the church authorities. The court looked into their behaviour and found Agnes to be in the wrong. She had slandered her neighbours, they determined, and so she was ordered to pay a fine. Agnes and James were required to patch up their quarrel and both had to find a sponsor or 'cautioner' to guarantee their good behaviour. Agnes' husband, David Jack, served as her cautioner and the matter was closed – for now.[4]

As this quarrel shows, in the early seventeenth century, fears about charming and witchcraft were regular matters of concern in Scottish villages like Mid Calder, just as they were further south in Newbury, Berkshire, and indeed across Europe and North America. But, as often happened in the early years of the century, in 1618, Mid Calder's elders decided not to investigate such accusations further, or have Agnes or James imprisoned or executed for charming or witchcraft. This was despite being presented with an ideal opportunity: Agnes Bishop and James Aikman had traded slurs, including the word 'witch', and at least one of them was definitely a charmer: why not hold a witch trial? But on this occasion, the kirk session did not decide that magic had actually been practised – or, even if it had, it was not evidently evil. They were more concerned about slander and its impact on community harmony, which may seem surprising. In fact, many seventeenth-century courts, both religious and state, would have responded similarly. Charming was often judged harmless, ineffective or unimportant, as it would be today in most places. In 1618, the elders of Mid Calder decided that no further action was needed. Agnes Bishop and James Aikman went home and got on with their lives.

Twenty-five years later, however, things had changed in Mid Calder – slowly at first, and then with frightening speed. Mid Calder's new minister, Hew Kennedie, arrived. Elders came and went. And the kirk session, like any council, adapted to its new members' views. On 3 September 1643, Agnes Bishop's fellow villager, Jean Anderson, was sentenced to perform a public penance for her magical practices. Unlike Agnes, she had been formally judged to be guilty of using charms. On that Sunday, she stood in the Kirk of Calder dressed in an ugly, coarse shift made of sackcloth while minister Hew Kennedie upbraided her and prayed over her sins. Even more troubling, though, was what he told Jean and the assembled congregation before he let her shuffle back to her seat: that if ever she should be found using charms hereafter, he would judge her to be a witch.[5] Hew had been in post for six months and was beginning the work of purification and edification that he intended for Mid Calder, purging sin and encouraging his congregation to lead more perfect, godly lives. That included ending fornication, swearing, lying and adultery, holding the kirk's worshippers to account for charming and, ultimately, showing them that charming was in fact witchcraft. So, three months later, that's exactly what he did to Agnes Bishop.[6]

This time, Agnes alone was accused formally of witchcraft, and her accuser was Hew Kennedie himself. After making the charge, Hew also escalated the process of trying Agnes beyond his local kirk session. He was satisfied that what he'd heard from witnesses in his parish – although the exact charges are not recorded – should be dealt with by a higher authority. The powers of kirk sessions were limited and had been since the Scottish Reformation of the 1560s, and witchcraft was a serious charge needing careful investigation. So it made sense that Hew reported Agnes to his local presbytery, the superior church court based in the market town of Linlithgow. The Linlithgow presbytery managed church affairs across Linlithgowshire, including West Lothian, holding regular meetings dealing with church administration, disputes and sin. Agnes, Hew Kennedie told the presbytery court, was 'a common charmer and a witch' – the two categories of magical activity had collapsed into each other in his accusation – but she denied she'd done anything wrong. The court agreed that accused and accuser should come back to a formal hearing after Christmas. Agnes would be indicted, or charged, with charming and witchcraft in January, and then Hew should produce his evidence.

On 31 January 1644, the presbytery therefore met again. Minister Kennedie was the chief witness and presented a dossier of written evidence. Agnes had, he said, used charming 'many times and sundry manner of ways' so that her activities had 'great appearances of witchcraft'. Then he asked the 'brethren', his Christian brothers of the presbytery, not just to consider her sins themselves, but to 'supplicate the Lords of his Majesty's Privy Council to grant commission to put her to further trial and to an assize [a formal, secular court hearing with a jury] and punishment of her'. Hew was pushing for further escalation. The kirk's jurisdiction over witchcraft was limited, but the members of the Privy Council – the Scottish monarch's advisory group – could commission anyone they chose to set up a witch trial. They could pick landowners, churchmen and local gentlemen, who would then form a criminal court. Supposed witches could be investigated and tried by this court composed of the Council's nominees: as part of the process, suspects could be tortured and, if found guilty, executed. In approaching the Privy Council, Hew was therefore asking for a national, governmental response to his and his colleagues' contention that charming was the same activity as witchcraft and that both were devilish sins against God, punishable by death. Poor Agnes Bishop would be the Mid Calder test case, and if Hew could get her convicted and killed, she might even propel him to national importance as a godly expert on witches.[7]

Unfortunately for Agnes, the presbytery's brethren were open to considering Hew's insistent request. They listened to his evidence and called before them witnesses from Mid Calder, whose verbal complaints against Agnes had also now been written up – although sadly this document is now lost, so we don't know who else accused her besides her minister. Based on their survey of the case, the presbytery decided there were 'great presumptions' of Agnes' guilt in the evidence, meaning they thought it reasonable to allege she was a witch. Responding to Hew's suggestion that they seek additional powers, they therefore pledged they would approach the Privy Council to ask for a commission to try the matter further.

In the meantime, Agnes remained imprisoned in Linlithgow Tolbooth – the meeting hall, courthouse, tax office and jail of the town – to await political developments. So far, it does not appear that she'd confessed anything, but she must have been terrified. Now she was set to appear before the king's ministers or their nominees, some of the wealthiest and best-educated men in her country, to be accused and interrogated about witchcraft. If found guilty, she would likely be strangled and her body burned at a stake. Poor Agnes would have heard stories of such executions and known what horror she was to expect.[8]

However, back in Mid Calder, despite their success in escalating her case, Hew Kennedie, the Sandilands and their fellow elders were still dissatisfied. They were itching with curiosity to know what Agnes had to say and, hardened by moral rectitude, they really wanted to investigate her themselves – soon. They and their neighbours had some thoughts about how to make her confess. After all, they were sure she was guilty: a secret enemy of her community and its pious people, just like the now-famous 'Witch of Newbury'. What was needed was a trick to break the devil's hold on such a woman, loosening her tongue so she could tell them about her evil deeds. Agnes had been imprisoned over the grim Christmas of 1643 in the Tolbooth, 'kept in ward till trial', as the Mid Calder elders noted. They now requested she be brought back to Mid Calder and imprisoned there instead – just while awaiting trial, of course. The presbytery did not object, and Agnes was brought home on 11 February. Then she was 'examined'. The process all looks orderly enough as the Mid Calder elders recorded it, neatly in brown ink, in their session book – but in reality it was not. What was unfolding was a private witch trial, a confused and volatile situation complicated by multiple layers of competing authority and driven forward by self-important agitators: James and William Sandilands and their minister Hew Kennedie.

Once Agnes was back at Mid Calder, these members of the kirk session examined her – we'll come back in a moment to what that meant – and, at last, she confessed she had used magic. On the evidence of 'her own confession and relevant probation' – proving or trial – Hew Kennedie and the elders decided she was guilty of being both 'a charmer and a heinous and notorious witch'. In theory, they were still waiting for the presbytery to get authority from the Privy Council to try her further. In the meantime, though, they seem to have acted themselves – *Why not?* they must have thought. They had enough evidence to satisfy themselves as the kirk's experts on religious crime. So they asked a 'civil judge' – a secular authority from the state courts – to condemn her to death. He did. Agnes was now caught between legal systems, in a web of conflicted, chaotic jurisdictions. She had no court representative to speak for her, no one to ask by whose authority she was being threatened with death. There was nothing she could do to protect herself. But Hew and the elders were canny enough to know they might be in trouble if they went ahead with an execution while they were supposedly waiting for royal authorities to step in. Agnes was therefore not killed immediately. Instead, she continued to be held captive in the Kirk of Calder.[9]

On 28 February, the session members recalled that it might be important to provide regular food and drink for her while she was imprisoned: they recorded the arrangement of funding for that in their sessions book, and later also a payment to its supplier.[10] These simple statements raise some horrifying questions, of course. We can only imagine what Agnes had been – or not been – eating and drinking before that, and how infrequently. In addition to providing subsistence for her, a guard named Andrew Ferguson was also appointed to watch her, and the kirk session agreed he was to be paid eight shillings a day, with the day specified as lasting twenty-four hours – one assumes he must have had assistance. So Agnes was to be watched full-time, through the night as well as during daylight hours. What was going on at Mid Calder? What was her guard looking for? Why, too, had a call been put out for volunteers to guard and watch more suspected witches at South Leith, fourteen miles east and a little north of Edinburgh? That order was recorded in the sessions book there. And why had Agnes Bishop suddenly confessed when brought back to her hometown from the Linlithgow Tolbooth?[11]

We can guess why, because in January 1644 another woman was also accused of witchcraft at Mid Calder, and she has left us a record of what happened to her there. Margaret Thomsone was the wife of Archibald Gray of Calder Muir. As well as being suspected at Mid Calder, she was also accused before the South Leith kirk session. If this was the same woman, apparently Margaret was feared across a wide area of eastern Scotland. Like Agnes Bishop, she had a reputation as a charmer, and hers was extensive enough that people across several of the districts surrounding Edinburgh knew of her work and had been using her services for many years. Eighteen years ago, said Margaret Williamston of Mid Calder, she'd called in Margaret Thomsone to examine her sick cow. That day in 1626, the charmer had inspected the animal, assessing symptoms and asking questions. Like a modern vet, she might have had a list of diagnostic queries: Was the cow eating well? Was she yielding ample milk, or was there less than usual? Did the milk smell odd or carry traces of blood? Was the cow listless or skittish? Had she kicked over the milk bucket, lowed all night or barged her owner off her feet? Any of these things could indicate natural disease, such as mastitis that might be treated with herb poultices. But Margaret Thomsone suspected this cow's disease was unnatural in its origin, and she told the worried farmer that her cow was 'forespoken'. This meant she thought the cow was bewitched, by someone who had a grudge against Margaret Williamston and her farm.

Luckily, Margaret Thomsone had a solution. If the farmer would ask her to help and 'for God's sake charm the cow', then she would be able to undo the malicious spell, with God's blessing. And so she did, Margaret Williamston reported. But then Margaret Williamston herself immediately fell ill: the cow was cured but her owner was sick instead. Perhaps she began to worry: had she done the right thing in calling in a magical veterinary consultant? What if, although she claimed to be acting in God's name, the charmer had wickedly transferred the cow's illness to her keeper? What if she were not a harmless healer but a malevolent witch? That was the sort of thought that could get charmers into trouble by making clients suspicious and sometimes keen to discuss the matter with ministers and elders. In fact, Margaret Williamston did nothing about her concerns for a very long time. Perhaps she really believed the charmer's actions were behind her own disease – and if so, this fear festered for eighteen years before she gave it voice – or perhaps she didn't. But now, in 1644, with rumours of witchcraft flying about and the trial and remand of Agnes Bishop proceeding slowly at Mid Calder, she and others were called to give evidence about Margaret Thomsone's past. Margaret Williamston made a formal statement about what had happened and waited for the kirk to sort the matter out. The witch hunt was beginning to spread.[12]

Another Mid Calder accuser who came forward was young John Forrest. His worries about Margaret Thomsone were more recent, although apparently also reluctantly expressed. About a year ago, he had fallen ill and Margaret Thomsone had come to him – uninvited, he said, exculpating himself from any criticism – to offer help. She told John she'd heard about his illness and that she had a son who suffered from the same disease. Margaret explained that she'd walked to Edinburgh to get help for her son from another woman more skilled than herself. This Edinburgh woman had given Margaret a drink to administer to her son, which had worked, curing him. Now Margaret offered this same drink to John Forrest, coming to visit him each morning for several days to dose him with the liquid. On top of this medical treatment, she also had a more obviously magical remedy for him to try. It meant sacrificing his belt, she explained, but it would pay back dividends in good health, and so John agreed to her plan. To him it must have made sense: belts encircled the body and so, in magical terms, might represent a person's self or self-protection. What Margaret did next, then, might have alarmed him: she took his belt and snipped it into nine pieces, a magical number of three times three. Then she gathered up the nine severed sections and carried them out of John's house, explaining that she would bury them in several different places. These locations would be along a boundary between two noblemen's lands, she told him, a place of magical power. Fascinated, John went with her to watch.

Charmer and patient tramped together over the pastures and heaths to the places Margaret had chosen for her healing rite. The areas around Calder and Leith, the villages and suburbs around Edinburgh, would have been criss-crossed by boundaries dividing different people's landholdings from each other. There were boundaries between open grassland and private houses' gardens, between adjacent fields and common lands, between estates at

Pumpherston, Hilderston, Linhouse and Broadshaw. Margaret could have chosen any of these. Perhaps the boundary she picked was indicated by a fence, ditch or wall, but perhaps it was also marked by older landscape features. Many boundaries incorporated ancient earthworks or standing stones, places that stood out enough to be named in legal documents stating that the lands of such-and-such a lord extended as far as the old stones on the east and the long mound on the south. Sometimes the boundary marker was a very old tree or a clutter of fallen slabs that had once been a chamber tomb. These were places where people thought ancient pagan religions had been observed and maybe now, they imagined, fairies, spirits and demons lurked. The sites' ancient spiritual energy made them seem powerful.

Once she reached the boundary between the two noblemen's lands, Margaret Thomsone knelt down and scraped at the earth with a tool and her hands until she had dug several shallow holes. Into these she laid the pieces of John's belt, and as she did, she chanted a charm to the belt: 'God let the boy never take that disease again until I take thee up again'. Then she earthed over each piece of the belt and moved onto the next one. Once she had buried all the lengths to her satisfaction, Margaret instructed John on his follow-up treatment. He was to go to her fellow charmer in Edinburgh himself, she said, and there he could buy more of the drink Margaret had given him. He would need to keep taking this medicine to heal himself. Perhaps it healed him or perhaps it didn't – John didn't tell the kirk session, so we don't know. Perhaps he just got scared by Margaret's magic: after all, the holes she had dug were awfully like graves and the boundary seemed like a haunted place. Had he done right in seeking a cure there? Did Margaret mean him harm? Anxious stories like John Forrest's were circulating freely in Mid Calder and South Leith by spring 1644, and they continued to spill out into the autumn of that year.[13]

On 7 March, the South Leith kirk session decided to be proactive: they put out a general call for further evidence against Margaret Thomsone. In the kirk on Sunday, an announcement was made that 'if any person hath any deposition to give in against Margaret Thomsone, who is apprehended for a witch, that they come judicially before the bailies and ministers in the Tolbooth [South Leith's town hall] and depone' – record a deposition, an accusation – against Margaret.[14] Meanwhile, Margaret was held in custody at Mid Calder, along with Agnes Bishop. She would now be part of the experimental examination under guard that Hew Kennedie and his elders had arranged. Perhaps she shared her cell with Agnes, or perhaps the women were rotated in and out of the vestry space; we don't know. We *do* know what happened to Margaret inside Mid Calder kirk vestry, however – and it sheds light on what may well have happened to Agnes there too. It likely explains why Agnes confessed to witchcraft shortly after she was taken from Linlithgow Tolbooth and sent to Mid Calder at Hew Kennedie's request.

In Mid Calder's vestry, among the books, robes and the physical props that helped the minister perform Holy Communion, Margaret Thomsone tells us in her legal deposition that she was stripped naked. In the room where Hew Kennedie and his fellow godly men dressed for their public appearances, she was ripped out of her clothes. After the humiliating undressing, she was redressed in a kirk gown made of sackcloth – likely the same type of penance garment used to shame Jean Anderson back in September of the previous year. Shivering in this scratchy, dirty shift, Margaret was forced onto one of the stools used by the congregation when they sat to hear sermons. There she stood intermittently for twenty-six days and nights (let's just repeat that: *twenty-six days and nights*) with 'men daily and nightly attending upon her'. These were men like Andrew Ferguson, the guard, who would force her to remain on the stool, awake and standing up. She was not given 'any leave [permission] to sit or lie down' and was 'ordain [ordered] to be held waking all that space [for the length of twenty-six days and nights]'. Such treatment is today classed as torture and prohibited under international law.[15]

During this hideous time, Margaret was questioned by Hew Kennedie and the two interested members of the Sandilands family, the baillie James Sandilands and the elder and Tutor of Torphichen William Sandilands. It is possible that she was also tested by a witch pricker for a numb demonic mark, though there is no definite record of this. However, we do know that both Sandilands men physically attacked her during their interrogations. James Sandilands hit her 'with a staff ... when she fell for [because of] weariness, to compel her to stand up'. Hew Kennedie struck her with his 'wand' – not a magical pointer, but a long stick carried as a sign of office by religious officials – and then 'because the same was not of great force he did strike her with a rung', a heavy cudgel. He'd failed to motivate her with his thin cane, so he had gone to find something more hurtful so that he could beat her with that. And, of course, during her sleep-deprived balancing on the stool, Margaret said that she 'did sundry times stumble and fall down to the ground, where she did break her face and head', as well as being beaten and told to stand up. Bloodied and bruised, she was wretched and panic-stricken, fearing she was 'in peril of her life by dinning [knocking] out of her brains by falling so oft'.[16] No wonder Agnes Bishop had confessed to witchcraft under this type of pressure. Astonishingly, however, Margaret Thomsone refused to do so: bravely, she somehow held out against her torturers.

As Margaret struggled to survive her ordeal, at South Leith another suspect was now being held: Margaret or Marion Ramsay, whose name varies in the records. When she was questioned in late

March, she was likely subjected to similar abuse. She, however, not only confessed, but also named other people as witches. On 4 April, the kirk session ordered these new suspects be arrested. Hearing of the additional cases, the presbytery at Linlithgow recorded its alarm at its meeting in May 1644, worrying not (as it should have done) about the torture being practised in its name, but that the use of charming appeared to be very 'frequent within our Presbytery'. The court's members resolved to seek advice from the church's synod – a further superior court of the Lothian kirk – about how to deal with this. Their witch hunt was gathering pace, just as Hew Kennedie had hoped.[17]

In June, Margaret/Marion Ramsay cannily escaped from the prison at South Leith and fled. She was right to run away. Although the records are silent about what had happened to the remaining suspects, by 18 July at least one woman had been burned as a witch. At Mid Calder, Jonet Bruce – about whom we know nothing beyond her name and death – had been killed and on the 18th her widower, David Aikman, paid about eighty marks or merks, several hundred pounds in today's money, to the kirk session to clear her debts. These included charges for her imprisonment, 'examination' and trial: Jonet's widower had to pay for her torture. Part of their fine was also spent on 'the remnant of the witches' who'd been imprisoned with her. Sadly, by 17 November, Agnes Bishop was not among them: she had been executed, a fact recorded in passing by her kirk's elders. In their session book, Agnes was described as a 'confessing and suffering witch': 'suffering' was a specific legal term meaning that she had suffered death for her crime. Qualms about the legality of her killing had been set aside, and Agnes lost the fight she'd been conducting since 1618 to defend her magical activities from suspicion and save her life.[18]

Meanwhile, the hunt was continuing to spread. At Lanark,

twenty miles southwest of Mid Calder in Lanarkshire, two women from the nearby village of Carnwath were called before the presbytery on 1 August. One of them, Katherine Shaw, had been named by some of the growing number of detainees at Mid Calder. From there, Hew Kennedie wrote to the minister at Carnwath, to give details of these accusations and extend his witch hunt further. Helen Stewart, he said, whom he'd been interrogating at Mid Calder, had named Katherine Shaw as a witch. Helen was questioned again. She confessed that she and Katherine had been present together 'at their solemn meetings with the devil': now it was not just attacks on neighbours that were being alleged, and confirmed by suspects, but a Satanic conspiracy involving multiple witches. By the last week of August, Katherine had confessed that she 'had sundry times [had] conference with the devil, had renounced her baptism for him, had received a mark from him'. Katherine's fellow villager Margaret Reid also confessed. She was another user of charms, some of which she described during her confession. Margaret was modestly wealthy – enough to be able to post bail, raised by her son Robert Russell, to guarantee her appearance in court and allow her to be released from prison to await trial once that had been agreed by the Privy Council. Two other women were also accused and confessed: Margaret Watson and Jean Lachlan.[19]

By late summer 1644, several of the accused women across Lothian and Lanarkshire were fighting back using whatever resources and legal processes were available to them. One of them was Margaret Thomsone, who still refused to confess. After months of detention and abuse, Margaret had still not been tried, so in August she and her husband Archibald Gray sent a letter of complaint to the Privy Council, accusing Hew Kennedie, James and William Sandilands of illegal torture and assault. In October, Margaret and Archibald produced seven witnesses to confirm her story of sleep deprivation and injury at the Kirk of Calder. At least five men had been involved in abusing her, and one of them was Baillie James Sandilands. When he was questioned about what he'd done, James retorted that he had only had custody of Margaret for two nights and 'he knows not how long she was kept that way'. Pressed, however, he admitted that 'he believes it was above fourteen days' – a severe underestimate. The other men questioned about their treatment of Margaret Thomsone contradicted his half-truth: they thought twenty to twenty-six days a more realistic reckoning of the time she had been held, subjected to questions, insults and beatings. That was what she had claimed herself, and it was clearly true.

Other women also resisted the churchmen's bullying and refused to be silenced. Isobel Ewart, wife of the wealthy laird William Douglas of Pumpherston (one and a half miles north of Mid Calder), shouted at the members of Mid Calder kirk session in public, 'scolding and railing' at them in what they called 'opprobrious and scandalous speeches'. Minister Kennedie, his baillie and elders had 'done many things behind souls' backs that he durst not do before their face', Isobel alleged, and she also made accusations that the kirk session's members were profiting from the witch hunt. They had tortured suspected witches, Isobel rightly stated, 'and beaten them with rungs, of purpose to extort of them the branding of honest women in the parish with witchcraft', which meant 'putting innocent women to death'. This was brave, dangerous stuff for Isobel to say, even as a well-off gentlewoman. But she and her husband, William, were formidable opponents.

William was a cousin of the Sandilands family, an early Scottish colonist in northern Ireland. He had twice assaulted an enemy with a cudgel in 1616. In addition to her bold attack on the witch hunters, Isobel was the survivor of two family feuds, against her birth family and her husband's, an heiress in her own right and the mother of at least nine children. The Mid Calder session and the Linlithgow presbytery, meeting to hear her accusations, were further told she had said four hundred marks had been taken from suspects and their families in charges for imprisonment and trial, including the hundred marks paid by David Aikman to the men who had tortured and killed his wife, Jonet Bruce. That was a huge sum, around £700 today, and its current location was worthy of investigation. But, of course, the session and presbytery members retorted that such monies had been given 'voluntarily' and the session subsequently censured Isobel Ewart, ignoring her perfectly correct claims.[20]

Margaret Thomsone was more successful in holding her torturers to account. On 9 October, she had Hew Kennedie and William Sandilands summoned to the Privy Council, as well as all the men who had given evidence of abusing her or observing her during her detention. By 20 November, the Privy Council had ordered that she be freed. The Mid Calder authorities, they judged, had acted unlawfully in holding and torturing Margaret without a warrant, rushing to trial without authorisation because they thought they could get away with it. Astonishingly, however, the Mid Calder minister and Torphichen Tutor tried to defy the royal Council. Claiming their own authority over religious matters in the same way they'd done with the execution of Agnes Bishop, they asked the Linlithgow presbytery for advice about Margaret Thomsone and received, in part, the answer they'd hoped for. 'The brethren think it most expedient that she be kept still in prison', the presbytery replied. But, realising the danger of open conflict with royal advisors, they hedged their bets: the presbytery members said they would make the request to the Privy Councillors that they be allowed to keep Margaret in the vestry, but in the meantime demurred that it would be best if she were freed.[21]

Sulkily, the Calder authorities desisted from watching and beating Margaret and let her out, but they did not free her. Instead, they put her in the stocks – a frame that held the legs of offenders in wooden restraints. Such humiliation could be employed as pre-trial detention or as a punishment the kirk was authorised to use for offences within its jurisdiction, such as drunkenness or Sabbath-breaking. But witchcraft was not one of these. Margaret petitioned the Privy Council again, pleading for their help. She was being 'kept in great misery', she said, 'separate from all company and worldly comfort', and she could 'see no end to her misery but lawful trial'. Even a properly authorised witch trial, she had come to think, would be better than this endless extra-legal torture. The Council, angered by the churchmen's defiance of royal authority, ordered once again that Margaret be freed – and this time the penalty for non-compliance would be five hundred marks. She was likely released – we can only hope, as no record was made. Nevertheless, new accusations of witchcraft continued to be made against her. On 17 November, Mid Calder kirk session was told that not only Agnes Bishop but two further accused women, Agnes Vassie and Marion Gibson, had said in their confessions that Margaret Thomsone had been with them when they attended witch meetings. However, the document in which their words were recorded also states that Agnes Vassie and Marion Gibson had already been executed, so no one could ask them what they had or had not said, or why.

So there she is, my namesake, the Marion Gibson of 1644 – accused, tried with dubious legality, briefly named on a few pieces of paper, and killed because she had been judged to be a witch. Blink and you'd miss her. This is so often the fate of accused witches in history, barely any better remembered than the nameless woman who became the 'Witch of Newbury'. Such suspects as Marion Gibson are hardly recorded at all, and when they are, it is often as bit players in somebody else's drama. Unsurprisingly, therefore, we know very little about Marion's life. Mid Calder's kirk records tell us that she was married to John Mailling or Malling on 1 August 1624 – the only event between 4 July and 24 August to be recorded in the then-quiet Mid Calder parish. Marion seems to have had a sister or other relative, Isabel Gibson, who was married to Robert Forrest in 1625 and who was also accused of witchcraft in 1644. Like Marion, Isabel is only mentioned briefly in the records, and again only insofar as she related to her accusers; in April 1645, a payment of nine pounds, ten shillings and fourpence was recorded to one of the men for his work keeping Isabel in prison for three months, paid by Mid Calder kirk session.[22] Probably Marion and Isabel were among the suspects imprisoned and tortured in the Kirk of Calder vestry along with Agnes, Margaret and some of the other victims of the Lothian and Lanarkshire witch hunts.

Before the hunt was over, many more women were accused – at South Leith, Lanark, Carnwath, Queensferry, Livingston, towns and villages across central and southeast Scotland and beyond – and some trial commissions were granted by the Privy Council, meaning that the imprisonment, torture, trial and execution of witchcraft suspects became legal in these cases. At South Leith, Lilias Barrie was accused and imprisoned for thirty-six weeks without trial, until her son-in-law and daughter petitioned for her release. At Lanark, it was Mailie Patersone and Jonet Lockie. Helen Stewart and Katherine Shaw were burned, with Privy Council approval. By the end of May 1645, this particular outbreak of witchcraft trials seems to have ended, but they were large in scale, killed many innocent women and left a terrible scar across the small communities that surrounded Edinburgh.[23] Yet they are only partially documented. We do know, however, that young Hew Kennedie went on to live a long and prosperous life.

He married into the family of the Lords Torphichen and became Moderator of the Church of Scotland, the national kirk's top official. He died in April 1692, just as the Salem witch trials were getting started three thousand miles away, a legacy of the British witch hunt that Hew had helped to begin. Hew was one of the first witchfinders of the 1640s, but soon he would be joined by English counterparts, four hundred miles south in Essex. There, building on the growing forebodings about witchcraft in 1643 and 1644 across Britain, a series of comparatively well-documented and very extensive witch trials began in 1645.

PART 3

Finding a Fantasy: Essex

CHAPTER 4

The Greatest Enemy

Anne and Rebecca West of Lawford, Essex, 1645

It's a hot summer and overdressed sheep loll in their fleeces under hawthorn hedges. I'm on my way to Lawford church on the Essex coast. It stands on a steep, rounded hill, smoothed by streams feeding the River Stour. Along the path to the church, which threads through a housing estate and then fields, the wooden stiles are wobbly. Giant fallen trees rot like Henry Moore sculptures among brambly thickets and nettles. Nearly four hundred years ago, this unassuming village was the site of events that saw personal tragedy and religious theory combine, turning neighbourly frictions into suspicions of a Satanic cult that strongly echoed the accusations made the year before in Scotland. At Lawford, however, these suspicions went further: they sparked a mass witch hunt that would spread across eastern and central England over the next two years.

When I reach the flint and brick church and open the door of its white-painted wooden porch, cool air rushes out: a blast from the past. Inside the church, I imagine the villagers of the 1640s ranked in front of their minister, stilled and tensed by his version of God's word. Today, the cream walls and plain glass windows cast a chilly light, despite the summer heat. I suspect the minister, John Edes, was a chilly man. He was certainly a puritanical reformer, raging against the comfort and colour of medieval Catholicism, against sin and the devil. His church dates from the fourteenth century and would originally have been decorated with brightly coloured glass and carved wood – but by Edes's time, by the 1640s, that was all gone, ripped out in fundamentalist rage. So much is gone, but where can I find the heart of the old village if not here? The church sits proud and lonely on its hill, but there are cottages down the lane. I follow a narrow path at a wood's edge and emerge onto a fast road. Here are the oldest homes in Lawford, built beside the ancient track to Manningtree. A long-closed pub, a row of thatch and slate, a wellspring bubbling water. A corner plot that could have held a wheelwright's shop.

Now it's 1645, the February of an icy winter: snow sifts from grey skies, larders run low, hacking coughs spread from neighbour to neighbour, and the Lawford wheelwright, Thomas Hart, is a worried man. As he labours by his furnace, hammering iron strips onto wheel rims, chiselling wooden hubs and spokes, Thomas broods on the threats to his family and livelihood. Some of his anxiety is focused on his wife, Prudence, five months pregnant, and his children. In the last few years, at least one of his young sons has died. Perhaps it was Nathaniel, baptised in 1632, or Daniel, baptised in 1635, or another son, John, who is mentioned in a later news report, but the parish register of Lawford is poorly kept by John Edes and his clerks. It's full of gaps where its children's short lives ought to be remembered. On top of his grief, some of Thomas's present fretting concerns his animals and crops: the fine white pigs he rears for pork, bacon and blood pudding, and the allotment garden he rents in the village. But much of his anxiety is turned outward in hatred of his neighbour Anne West, a widow known as 'the beldam West' because of her advanced age – beldam means 'good old woman' or 'grandma'. Thomas does not believe Anne West is a good old woman, however. He's convinced she's a witch.[1]

Thomas's suspicions about Anne stretch back at least to March 1641, when his prize sow died. She was worth ten shillings, in her own right and as the mother of piglets. Thomas was furious, because he believed Anne West had killed the sow by witchcraft. He reported his suspicions to his local magistrate, the magnificently named Sir Harbottle Grimston. Anne was arrested, taken to Colchester Castle, imprisoned and tried. But, much to Thomas's disgust, the twelve-man jury acquitted her.

It seemed unfair: Anne had served jail time before for a minor witchcraft offence and another conviction would have rid Lawford of her forever. The 1604 Witchcraft Act mandated that for a second offence, a convicted witch should be hanged. What was the jury thinking? Harbottle Grimston agreed and, as a respected public official – a Justice of the Peace in his seventies – his word carried more weight than Thomas's. At his request, Anne was re-imprisoned to await further charges, on the pretext that during her trial her neighbours said she'd threatened 'to fire some of the houses' in Lawford as payback if she survived. Thomas feared his property would be the first to burn. He'd travelled all the way from Lawford to Colchester for the trial, almost nine miles, paying his own bills, and risking much. Now it looked like he'd achieved nothing more than inviting revenge. Although Anne remained in jail for a while, nothing further was proven about the arson threats and she came home to Lawford. Thomas feared that, if she didn't burn down his house, she intended to bewitch him, his wife and children just as she'd killed their sow. Witchcraft was harder to fight than fire.[2]

Thomas Hart was not alone in his suspicions of Anne; several other Lawford villagers had long harboured concerns about her, without being able to make their suspicions stick. The influential landowner John Cutler thought she'd bewitched his son John, who had died suddenly, as far back as the late 1620s. In May 1643, George Francis, son of the wealthy Presbyterian farmer George Francis and heir of an old Lawford family, had also died aged twenty-three. Both had been buried close by the village's little hilltop church, St Mary's, overlooking the River Stour. Some of the talk at the funerals might have been about how both the boys' fathers had fallen out with Anne West over the years. Then, in October 1643, the sailor Thomas Turner drowned when his hoy – a sailing barge – foundered at sea off the Essex coast. Thomas's brother George attributed the shipwreck to witches, who were thought to be able to cause violent storms or unexpected winds that blew up out of nowhere and capsized perfectly seaworthy ships. Eventually he too blamed Anne West for his brother's death.[3] By the mid-1640s, people in Lawford and beyond had begun to compare notes; gossip was spreading, building towards a formal accusation in which Anne would be denounced (again) to a magistrate by multiple neighbours.

It was easy for suspicions to be shared from family to family. Lawford was a tiny village in the seventeenth century, where neighbours chatted regularly after church and in parish meetings. Anne West's supposed targets Thomas Hart and George Francis had sat together on the jury of the Lawford Hall manor court since the 1620s, hobnobbing with Manningtree-based farmers like Richard Edwards, who also farmed land in Lawford. Later, that connection would play a part in spreading the witchcraft accusations further afield. Lawford's rector, John Edes, sat on the manor court jury too because he was a tenant of manorial lands. The manor's jurymen worked together to make legal decisions about disputed land rights and to report dangerous bridges, broken floodgates and neighbours who did not unclog their ditches. Before and after the court met, they would have shared stories, including ones about Anne West. Her latest supposed victim, Thomas Hart, was among the most reliable tenants: one of the select few trusted to witness land transactions on behalf of the manor's bailiff – a senior estate manager – when the bailiff was busy elsewhere. Thomas probably couldn't write (we don't have his signature on any documents), but his word was good and he had a reputation as a sensible, honest neighbour. In the Lawford Hall manor records, we see him working closely with fellow witch accusers George Francis and John Edes over the decades leading up to 1645. When their neighbour Robert Adams died in 1630, these three men handled the transfer of his lands to his wife Katherine. In 1631, Thomas and George did the same neighbourly work for the family of the late Thomas Manning. And so on down the years. As they comforted widows, interviewed witnesses to wills and processed the necessary paperwork, imagine what tales of trouble they might have shared.[4]

John Edes was a particularly powerful figure, a big fish in a small pond with influence in both the religious and business communities. Educated at St John's College, Cambridge, as rector of Lawford he led villagers in prayer at St Mary's, christened, married and buried parishioners, and worked with senior villagers – men who became elders as the English state church moved towards and into Presbyterianism – on shaping doctrine and rites. He owned a mill on Lawford's Sherborne stream, charging fees to all the local people who ground their corn into flour there. John's village was no more than a cluster of cottages on the ancient highway Wignall Street, which led west from the growing port of Manningtree on the coast to Essex's county capital, Colchester, but his rectory was an important landmark and meeting place. He'd been there since 1615 and knew everyone, and he had a large family, active in all areas of local life. In 1645, he was living with his wife Thomasine, whom he'd married in 1616 when he was twenty-seven, and with whom he'd had many children: Sarah (born 1618), John (1620), Jemimah (1622), Hannah (1624), Martha (1627), Henry (1628) and Thomas (1631). Sarah and John had both married Lawford spouses: William Buckingham in 1640 and Elizabeth Gladwin in 1644. So if someone in Lawford had a problem with witchcraft, John Edes was bound to hear of it almost at once.[5]

In fact, the witch attack that changed Lawford forever probably happened before his eyes: certainly it happened in Lawford church. One Sunday in February, Thomas Hart's forebodings tragically came true. Thomas and his wife Prudence, dressed in their cleanest linens and thickest coats, walked from their cottage along the wooded footpath to St Mary's to hear the Sabbath sermon. Quietly, they sat in the white light, their feet chilled by the stone-slabbed floor. Perhaps they remembered how St Mary's was once illuminated by colourful glass: the new glazing was intended to cast a clearer light, focusing pure, compliant thoughts. The religious ideal of Lawford parishioners was recorded in their church court book in 1613: that worshippers attend St Mary's 'orderly and dutifully . . . as by law they are bound'. Orderly and dutifully, Thomas and Prudence sat silent during the sermon, joining their friends at the Communion table to eat the bread and drink the wine that represented Christ's love. But as the service droned its customary rhythm, Prudence's belly cramped. The spasm repeated and she knew she must leave. The minister – John Edes, if he was preaching that Sunday, or perhaps a visiting preacher – might have paused in his sermon. If it was John, as the father of seven children he would have known that pregnant women might suddenly feel pain. Women were frail, prone to sickness – and sometimes to sin. Prudence struggled to her feet. Bleeding, she was helped through the neat wooden porch but collapsed on the grass among the gravestones or in the lane outside the church gate. There, she lost her baby. Her friends walked her home in sober shock. It was a dreadfully public bereavement.[6]

Was Anne West in St Mary's church that day? Legally, she ought to have been, and probably she was. Indeed, she might have chosen to be there regardless of her legal duty. Anne was an outwardly pious woman, fond of prayer and sermons, despite her reputation for witchcraft and her supposed threats of arson – and perhaps she really was godly, even if she had a reputation for quarrelling. The two weren't mutually exclusive: anxious neighbours judged each other's morality or fell out over points of theology just as often as they fought over land, work or relationships. So, orderly and dutifully, Anne would have often taken Communion with the Harts, knelt beside them with their voices mingling in prayer. But were there cold stares between the families that Sunday, in an atmosphere of unchristian hate? It seems likely, because in the days after Prudence Hart's miscarriage, Anne's daughter Rebecca West candidly described Prudence as her 'greatest enemy'. That stark phrase suggests a long-held grudge. Rebecca, baptised on 11 February 1615, was around thirty, and she remembered Thomas Hart's 1641 prosecution of her mother as well as, possibly, previous clashes over the preceding decades. She had no reason to love Thomas or his wife, and she had ample evidence they hated her mother.

It was this feeling of mutual enmity that prompted Thomas and Prudence to blame Anne and Rebecca West for the loss of their baby. After its untimely death, things grew even worse for the bereaved parents: Prudence fell ill with burning pains in her right side. Perhaps it was a stroke, made more likely by the thickened blood and higher pressure of pregnancy; perhaps it was a post-natal complication or the psychological impact of grief. But Prudence did not know of any medical cause; she suffered in confusion and sadness. She might have wondered if she had done something wrong and was being punished for sinning, but a more plausible explanation – to her – was that Anne West had cursed her and her husband. At last, seeking guidance, Prudence spoke to Rector John Edes and confided her fears: if she thought the Wests had bewitched her and her lost child, what should she do? John would have advised her to go to her local magistrate; Justices of the Peace made themselves available regularly at home or in public places to hear such complaints. So, on 23 April 1645, Prudence went to Harbottle Grimston, who was holding court that day with his fellow magistrate Sir Thomas Bowes, to accuse both Anne and Rebecca West of bewitching her body and killing her unborn child.

As Prudence's suffering delayed her accusation, however, events had moved forward without her. People had talked, and fear had spread down Wignall Street into nearby Manningtree. By late April, Prudence was joining a chorus of other complainants – people who had begun making witchcraft accusations in earnest a month before. As part of these stories, Anne and Rebecca West's names had already come up – probably in relation to Prudence Hart's loss and definitely in relation to other suspected crimes. Because of Anne's previous jail time, the Wests had been regarded as nightmare neighbours for years, and now all their community's fears about them came spilling out. The people of Manningtree knew the Wests' reputations just as well as the people of Lawford, a mile and a half away. How fearfully they must have observed Anne and Rebecca's visits to their town's markets, shops and wharves! By the time Prudence was well enough to speak to the district's magistrates in April, she and her husband Thomas were pushing at an open door. What relief they must have felt; in contrast with their attempt to prosecute Anne in 1641, now they had a groundswell of opinion on their side.

On 21 March – a full month before Prudence Hart told her story of miscarriage to Bowes and Grimston – Rebecca West had been questioned by the magistrates. What she told the two men was not, however, all about ill-wishing babies. Instead, partly prompted by a conversation she'd already had with minister John Edes, she confessed to an astonishing conspiracy. Rebecca had told Rector Edes and now repeated to the magistrates how, around the time of Prudence's tragic miscarriage, she had met with her mother Anne West, Anne's friend Bess Clarke and three other local women – Elizabeth Goodwin, Anne Leech and her daughter Helen Clark – in Bess's home at Manningtree. Rebecca and Anne West had walked over to the town from Lawford, past Dale Hall Farm, skirting the marshy ground at Causeway End, tramping up Old Chapel or Wormwood Hill, now South Street, to Bess's cottage. When they arrived, Rebecca had been amazed to see strange animals skipping about among the assembled women. They were familiar spirits, she was told, little devils in the shapes of animals. Witches were said to keep them because the creatures could do magical harm to their enemies.[7]

This was alarming enough, but the magistrates were even more excited by Rebecca's next claim. She, her mother Anne and the others had 'spent some time in praying unto their familiars', she explained. Their spirit animals were a demonic alternative to God, to be prayed to and worshipped. Then some of the women 'read in a book', Rebecca said, which belonged to Bess Clarke. Perhaps it was some sort of alternative Bible or prayer book, speculated the magistrates. Rebecca could not read, and so she could not tell them more. But to Grimston and Bowes, her story seemed clear evidence of a Satanic cult. Having petitioned their false god, the witches then ordered their spirits to do damage. Anne Leech wanted to lame a cow. Bess Clarke wanted gentleman farmer Richard Edwards to fall from his horse. Elizabeth

Goodwin wanted to kill a horse belonging to shopkeeper Robert Taylor. Helen Clark wanted to kill pigs. And Rebecca's story of what her mother Anne West requested from her familiar rang true to Grimston and Bowes when they heard the Harts' tragic tale. During her questioning on 21 March, Rebecca had admitted that Anne asked the spirits 'that she might be freed from all her enemies and have no trouble', but she also wanted to 'be revenged on Prudence, the wife of Thomas Hart'.[8] All Prudence had to do when she met the magistrates was confirm the outcome: her bitter bereavement. Everything came together for Grimston and Bowes: Anne and Rebecca West had killed the Harts' baby and their attack was – astoundingly – motivated by an anti-Christian witch religion.

Rebecca's self-incriminating accusation of her mother Anne allowed charges to be drawn up against them both for the Assize court, stating who had bewitched whom, when and why. Bess Clarke was arrested too, on the same day that Rebecca levelled her accusations against her, and a few days later she confirmed Rebecca's claims and her charges against Anne West.

Legally speaking, it all seemed sound: witches were attacking their neighbours in Lawford and Manningtree and the harm they'd done could confidently be demonstrated to a jury. But as well as doing their judicial job as magistrates, forwarding accusations of harmful magic to the Assizes, Harbottle Grimston and Thomas Bowes had other, spiritual interests. Both were Presbyterian-leaning, broadly puritanical men who by 1648 would be elders in their local churches: they would have been curious about the power behind witchcraft in the way that godly people usually were: people like the Earl of Essex, the Sandilands family and Hew Kennedie. Knowing the wiles of the devil, such reformers thought, helped Christians to avoid them and to better understand God's plan. For pious people like these, petty human enmities were secondary to the cosmic conflict of human versus devil. The devil was the greatest enemy of humankind, a far greater foe than any mere mortal. Prudence and Thomas Hart's suffering at the hands of the Wests was important, but more significant was the witch religion that had enabled it and the enemy agents who were the soldiers of that Satanic anti-church.

So Lawford's rector, John Edes, and the magistrates Grimston and Bowes met on 29 March to talk over the stories told by Thomas and Prudence Hart, George Francis and the other accusers, and to share what Rebecca West had said about the witches' cult. She had told them all a similar story about a forbidden prayer meeting and demonic animals, but she had also told John Edes the backstory to her witchcraft career – in response to his questions and perhaps his threats. There's no evidence that John beat Rebecca, but he might have applied other kinds of pressure, as we'll discover shortly. And even if he merely asked Rebecca questions, the rector would have been an authoritative, persuasive speaker: all Rebecca would have had to do was confirm his suspicions. She was a poor, illiterate young woman; probably a servant, a job that was often the only choice for the children of widows like Anne West. We know she'd lived away from home at Rivenhall in the past, perhaps as a maid or nurse. How could this lowly person resist the suggestions put to her by a learned, wealthy, older man? So Rebecca had told John what he wanted to hear. And he was happy to share it with Grimston and Bowes.

Rebecca's life as a witch had begun seven years before, in around 1638, when the devil had appeared to her in a variety of shapes, including on one occasion 'a proper young man'. 'Proper' meant pleasing or handsome. This young man wanted to have 'familiarity' with her – a term that could mean anything from acquaintance to sex – and she told John she had agreed, because she hoped the devil could improve her life. Like her widowed mother Anne, Rebecca must have been a rather lonely, vulnerable person. She was unmarried, had hardly any money and no access to education nor any experience of the world beyond the most functional travel to and from employment. There would have been little lively entertainment in her community, which had discontinued many of the sports, plays and feasts common a hundred years earlier, before religious reformers took over society. Being a woman ruled out most professional work beyond being a servant: in that role, all Rebecca had to look forward to was cooking, washing, milking the cows of wealthy employers, plucking their chickens, brushing their clothes or scrubbing their floors. Since Rebecca was still single, she had no husband to give her a defined social status or the comfort of love and domesticity in a home of her own. It's likely no one paid her kindly attention or granted her any respect. All this made her a perfect target for the devil to recruit – at least in the eyes of her accusers. And it made her likely to confess to fantasies of intimacy, friendship and sex with demon lovers: ideas that haunted the folktales she would have known, the ones about tempting devils, fairies and elves that carried off human women, showering them with fine clothes, gold coins, rings, ribbons, love and pretty things. If those were the stories ministers and magistrates insistently demanded, it was not surprising that she would submit and tell them.

For Rebecca, these stories might have appeared harmless: the prompted, penitent recital of a well-known genre woven with elements of a pleasing daydream. But for men like Edes, Grimston and Bowes, they incarnated a gnawing fear. What if Satan could provide people like Rebecca with the decent life their church and state had failed to offer her? Lurking behind the paranoia of the Parliamentarians who executed the Newbury 'witch', the brutality of Hew Kennedie and his men at Mid Calder, and now the fears at Lawford, was the recognition that many women, particularly poor ones, led lives that were wretched, powerless and frustrating. Why, the educated, comfortable, potent men of their society wondered in the small hours of sleepless nights, shouldn't they become envious and vengeful? They would have every right. And Rebecca accepted these men's estimate of her life: yes, she did feel angry, marginalised and hard done by. Yes, she'd like something better.

So, under John Edes's pressure, she readily imagined the devil might have tempted her and she might have agreed to be his friend. Rebecca explained to John Edes that she'd acquiesced to the devil's demand because he'd promised she could 'rely upon him'. Then, she said, she'd wished evil to Thomas Hart, asking Satan to 'avenge her on the said Hart by killing his son'. The little boy – Nathaniel, John or Daniel – was just a few years old, and he died soon after. Of course, there was a price to pay: in her account of their conversation, Satan told Rebecca she must 'deny God'. That meant rejecting his power and love, and the baptism that had inducted her into the Christian faith. She would turn away from the church on Lawford's hill, its tower pointing the way to heaven. She would lose her soul and her hope of an eternal afterlife. But what did she have to lose right now, here on earth? Not much. And everyone seemed to know it.

As the culmination of their rebel love story, Satan and Rebecca had sex. Her fall was complete, yet she imagined herself empowered: Satan had granted everything she asked; she was loved and valued, served by a potent demon. And at this moment, the point of the shared fantasy that John Edes had extracted from her emerged. 'She conceived he [Satan] could do as God', the rector summed up as he presented his evidence of Rebecca's guilt to the magistrates Grimston and Bowes.[9] John Edes meant that Rebecca had confirmed to him she thought Satan had the same powers as God, powers he'd graciously devoted to her. Satan had become the deity of this underpaid, unappreciated woman. It was an eye-poppingly blasphemous, heretical claim, one John Edes may well have spoken with awe. Hearing his tale, the magistrates nodded wisely, their clerk's pen scraping Rebecca's story into ink. Now they understood how the devil was working along the Stour estuary, what it was that local witches were doing as the secret enemies of reformers in wartime Britain. At last they knew hard, verified facts about their enemy and could fight back.

~

Rebecca West's fantasy of heresy was exactly what many churchmen and magistrates both dreaded and wanted to hear, building on over a hundred years of suspicion about the devil and fears that some imagined Satan was God's spiritual equal, or even competitor. The concern was that the demonic feats demonstrated by witches appeared to substantiate these claims of power. If the devil was not as powerful as God and didn't cede power to heretics who worshipped him, then how were the witches doing any harm? The vicar of nearby Maldon, a Puritan called George Gifford, explained this away by claiming that Satan would fool the witches by sending blasts of spiritual energy to wound his victims, then allow accused people like Rebecca West to take the blame. That way he set humans against each other and ideally got some of them executed. But, Gifford was careful to remind his readers, even though the devil was really to blame for magical harm, people who signed up as witches did believe they were going to hurt and kill innocents when they made such Satanic deals. Rebecca West would have killed the Hart children herself if she could. That evil impulse, enacted by the devil, made her a witch who should be punished. And it made her mother, Anne, who had introduced her daughter to Lawford's heretical cult, a witch too.

Of course, it was all untrue. But maybe it also had roots in reality. Perhaps Rebecca had taken a lover at Rivenhall while she was away from her mother. And the formal witches' meeting she described, with its prayers, books and statements of belief, sounds in many ways like a real community gathering. Rebecca lived among reformist sectarians who did indeed hold meetings of this kind. They would attend Communion at the official, state church to satisfy the requirements of the law, but they would then hold additional private services, where they debated points of doctrine and God's will, claiming their own access to religious truth. Some of the new sects of the civil wars encouraged women to learn about theology in this way and allowed, even favoured, women preachers. Around 1613, Lawford's former rector William Hawes had written proudly that 'we have not in our town and parish any popish recusants ... nor any Anabaptistical Brownists to our knowledge' – neither Catholics, he meant, nor radical reformers. By the 1640s, however, that religious unity was long gone. Perhaps Lawford had a reformist group that met in Bess Clarke's cottage. Men like John Edes thought such unsupervised religious activity could easily turn subversive. 'Rebellion', the Bible told him, 'is as the sin of witchcraft'. So if Anne and Rebecca West were rebellious, freethinking heretics, then men like John Edes would readily suspect them of witchcraft too. Such people could be imagined as combining every type of evil.[10]

In important ways, the clergymen, magistrates and witchfinders of the 1640s in England and Scotland were not looking for real people – ordinary folk with names, families and lives like Agnes Bishop, Marion Gibson or Anne and Rebecca West. They were looking for The Enemy, the single demonic antagonist behind every human misery: sin, subversion, civil war, sickness, heresy. That person could be nameless or named; it didn't matter much. When, later in 1645, an account of the Essex witch hunt's origin at Lawford and Manningtree was published, it revealed clearly the paranoia that had gripped Britain. The little book began simply: 'Ingenuous readers, thou hast here presented to thee a sad emblem of the strange sleights and cunning subtleties whereby Satan labours daily to ensnare souls'. Anne and Rebecca were just an emblem, a symbol of demonic wiles, not rounded, individualised fellow humans. Satan, the writer went on, was 'that grand imposter' who had begun his attack on such emblematic people immediately after God had created Adam and Eve. Then, 'in the morning of the Creation, in the body of a serpent [he began] miraculously to reason, dispute, speak and confer with Eve', causing her to tempt her husband Adam by offering him God's forbidden fruit and eating it herself. Satan 'never ceased till he had laid the honour of those glorious creatures in the dust' and now he had tempted Anne and Rebecca West, Bess Clarke, Elizabeth Goodwin and the others in the same way.

'Poor silly creatures', lamented the writer. In the seventeenth century, 'silly' meant innocent as well as foolish, and the writer seems to have genuinely pitied the Essex women, Eve's daughters who had fallen for Satan's lies. But the fact remained that they had committed 'horrid and detestable practices of renouncing God and Christ, and entering into a solemn league and contract with the devil'.[11] This meant they should be tried as witches, and if found guilty, they should be condemned to death. And, of course, that was also the outcome that Thomas and Prudence Hart wanted for the Wests. They believed it would free them from the fear that stalked their lives. Perhaps, they must have thought, it would save their remaining children from inexplicable illness and early, painful death. Perhaps Prudence's next pregnancy would progress smoothly to a happy birth: another heir for Thomas's wheelwrighting business, another little soul to bring up in the joyous knowledge of God. And their personal, heartfelt hopes and fears clicked neatly into place as part of a plausible theology as they made their statements accusing Anne and Rebecca West of witchcraft.

In reality, though, Anne and Rebecca West were ordinary women going about their daily lives. Like other poor widows of her time, Anne would have sold vegetables, herbs or handicrafts at the market in Manningtree, cleaned rooms in an inn or served ale to visiting sailors, spun wool, pulled weeds or sewed shirts for a living – whatever kept a few pennies in her pocket and food on the table. Some women made brooms from twigs they scavenged from farmers' hedgerows; some beat hemp or flax fibres to ready them for weaving; some took in washing or dyed clothes or sold foraged fruit. They hoarded their meagre supplies of milk, cheese, butter and flour, gathered resources to hawk in the street, baked bread in a communal oven. They cadged a little beer and borrowed a sieve or a saw where they could find a neighbour kind or unwary enough to lend it to them. They sent their daughters away to work in richer households, hoping they would bring home part of their wages to support their elderly mothers. Rebecca West was perhaps lucky to have left her home village in such a manner, to have had experience doing different work elsewhere, however unwelcome her tasks may have been. Like her mother, she would have tried to earn every penny she could.

All across eastern England in that turbulent year of 1645 there were Anne and Rebecca Wests, hoping for the best but also, as spring became summer, waiting in dread for a finger to be pointed, a witchcraft accusation made. Every community had its John Edes, concerned about Satanic threats, and its Harbottle Grimston or Thomas Bowes, sending witchcraft suspects to court to be put on trial for their lives. And there were men and women like Thomas and Prudence Hart up and down the country, ready to make accusations, hoping to ease their own pain. Their neighbour Richard Edwards, who sat with Thomas on the Lawford manor court jury, was just such a man – richer than Thomas, but with his own troubles at home.

Richard often rode back and forth between his lands in Lawford and Manningtree, and over the River Stour to the town of East Bergholt in Suffolk or upriver to Dedham, where he had business with his sister-in-law's family. One night, as he was riding from East Bergholt to Manningtree across the Middle Bridge (one of three that spanned the mud and marshy islets of the Stour in the valley below Lawford church), Richard's horse stumbled and he was thrown from his horse, very nearly pitching into the oozing slime and dark water of the river. He blamed witches for his accident, perhaps with the memory of recent gossip in mind – as you may remember, Rebecca West had claimed that Bess Clarke petitioned the devil that Richard would fall from his horse. Like the Harts and many other neighbours in the Stour Valley, Richard talked about his suspicions and, because he was a wealthy and well-connected man, stories spread across his hometown of Manningtree. There, some friends and relations who aspired to professional witchfinding were waiting and, like Hew Kennedie, they had innovative ideas about how to fast-track suspicions into confessions and executions.[12]

CHAPTER 5

Fatal Changes

Bess Clarke and Elizabeth Goodwin of Manningtree, Essex, 1645

When, following the trail of Richard Edwards, I arrive in Manningtree, I'm worried there will be no room at the inn. But the manager checks her calendar: the Georgian pub on the High Street has an empty suite in its old mews, where once horses dozed among the hay. Am I on holiday? the manager asks. 'I'm researching seventeenth-century witch trials,' I tell her. She takes that in her stride and offers me a story in exchange: 'I'm moving into the inn to live on the premises,' she says, 'and I'm sort of worried it might be haunted by witches!' We laugh, ambiguously. 'But,' she continues, 'I said that to my daughter, and she said, "Don't worry, Mum – you're one of them!"' We laugh again, properly this time.

Magic has been in the news in Manningtree lately, just as it was in 1645. There's a new blue plaque in the marketplace, commemorating the witch hunt. It hangs above another plaque dedicated to the Manningtree ox mentioned by Shakespeare in his play *Henry IV, Part 1*. The ox plaque was put up by the town's Rotary Club.

It was a positive claim to fame: Shakespeare's character Falstaff is described in a tasty double metaphor as a 'roasted Manningtree ox with the pudding in his belly', a stuffed joint of beef. In 2023, however, the Manningtree Museum and Local History Group was feeling less bullish. Their plaque is dedicated to 'all people who have suffered intolerance and persecution on account of their gender, religion, ethnicity or social standing', and it names each local person hanged for witchcraft in 1645. Manningtree, after all, is famous for one of the most dogged witch hunts of the seventeenth century – and was home to the witch craze's most famous hunter, Matthew Hopkins. As I read the plaque in memory of those he victimised in this town and beyond, a young woman sits down on a nearby bench and absorbs the text slowly before getting up to continue her shopping.

Despite alterations to shopfronts, road surface and signage, Manningtree High Street is little changed since 1645. Rambling half-timbered houses survive as restaurants, cafés and charity shops, thinly disguised by modern facades. They continue into South Street, which meets the High Street at a crossroads by the marketplace. South Street curves left, past a triangular green that used to be at the edge of town and has been suggested as a gallows site: it fronts the Red Lion pub and cottage driveways splashed with hollyhocks in blackberry and watermelon pinks. A sleek black cat strolls in the road. It runs up to a passing woman, yowling and looping round her legs. I walk back down South Street towards the river. The mud is flat. The River Stour is flat and barely moving beyond the flat marsh that borders it. There's a lot of sky. The Manningtree area is often named 'Constable country' after the Stour Valley painter John Constable, but today it looks unlike his canvasses: no cushioning clouds, few shady trees. The first time I visited, a witheringly cold wind lashed snow flurries off the grey water. Sky, waves and land were stacked slabs of ice, swans bobbing, huddled in their feathers. The east wind was undeterred by coats, gloves or walls, and there was no hiding place. Manningtree is a beautiful town, but in 1645, four townswomen were hanged there and still more killed at Chelmsford, because their neighbours – people who lived in these houses and walked these streets – accused them of witchcraft.

Thomas and Prudence Hart's accusations and Rebecca West's confession were important in beginning this witch hunt, sparking fears that a devil-worshipping cult was active along the Stour. But earlier events mattered too. Some concerned the family and friends of Richard Edwards, the apparently cursed Manningtree farmer who fell off his horse on the Stour's Middle Bridge as he passed Lawford homeward bound. These events appear at first to be unconnected to witch hunting, but actually they created the perfect preconditions for it – and without them perhaps the Stour's witchfinders would have struggled to plant and grow their poisonous seeds in Manningtree, building on the stories coming out of Lawford and drawing in people from other riverside villages to accuse more and more witches. One of the most important precursor events happened in Great Bromley, five miles south of Manningtree, in 1643, when Thomas Bowes, the lord of Great Bromley's manor, made a decision. He appointed his old friend Thomas Witham, rector of the joint parish of Mistley-with-Manningtree, to a prestigious post far away in the City of London. This simple act made a big difference in Manningtree, one that would mean it was easier for a witch hunt to get started. In 1645, Thomas Bowes would see the consequences of his decision when, along with his friend Harbottle Grimston of nearby Bradfield, he became one of the witch-questioning magistrates who arrested Anne and Rebecca West.

Thomas Bowes was not just a country squire. He was a wealthy magnate, knighted in 1630 and buying the Great Bromley estate in 1618. Funding came from Bowes's family business in London. Thomas's great-grandfather had been Sir Martin Bowes, Lord Mayor of London from 1545 to 1546 and a goldsmith of the Royal Mint – the smelting and stamping plant that created the nation's coinage. The Bowes fortune grew with Martin's son, Thomas, and grandson, also Thomas. Soon the Bowes family held the licence to appoint the rectors of the church of St Mary Woolnoth, near their London home in Lombard Street. Sir Thomas Bowes, now of Great Bromley as well as London, inherited that right and used it to move Thomas Witham from Mistley-with-Manningtree to St Mary Woolnoth in 1643.[1] In late June of that year, Bowes had received an unexpected letter suggesting he select another cleric for the London post: Walter Bridges. Flatteringly, the letter was signed by eight of England's most powerful noblemen, the Earls of Northumberland, Bedford, Pembroke, Rutland, Holland and Manchester, Lord Howard of Escrick and Viscount Saye and Sele. They wanted Bowes to choose Bridges because he was an ambitious evangelist. Instead of a noisy preacher, however, Bowes picked country parson Thomas Witham, a hard worker who had been rector of Mistley-with-Manningtree for thirty-three years.[2]

Although he was a dutiful rector, Witham wasn't a craven conformist. In the first years of his ministry at Mistley-with-Manningtree, he had refused to wear the priest's uniform of cassock and surplice, a black gown covered by a white tunic. This was because Christians on the puritanical wing of the Church of England considered these garments too Catholic-looking. Thomas Witham's first wife may have held such reformist views – she had a Puritan-sounding name, Free-Gift, referring to God's 'free gift' of salvation. However, despite his godliness, her husband was no dogmatic sectarian or republican fanatic. Writing in 1642, he looked back on the building of a new chapel in Manningtree, describing it in comfortably monarchist terms as built 'under God and King James' and consecrated by Bishop William Laud, an arch-conservative. He also agreed to go back to wearing his surplice when the Church of England told him to. Thomas's pupil John Angier described him as thoughtfully quiet, 'a better scholar than preacher'. Such moderate reformism appealed to Sir Thomas Bowes. He was a Presbyterian-leaning reformer himself, but as a magistrate, he was keen to promote calm. Thomas Witham had certainly kept Mistley-with-Manningtree orderly for decades, despite increasing sectarian division across Britain; now he could do the same in London.

Whatever his exact doctrinal position, Thomas Witham was a sound pastor. He cared deeply for his congregation, writing the parish register entries himself. He rode attentively back and forth between the two halves of his parish, Mistley and Manningtree, through the little fields of Manningtree Pightles and the Teynterfield, where newly made cloth was stretched on frames, passing through his own corn and cabbage fields along the marshy bank of the Stour. He shared in three decades of Mistley-with-Manningtree's joys and griefs. But Sir Thomas Bowes's choice of him for St Mary Woolnoth meant he left suddenly in summer 1643.[3]

Unfortunately, no new rector arrived to replace him. This was because Sir Paul Bayning – patron of the Mistley-with-Manningtree church, who nominated rectors there just as Sir Thomas Bowes did in London – had died in 1638, leaving his estates to his infant daughter. She was in no position to appoint a clergyman. The congregation of Mistley-with-Manningtree was left leaderless. Church services faltered and no one wrote up the parish register. Those blank pages, where the town's spiritual life should have been recorded, indicated a community of souls in peril. When residents heard Rebecca West's stories of a witch conspiracy spilling out of Lawford, they concluded that witches were adding to the danger.

Rebecca's statements had named Manningtree resident Bess Clarke as a particular threat. According to Rebecca, her own initiation into witchcraft had happened at Bess's house on Old Chapel or Wormwood Hill, now South Street. Bess was a middle-aged, disabled single mother, born in 1606 in the village of Bradfield, three miles from Manningtree. Her mother, whose Christian name we don't know, had been hanged for witchcraft along with some of her other relatives – when, we don't know. The family relocated to Manningtree and Bess's sister Jane married Richard Benifield or Bedingfield in August 1621. Bess probably shared their home and was soon known as Bess Bedingfield as well as Bess Clarke. She would have needed to live with caring relatives because of her disability; she had only one leg. But Jane Bedingfield died in 1640, her husband remarried, and by 1645 Bess Clarke lived alone in poverty. She had become pregnant in 1642 and in February 1643 she gave birth to an illegitimate daughter, Jane.[4]

Jane Clarke was baptised in a newly built chapel recently opened on Manningtree High Street. This new chapel was a focus for religious reform within Mistley-with-Manningtree parish, and the fact that Bess took her child there suggests she was a pious Christian, outwardly at least, like her friend Anne West. In 1616, Richard and Priscilla Edwards, the uncle and aunt of that Richard Edwards whom witches would one day push off his horse, had given the land on which to build it, with a curate's house and burial ground attached. Their nephew Richard Edwards the younger was as pious as they were – 'my wellbeloved in Christ', his uncle Richard Edwards called him – and he joined the chapel's project team as he grew to adulthood. In 1639, he married Rector Thomas Witham's daughter, Susan.[5]

It was one of several important changes in the Witham family that propelled them, Richard Edwards and Bess Clarke to the centre of Manningtree's witchcraft crisis. Thomas's first wife, Free-Gift Witham, died in 1633, and by 1641 Thomas had re-married, choosing a Suffolk minister's widow, Marie Hopkins, whose first husband had died in 1635. Then, in 1643, Thomas left Mistley-with-Manningtree, creating a leadership void that was unpredictable in its consequences. Perhaps anxious townspeople turned to nearby Lawford's minister John Edes for advice, since they now had no rector of their own. And they also turned to Thomas Witham's son-in-law, Richard Edwards.[6]

Richard was wealthy, energetic and effective, a godly man who called Sunday by its biblical name 'the Sabbath' and structured his days around attending multiple sermons. When not in church, he farmed cows and pigs at Mistley, Bradfield, Lawford and in Manningtree, where they grazed at Hillfield and Hopping Bridge. He paid twenty-eight pounds in rent, around £5,500 today. But, though wealthy, his life was not easy. He was a hands-on tenant farmer and – just like Thomas Hart in Lawford – he'd suffered family tragedies. Richard and his wife Susan Witham-Edwards lost six-week-old baby Richard in August 1640 and nine-month-old Susan in March 1642. A daughter, named Free-Gift after Susan's mother, was born in July 1643 and may have survived. But in summer 1644, another child, John, died after suffering fits. Child mortality was, of course, high because of poor sanitation and ignorance of how to treat common illnesses, but adults were also vulnerable, and in September 1641 Susan and Richard Edwards's stepbrother John Hopkins – the son of Thomas Witham's second wife Marie Hopkins, who lived with his stepfamily at Manningtree – died in his twenties. The cause may have been tuberculosis, a diagnosis suggested by his age, his family's medical history and the spread of this disease across

Europe in the seventeenth century.[7] Whatever the sad circumstances, John's death and those of his stepsister's infant children decisively ended what had been comparatively good times for the Witham-Edwards clan.

The Hopkins boys, however, had been brought up to expect trials at the hands of a stern God. John and his brother Matthew Hopkins – later to become the most infamous witchfinder in Britain – had been raised by a hardline Puritan, their father James Hopkins, who until his death in 1635 was rector of Great Wenham in Suffolk, seven miles north of Manningtree. James's will had insisted his elder son Thomas sail to the godly colonies of 'our friends in New England', and stay there until he was twenty-two, or else he was to be disinherited. That was harsh, manipulative parenting even by seventeenth-century standards, and no doubt John (born in the late 1610s) and Matthew (born about 1620) felt equally obliged to dedicate their young lives to piety. Then John died, leaving Matthew to carry his father's legacy alone in Manningtree.[8] He inherited the impulse to control others, to reform and cleanse the world and colonise it for Christianity – and with such traits often came suspicions about witches. Especially when family tragedy struck, as it did, yet again, with the news that his stepfather, the Rector Thomas Witham, had died in London, shortly after his arrival there. Mistley-with-Manningtree had been left in chaos by Rector Witham's departure and was now further damaged by his death. It's no surprise, therefore, that by the mid-1640s Richard Edwards and his stepbrother-in-law Matthew Hopkins had become convinced that Satanic plots were killing the people of the Stour Valley.

In adjacent Lawford, the Harts had begun to suspect witches were at work, in particular the West family. And just as Lawford turned on the Wests, so the people of Manningtree began to fear their associate Bess Clarke. Though she attended the new chapel, she had an illegitimate child, and her mother had been hanged as a witch. By autumn 1644, Matthew Hopkins had come to believe Bess was a witch as well. He'd overheard strange conversations with and about animals, whispered in the nighttime outside his house – surely, he thought, these were witches' sabbaths and the animals were familiar spirits. Hopkins knew about sabbaths and the Satanic covenant imagined in theological theory: he had read textbooks like the 1597 Scottish witch hunter's guide *Daemonologie*. Now he said he'd overheard one attendee of a supposed witches' sabbath telling her demonic animals to go to Bess Clarke's house.[9]

Perhaps Rebecca West was asked about Hopkins's suspicions by John Edes, or perhaps she'd heard other rumours about Bess by the time she was questioned in March 1645. Either way, when she described Bess as the host of a meeting attended by witches from both Manningtree and Lawford, Hopkins was encouraged to tell his own story. And on 21 March, as Rebecca's accusations began to spread, a South Street tailor also complained about Bess's supposed witchcraft. The tailor, John Rivet, told Grimston and Bowes that his wife had begun to have fits, 'more than merely natural'. He'd been to visit a 'cunning woman', a diviner with magical knowledge – someone like Agnes Bishop or Margaret Thomsone – who told him that two women had bewitched his wife. One lived on the hill above John's house and one below, the diviner said. Well, Bess Clarke lived up the hill. She was arrested that day, and it was Grimston and Bowes's duty to commit her to prison for trial at the county's Assizes. Ultimately, they would do that. But first, they agreed to a plan for extracting a confession from her using local volunteers.

It's not clear who originated this amateur interrogation, though my money would be on Matthew Hopkins – who read Scottish witch-hunting manuals and was already interested in Bess – and his friend John Stearne, who was soon revealed to be a keen experimenter in the detection of witches. Grimston and Bowes backed them with the authority of their offices as Justices of the Peace – not something they should have done. Magistrates were supposed to question suspects themselves, not delegate it to other people. Yet this is what they did, giving John Stearne written authority to set up watching and bodily searches of the suspects, starting with Bess Clarke and moving on to other women who were to be arrested because they'd been named by Rebecca West.[10] Perhaps this democratising of religious investigation appealed to the magistrates, both of whom held Presbyterian views: it recalled the devolution of church power to presbyteries of elders as at Mid Calder and the way the Scottish Privy Council commissioned groups of ordinary citizens to investigate witchcraft. With Thomas Witham gone, there was no rector, and the magistrates themselves were busy men: so why not entrust the investigation of spiritual matters to decent, godly parishioners?

Ten people stepped forward. John and Grace Norman were traders with premises on Manningtree's quayside; Edward and Mary Parsley were a bricklayer and his wife. These volunteers were of lower social standing than men like Matthew Hopkins, and they were also older than him: the Normans had married in 1617 and had a large family between 1618 and 1637. The Parsleys were a little younger, starting a family in 1626. Then there were John and Mary Banks, married in 1633, and Frances Mills, married in 1641 to her husband John, as well as a widow, Mary Phillips. All the watchers had reason to be interested in the safety of their community, but for some the fear of magic was personal, just as it was for couples like Richard and Susan Edwards. Edward and Mary Parsley had recently lost their daughter Mary, baptised in May 1637. She died on or about 1 March 1645, just three weeks before Bess Clarke's arrest on 21 March. The Parsleys had lost many children before: John, another Mary, Susan, Dorcas and another John in the 1620s and 1630s and Anne in 1643. They explicitly blamed witches for killing Anne, and with their recent grief for her sister Mary so raw, no wonder they were committed to finding a culprit. Their neighbours – other mums and dads fretting over their children – were keen to assist them.

Working in relays, the Parsleys, Bankses, Normans, Matthew Hopkins, John Stearne, Mary Phillips and Frances Mills spent the three days and nights following Bess Clarke's arrest keeping her imprisoned and under constant observation. They stripped her and searched her, then watched her. She had no privacy and they would not let her sleep, just as Margaret Thomsone had been allowed no rest at Mid Calder the previous year. They kept Bess in motion, walking her up and down the room. Eventually they must have been dragging her, because Bess's disability would have made it impossible for her to continue. Unlike the Scottish questioners whose technique they were echoing, they did not stand their suspect on a stool – perhaps her disability would have prohibited that, or perhaps they believed walking was a more effective stressor – and they did not admit to hitting her. But in other respects their methods were the same as their Scottish counterparts. Under this duress, they questioned Bess about her adventures in witchcraft. Matthew Hopkins later called the volunteers' experimental process 'trying ways' by which he and others 'gained ... experience' in witch hunting; they felt themselves to be pioneers of a new witchfinding procedure – new to England, anyway – and were genuinely excited to see the results.[11]

John Stearne was keen to contribute. Initially, he was unconvinced that watching and walking would be enough. Stearne proposed throwing Bess into water as well, an ancient folkloric practice with a pseudo-scientific rationale: if a suspect floated, the water had rejected them and they were guilty. It was vaguely theorised that because, as part of their demonic covenant, witches renounced their baptism, carried out by being dipped into holy water, then any other body of water would repel the taint and spit them out. Presumably John Stearne wanted to march Bess Clarke down to the Stour at high tide and push the disabled woman off the quayside. But his idea was vetoed, not because it was cruel, but because some of Bess's interrogators feared it was theologically unsound. Stearne backed off. He wasn't a Manningtree native, and if local people had their witch-hunting experiment worked out, who was he to dissent?

Stearne, originally from Long Melford, twenty-three miles to the northwest in Suffolk, was a relative newcomer to Manningtree. He and his wife, Agnes, had a son, George, who was baptised there, by Rector Thomas Witham, on 18 February 1642. John, likely in his early thirties, was probably known to Harbottle Grimston too, since he was in Bradfield, where Grimston was lord of the manor, in 1644. There, Stearne witnessed a manorial legal document for the wealthy tenant farmer Thomas Cooke. He seems to have been a trusted participant in legal matters and land deals, and by the 1640s he had done well for himself, acquiring assets across East Anglia.[12] None of that made him an expert on theology, however, so he watched with interest as the Manningtree volunteers worked through their tests. The four women watchers stripped Bess, looking for teats with which she fed her familiars, and reported back to the men. Today their technique would be classed as torture, just like Hew Kennedie's methods. The sleep deprivation, physical intrusion and constant disturbance to which the witchfinders subjected Bess would have reduced her to despair, shattering her concentration and lowering resistance to suggestion. Yet she held out for two nights without confessing anything.

It was not until Matthew Hopkins and John Stearne visited her on the night of 24/25 March that Bess cracked. Suddenly, she told Hopkins and Stearne, 'if you will stay, I will show you my imps!' She meant that she would summon her familiar spirits.[13] Delighted with her newfound compliance, her questioners pursued their own demonic fantasies. 'Hath not the devil had use of your body?' they demanded – meaning, had Bess had sex with Satan? Of course, because she had given birth to an illegitimate child, Bess's sexual history was one her community thought sinful, even demonic. Like Rebecca West, and very likely drawing on Rebecca's own story, Bess accepted the suggestion.

Then, to summon her spirits, she made 'smacking' noises with her mouth and beckoned with her hand. Supposedly, 'there appeared an imp like unto a dog', as Matthew Hopkins reported. Perhaps it was a real animal, but more likely the watchers simply relied on what Bess said she could see. Years later, one sceptical writer described how he'd seen intelligent people so deceived, their 'fantasy [being] so far deluded', that they would swear they saw 'real ducks squirming about the room' if they were told there were demonic ducks present. Often animal familiars were thought able to render themselves invisible to anyone but their witch. Yet in their descriptions of what went on in Bess's cell, both Hopkins and Stearne reported demonic presences as if they had actually seen them. Later on, someone commissioned an artist to produce a woodcut image of the dog and Bess's other familiars based on their testimony, which Hopkins used as the title page of his published account of his witchfinding, *The Discovery of Witches.* Next came a spirit whom Bess called Vinegar Tom, 'a greyhound with long legs', much like a greyhound Hopkins himself owned. Hopkins later added that Bess's greyhound had a head like an ox – which was the image the artist, unsurprisingly, chose for his illustration of Vinegar Tom. Tom also apparently transformed himself into the shape of a child as the watchers continued to question Bess. Then came a black rabbit called Sacke and Sugar, and a polecat. John Stearne added that Bess referred to the spirits as 'my children' and said she had five of them.[14]

Bess told her interrogators she shared some of her spirits with Anne West of Lawford. *Excellent*, the watchers must have thought: the witchcraft stories of the Stour Valley were starting to converge! In their minds, they were piecing together the secret rites at the heart of the witches' anti-Christian religion. Bess said her familiars had pestered her until she agreed to let them kill pigs belonging to Richard Edwards. Later she would also be charged with killing his little son. In mid-March, she catalogued, Anne West killed a Dedham woman and Robert Oakes's wife from Lawford. Another recent victim of Anne's was Marie, the wife of William Cole of Manningtree, who had died in 1642. Finally, Bess named another co-witch, Elizabeth Goodwin of Manningtree, whose name had already come up in Rebecca West's confession. Elizabeth, she said, killed a horse belonging to the Manningtree gentleman Robert Taylor.

Robert Taylor was a wealthy Presbyterian grocer who, along with his wife Olive, owned a provisions shop in Manningtree and held lands in Mistley-with-Manningtree parish, in Bradfield and beyond. He was the son of a clergyman, just like Matthew Hopkins. Robert's father was Rector Thomas Taylor of Bradfield, the village where Bess had been born. The rector and his son Robert would have known Bess, both as a little girl and young woman, and they would also have known her mother, the convicted and executed witch. Although Robert Taylor married Olive Markes in Manningtree in 1619 and set up his business there, he still had a house on Bradfield's village green which he co-leased with his mother. When Rector Thomas Taylor died in 1617, Robert's mother Jane remarried. She chose a Bradfield man, Joseph Alderson, a regular juror for Bradfield's Nether Hall manor court alongside his neighbour Thomas Cooke – one of John Stearne's business acquaintances.[15] Through all these connections Bess's haunting past had followed her from Bradfield to Manningtree.

Although Robert Taylor did not immediately come forward when Bess confessed, when he did speak to Grimston and Bowes on 23 April, he began his evidence by referring back to Bess's accusation of Elizabeth Goodwin. About nine weeks before, Robert Taylor said, in early March, Elizabeth had come to his shop at Manningtree. She 'desired to be trusted for half a pound of cheese', meaning that she asked Robert's employees for some cheese on credit. But, Robert reported, she was 'denyed' and 'went away muttering and mumbling to herself'. This was thought to be a sign that a suspect was cursing her victim, the muttered words being a spell. Although a few hours later Elizabeth came back to the shop having raised the money to pay for the cheese, the shop assistants were on the alert. That night, one of Robert's horses was taken ill in his stable.

Robert called in four different farriers, one after another, to see if any of them could cure the animal. None 'could discover the cause of the disease' and, sadly, after four days the horse died. Robert decided that Elizabeth Goodwin had bewitched it. Now he had heard that she'd been accused by a fellow witch of just such a crime. He knew Elizabeth Goodwin 'kept company' with Anne West of Lawford too, who 'hath been suspected for a witch many years since'. Once again, all the stories were coming together. Robert said that Elizabeth Goodwin was 'a lewd woman', like Bess Clarke. 'Lewd' could mean ignorant or irreligious, but it usually suggested sexual transgression as well. Elizabeth was the wife of Edward Goodwin, a labourer: they'd married in 1621 when she was Elizabeth Roice. She was a churchgoer and the mother of at least three children (John, born and died in 1622, Elizabeth, born and died 1624, and Anne, 1625). If she was suspected of immorality, no record remains, but it was easy for such slurs to stick as the witch stereotype was applied. From Rebecca West to Elizabeth Goodwin, the Stour Valley witches now seemed to their accusers to resemble each other. They were not just demonic conspirators, heretics and anti-Christians, working together in a cult to harm their neighbours; they were also riddled with sexual sin.

By the time Robert Taylor gave his evidence against Elizabeth Goodwin, she had already been arrested, and on 11 April she was questioned. Whatever was done to her, Elizabeth refused to confess. She said simply that she was 'not guilty of any one particular charged upon her'. Anne Leech of Mistley was questioned on 14 April and confessed she had worked with Bess Clarke and Elizabeth Goodwin to send her imps to kill Richard Edwards's cows, and some of her fellow villagers. Another widow, Sara Bright of Manningtree, was accused of the murder of Anne, daughter of the mason Henry Woolvett, in June 1644 – her case seems unconnected to the other suspects as far as can be made out, with none of the same victims mentioned and no surviving statements.[16] But the original group of watchers were still making accusations: Mary and Edward Parsley had come to suspect that it was Anne Leech's daughter Helen Clarke who had bewitched their child Anne, so Helen was questioned on 11 April. She admitted keeping a familiar spirit, a white dog called Elemanzer. The dog had told her to 'deny Christ, and she should never want'. But Helen said she had not killed the Parsleys' daughter.[17] The experimental technique of watching and walking had cracked the resistance of most of the accused witches, but some were still capable of denying the allegations, heroically refusing to accept the guilt their accusers were desperate to load onto them.

Yet whether they confessed or not, all the accused women were sent from Manningtree to prison in Colchester Castle to await their trial at the summer Assizes. There, in mid-April, Matthew Hopkins visited Rebecca West to make her repeat her confession just for him, reporting it back to Grimston and Bowes in case that should help to convict the accused women. How he must have looked forward to their trial! It would be held in the market town of Chelmsford, thirty miles west of Manningtree. The Assize court met in the market hall in Chelmsford High Street, a two-storey, galleried building where on ordinary market days farmers sold vegetables and meat and merchants haggled over cloth and grain. Normally, the Assize judges processed to the court from their lodgings in one of the town's coaching inns, with a scurry of clerks carrying armfuls of official documents. After them came the magistrates, gentlemen like Sir Harbottle Grimston and Sir Thomas Bowes, who had examined the suspects. The Assize was a theatrical display of authority and learning, wealth, royal power and arcane legal rite. It was mysterious and solemn, an unbroken tradition of ceremony and process that had played out since the 1300s. This year, however, things would be somewhat different.

The outbreak of the civil wars meant that judges were no longer reliably riding out from London to the provinces to hold Assizes. Legal administration had broken down and individual officials had been displaced. Even if judges were still in post and accessible, a journey would sometimes have been too dangerous for them to attempt. Anyone representing royal or other state power might find themselves in difficulties in hostile localities. So Assize courts were reorganised, especially in Parliamentarian areas, to make use of the available authorities as judges and courtroom personnel. In summer 1645, the Essex Assizes were more like a general meeting of the magistrates' court, and would be presided over by the Earl of Warwick, Robert Rich, a Parliamentarian commander and puritanical reformer. He had no legal training and no experience of Assize trials beyond attending them as a magistrate. He was not professionally interested in legal precedents, impartiality, the rights of the accused or the rules of evidence. Instead, he was a tough, practical politician. He was also a cousin of the Earl of Essex, Robert Devereux, whose men had shot the 'Witch of Newbury' and whose ex-wife had narrowly escaped being convicted of witchcraft herself. It was unlikely the Manningtree women who assembled before the Earl of Warwick on 17 July 1645 would get a fair trial.[18]

Even if the Earl was able to keep an open mind about witchcraft, he was presented with an unusually complete, sensational body of evidence that would make it hard for him to do anything other than condemn most of the suspects arraigned before him. The Witchcraft Act of 1604, under which they were tried, stated that any contact with evil spirits and any magical attack on a human was punishable by death. Magical divination or an attack on an animal were in theory punishable only by imprisonment, with execution for a second offence, but in practice such crimes were thought to involve evil spirits – so they could easily tip over into the first category. Warwick was part of a reformist, militaristic regime under pressure to stamp out this sort of ungodliness.

Outside and within the courtroom itself, a mob of fretful spectators jostled, panicked by the wars, by talk of devils and witches. Into this nightmare situation were shoved Anne and Rebecca West, Bess Clarke, Elizabeth Goodwin, Anne Leech, Sara Bright, Helen Clark and the other accused felons of that summer, herded into court wearing iron fetters. They were frightened, tired and filthy after months in the cells at Colchester Castle. No doubt they shuffled into the hall with their heads down, avoiding everyone's eyes, shrinking from their persecutors. A grand jury of twenty-four men had already judged their indictments – the charges drawn up against them – to be plausible and confirmed their alleged offences had been correctly described, so that they could be tried at the Assize. For many people, that would have seemed good evidence of guilt, and the suspects must have looked guilty too – as anyone will wearing prison rags and shackles.

For all its unconventional structure, the Chelmsford witch trial of July 1645 is far better documented than any of the others in this book, just as the lives of its suspects are. We know Anne West was indicted for bewitching to death John Cutler, son of the Lawford farmer John Cutler, on 1 August 1629, and for interacting with familiar spirits on 10 July 1644. John Cutler senior appeared as a witness. Such dates and details as appear on Anne's indictments were, however, often rather arbitrary, added to the charges because the law required a specific date and place to be given for each offence alleged. Anne may also have been charged with other offences, although if she was, the documentation hasn't survived. But even if she was not formally indicted with bewitching Prudence Hart, we know that Thomas Hart was in court to give evidence against her. He stood up before the Earl of Warwick, the magistrates and the twelve-man petty jury to tell his story, probably contributing to a narrative about Anne's familiar spirits and the supposed harm they'd done. He was accompanied by the rector of Lawford, John Edes, with his stories based on Rebecca West's confession. Sadly, Rebecca was also called as a witness against her mother Anne. Rebecca herself was charged only with keeping familiar spirits, but she'd evidently elaborated on her fantasies about them, since now these creatures had names: cats called 'News' and 'Germany' and, tragically, a young man called 'Her Husband'. She was apparently still convinced the devil had seduced her and now thought he had married her too. Thomas Hart and the other witnesses were ready to confirm that she'd kept evil spirits and practised witchcraft with them.

Bess Clarke was also charged with keeping familiar spirits, a crime to which she had already confessed, although like all the other suspects she pleaded not guilty in court. She was further indicted, along with Anne Leech and Elizabeth Goodwin, for bewitching little John Edwards, the son of Richard and Susan Edwards, on 25 June 1644 so that he died on 5 July. Matthew Hopkins, John Stearne, Richard and Susan Edwards, Edward Parsley, Mary Phillips, Frances Mills and Robert Taylor gave evidence against Bess and Anne. In addition to bewitching John Edwards, Elizabeth Goodwin was charged with keeping spirits, two cats called 'Mouse' and 'Pease'. Perhaps she had confessed after all, and supplied these names in an undocumented interrogation, or perhaps they were attributed to her by another desperate suspect. Watcher Grace Norman gave evidence against Elizabeth, along with Susan Edwards, Mary Phillips, Rebecca West, Matthew Hopkins and John Stearne. Anne Leech's daughter Helen Clark was charged with killing the Parsleys' daughter Anne: Edward Parsley, Susan Edwards, Grace Norman, Matthew Hopkins and John Stearne spoke against her. With such formidable lists of witnesses against each suspect, it would be hard for any jury not to convict, and in most cases that was what happened. Anne West, Bess Clarke, Anne Leech, Elizabeth Goodwin and Helen Clark were all found guilty.

Rebecca West was indicted, but she may or may not actually have been tried. The grand jury approved her indictment, but there is no record of her plea (guilty or not guilty), a verdict or any sentence on the charge. These outcomes would usually be written on the indictment if a trial had been completed. A printed account of Rebecca's evidence suggests in a marginal note that she was acquitted, but it's not clear whether its author fully understood court procedure. Either way, Rebecca West probably survived her trial but would have lived with the knowledge that her evidence condemned many other people – including her own mother. The final Manningtree suspect, Sara Bright, was convicted of killing Anne

Woolvett.[19] And these Manningtree women were tried alongside suspects from other Essex villages – all of them women.[20] They were variously charged with keeping spirits, killing animals and children, and belonging to Satan's church. Some accusations linked back to the witch hunt's origin in Manningtree. Margaret Moone from Thorpe le Soken – a village nine miles south of Manningtree – was accused of participating in the murder of Richard and Susan Edwards's son John, along with Bess Clarke and the other Stour Valley women.

The number of accused people across Essex – and, soon, Suffolk – grew so large that the outcome of the Chelmsford Assizes was discussed in Parliament. Eventually those who had survived it were pardoned and ordered to be freed, after they had paid their jail fees. By that point, some had already died. Four Essex women suspected of witchcraft had died imprisoned before they even came to trial. In all, at least thirty-six women had been imprisoned by the Manningtree witch hunters and their Essex co-workers. Matthew Hopkins reported from the Chelmsford court that twenty-nine of these people were sentenced to death; John Stearne thought twenty-eight – with the reprieves, that would mean some nineteen or twenty Essex witch executions were planned for late July 1645. The unconventional court with its inexpert judges had taken just one day to decide their fate.[21]

And so, the day after the Assize trial, 18 July 1645, most of the convicted women were walked or carted down the lane out of Chelmsford towards the west. Here the gallows stood, next to a field of prehistoric burial mounds. The execution apparatus was a crossbar supported on two uprights, to which were tied rope nooses. Ladders were propped against the crossbar. Each condemned person would be helped up a ladder, the noose fitted around their neck, and then the ladder twisted away: this was known as being 'turned off'. The drop from the ladder would not kill most of them; instead, they would strangle. There were only a few nooses, so the women had to queue up to die in this dreadful way. Bess Clarke, Anne Leech, Elizabeth Goodwin and Sara Bright were all hanged. Anne West and Helen Clark were missing – not, unfortunately, because they had been reprieved, but because as part of its unconventional process of judgment, the court had decided they should be returned to the Stour Valley to be hanged at home. This was highly unusual. Almost all felons were executed close to the courtroom in which they'd been sentenced: it was cheaper, apart from anything else. A point was being made to the people of Manningtree and Lawford. So Anne West and Helen Clark, along with two other condemned women, were transported to Manningtree and hanged there in a display of localised vengeance.

But it wasn't only condemned witches who were travelling across the baking landscape of southeast England that summer. Also on the move were Matthew Hopkins and John Stearne, who – elated with their success after the killings that followed the Chelmsford Assizes – began a tour of England's eastern counties. They were taking their witchfinding show on the road – an unprecedented act of religious entrepreneurship which would have horrific consequences for hundreds of people. The two men, and some of the searchers who accompanied them, believed they had learned enough from confessing 'witches' like Rebecca West, and particularly from the Manningtree watchers' experimental, extra-legal questioning of Bess Clarke, to be able to detect witchcraft wherever it was hiding. Both Hopkins and Stearne had been born in Suffolk, and it was to that county they returned in summer 1645, flitting from one community to another, spreading their witch hunt and their witchfinding methods like the plague that also spread in such hot weather. As temperatures rose, so did the anxiety and aggression among Suffolk's farming communities and market town traders – tired by weeks of fretting over their parched root and grain crops, watching dairy products curdle and grass die, and worrying about the impact of drought on wartime prices. Their fears speeded the witch hunt on its deadly way north from the Stour.

PART 4

Fear and Frenzy: East Anglia and the English Midlands

CHAPTER 6

The Framlingham Witches

Mary Scrutton, Margaret Wyard, Ellen Driver and the Women of Framlingham, Suffolk, 1645

Under Union Jack bunting and green, red and blue striped awnings, stalls are selling pottery, vegetables, craft jewellery and beer. Around the triangular marketplace, Framlingham's narrow streets are patchworked with pink and primrose cottages. Swifts scream overhead against sulky clouds. There are sudden, thunderous blasts of heat. A Mercedes glides by, followed by a Range Rover and a BMW. Wealth has accrued in this Suffolk town for centuries, primed in the Middle Ages by takings from the wool trade. Cloth magnates – known as mercers – and sheep-rich nobles once haggled by the Market Cross House and in the Crown Inn. That's why the hill above the marketplace is dominated by an enormous church and an even bigger castle, built with their profits. Today I walk, as the sheep farmers, dairymen and mercers did, a hundred yards up the hill from the stalls to St Michael's. The church's walls and tower are patterned with contrasting flints: circles, mazes and checkerboards like the designs on an embroidery sampler. Inside the church hulk the marble tombs of an Earl of Surrey, two Dukes of Norfolk and their wives, Henry Fitzroy (an illegitimate son of King Henry VIII) and Attorney General and Assize judge Sir Robert Hitcham. Together they spell out in stone Framlingham's importance in the fifteenth and sixteenth centuries.

But by the 1640s, things were changing fast, just as they were elsewhere in Britain. The little town of Framlingham was less prosperous than a century before, and its citizens felt the loss. Across Suffolk, the wool business had collapsed due to changing textile trends, European war and competition. By the mid-seventeenth century, Framlingham was surviving on dairying, vegetable production, hemp and flax processing and weaving – a residual cloth trade, but nothing like the town's heyday. The Dukes of Norfolk had abandoned the leaky, draughty castle, and it was being used as a prison and brewery. In 1635, Sir Robert Hitcham – the Assize judge buried in the church – bought the castle estate, proposing to use its buildings to establish schools and an almshouse for the poor. But his well-meant plan was unclear, and for decades after his sudden death in 1636, his executors argued as the estate faltered. Some of its assets were held by local gentry, some by Pembroke College at the University of Cambridge, the main beneficiary of Sir Robert's will. There was friction over monies moving between institutions as town, university and church jostled. Manor courts ceased being held in 1643, leaving a vacuum in local administration. The castle crumbled and the town sagged further into decline, worsened by civil war.[1]

It didn't help that Pembroke College appointed one of Framlingham's churchwardens, the wealthy apothecary Francis Ireland, as the leading trustee who would run its Framlingham estate. The town's church community was riven by sectarian strife. Its churchwardens were often reformers, but their rector was a traditionalist – Richard Golty, who'd arrived as curate in 1624 and became rector in 1630. His congregation thought him old-fashioned and too often absent, and he made himself unpopular by raising the tax payments parishioners had to make to him and the church. He sued his debtors in 1641 and went to court in 1644 over churchyard timber that he claimed had been stolen from him. By then it wasn't just religious radicals who were discontented. One gentleman, Edward Alpe, went further: when at a session of the magistrates' court in October 1644 he and his neighbours were ordered to pay their debts to the rector, he said he 'cared not for the said sessions'. For this contempt of a secular, state court he was arrested, inflaming tensions which rumbled on into 1645. In January, magistrates tried to end the dispute, ordering a revaluation of lands in Framlingham, 'to the intent that all the differences within the town of Framlingham concerning rates might be ended'. But resentment remained, with the church at its centre.

The church tax issue fed into wider disagreement. Golty's churchwardens and overseers of the poor, who managed parish finance, wanted less spent on the decoration of religious buildings, which they thought Catholic-like, and they also demanded less deference to priests, bishops and kings and more attempts to combat sin. Before Golty, their rector had been Thomas Dove, who was Bishop of Peterborough (then in Northamptonshire, now in Cambridgeshire) as well as serving the Suffolk community. Locals questioned how effective that service had been, and as Dove's curate, Golty had facilitated the unsatisfactory situation. Now his congregation pushed him to invite neighbouring clergy to lecture in the town. In 1643, Thomas Witham of Manningtree came, and so did more radical speakers. Some lecturers stayed for months, offering a supplementary set of church services. The radical churchwarden Nicholas Danforth organised one such lecture series, and when he emigrated to Massachusetts in 1634 to found a Puritan settlement, his successors – including Francis Ireland, the Pembroke College trustee – continued his work. Trouble simmered: Golty insisting on his right to set the religious rules, many among his congregation refusing to conform.[2]

Parish officials were powerful in small communities like Framlingham, and their influence increased as the English state church shifted towards Presbyterianism and started to treat them as elders. As overseers of the poor, they administered welfare services, bringing them into contact and sometimes conflict with their neediest neighbours. In the 1630s and early 1640s, Framlingham was home to many middle-aged and older women with few ways of earning a living now that the wool trade had shrunk. The new almshouse – the charitable foundation promised by Sir Robert Hitcham – had not yet been built. Widowed and often caring for sick relatives, poorer women depended on parish funds. The overseers spent hours hearing their pleas: a few pennies for food, a few shillings for rent, a new coat for their orphaned grandson, a load of firewood to warm their homes in winter. If requests seemed reasonable, they would be granted. But this depended on whether the overseers judged the recipients to be worthy – not likely to spend the money on drink or fripperies – and on the church having collected enough tax to cover the parishioners' needs. There was ongoing argument over whether townspeople approved of the parish rates and accounting procedures, which, as we've seen, many didn't. Meanwhile, welfare claimants desperately begged for help.

All in all, Framlingham was a depressed, stressed and polarised community by the hot summer of 1645. On top of everything else, Britain's drift into civil war had made everything more expensive and most people poorer. In 1642, the overseers had to spend eighty-six pounds on charity work and expenses, but in 1643 that had risen to one hundred and five. People and resources were siphoned into political and military projects. Across the years 1640–45, many men were 'pressed' – forcibly conscripted – into the army instead of remaining at home to support their families. The overseers' accounts record grants made to pressed men, and the ominous purchase of weapons for the town: three snaphances (long-barrelled guns), swords and ammunition. Money that would once have gone into social welfare paid for the re-lining and varnishing of an old corslet (body armour) and the cleaning of other kit. Weapons that had been kept in the church for centuries – in 1631 there were four corslets, two pikes, a dagger, a sword and two muskets – were now to be refurbished and used, dreadfully, against fellow countrymen. Inevitably, the radical churchwardens and overseers were on the side of the Parliament, and traditionalist Rector Golty was on the side of the king. Framlingham's less partisan townspeople were stuck in the middle.

By 1645, many Framlingham men had left their hometown to fight for Parliament's rights, and their church officials backed them, literally to the hilt. They supplied men and weapons directly to the Parliamentarian army: 'two swords for John Clarck and Robert Bradshaw at their first going to serve in the wars', travel expenses 'to Robert Browne when an alarm was given to the Associated Counties [the Parliamentary alliance of eastern England]' following a Royalist advance. A member of the Danforth family who had remained behind when his cousins emigrated was given help: 'for healing of Nicholas Danforth's head, wounded in the exercise of soldiers' and 'at his going to the wars'.[3] As war raged to the west and north, refugees and wounded soldiers arrived too: Irish Protestants, veterans 'lamed at Newbury fight' in 1643, men 'out of Nottinghamshire lamed', Parliamentarians 'imprisoned at Oxford' by Royalists, or 'maimed in the Earl of Essex's army' or 'routed in the Lord General [Essex's] army in Cornwall and much wounded'. In June 1644, it was a woman and five children 'driven out of the west by the King's forces', then 'west country people that had their houses burnt', six people from Anglesey in Wales 'burnt with granadoes' (grenades) and a Southampton man 'with his arm shot off'. These refugees needed urgent help, and resources went to them rather than to the local widows who, yet again, needed a few pence to buy some bread, a shawl or weaving supplies.[4]

Some people, this hard-pressed community began to think, did not share the glorious wartime mission of creating a pure Christian country. Some were a drain on town funds; some were unproductive, would not fight or work; some had what others considered too many children or too much bad luck. Some supported the wrong army. These people sucked strength from the reformist war effort. And what if there were even more concerning enemies within, like the witches who'd been found in Essex, mobilising Satan against the forces of God? What if – a horrifying thought – there were even more of them: not just five or six spread across interconnected communities like Lawford and Manningtree, but ten, twelve, fourteen in a single town? What if most of that town's poor, troublesome women were witches? As tensions rose in spring and early summer 1645, between 17 May and 17 June, Framlingham's parish overseers paid out

> to 3 maimed soldiers viz Hudson, Harrington and Daines – eightpence
> to widow Howard – one shilling
> to one John Horne, wounded in the west – threepence
> to Scrutton's wife – one shilling

Expenses could not continue at this burdensome rate, townspeople felt, and when their patience finally failed, they began

Indictment of Henry Maggs.
Ref: C/S3/Box 36.

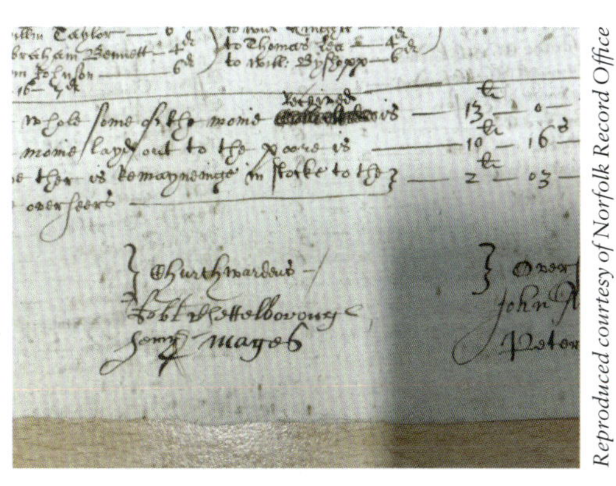

Henry Maggs's mark beneath his name on Hempnall's churchwardens' accounts.
Ref: NAS 1/1/2/152.

empnall church, Norfolk, where Henry Maggs was a churchwarden and worshipper.

Courtesy of the author

The ruins of Bury St Edmunds Abbey, Suffolk.

Courtesy of the author

Houses built into the Abbey ruins, Bury St Edmunds.

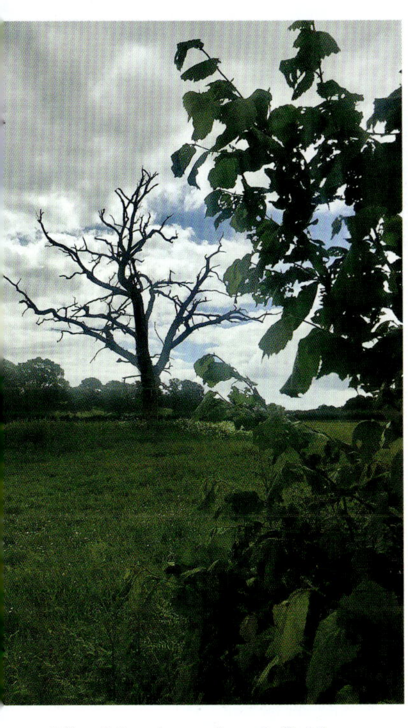

The Newbury battlefield, Berkshire, where the nameless accused 'witch' was captured.

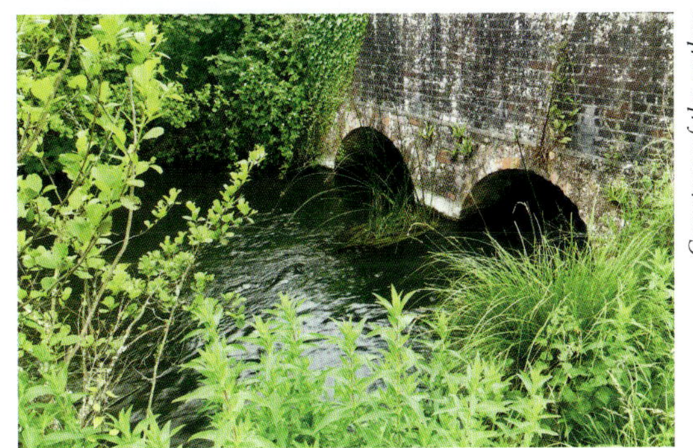

Courtesy of the author

The river on the Newbury battlefield.

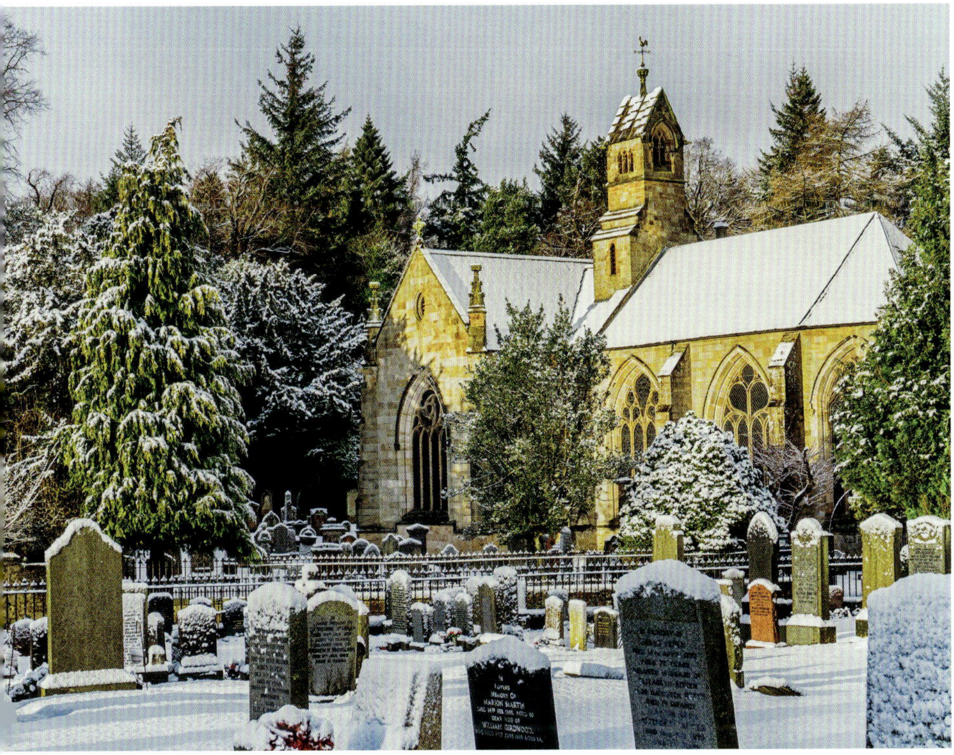

Dougie Milne Photography/ Alamy stock photo

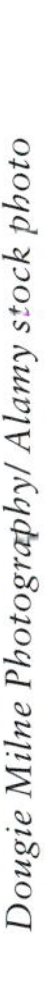

Mid Calder kirk where accused 'witch' Margaret Thomsone was held captive.

Courtesy of the author

Lawford church, Essex, where the accused 'witches' Anne and Rebecca West worshipped alongside their accusers, Thomas and Prudence Hart, and where Prudence suffered her miscarriage.

Courtesy of the author

Mistley village sign, Essex, showing the River Stour linking Mistley and Manningtree and the area's shipping.

Courtesy of the author

Mistley church, where Thomas Witham was rector, the Hopkins-Witham family worshipped, and witchfinder Matthew Hopkins is buried.

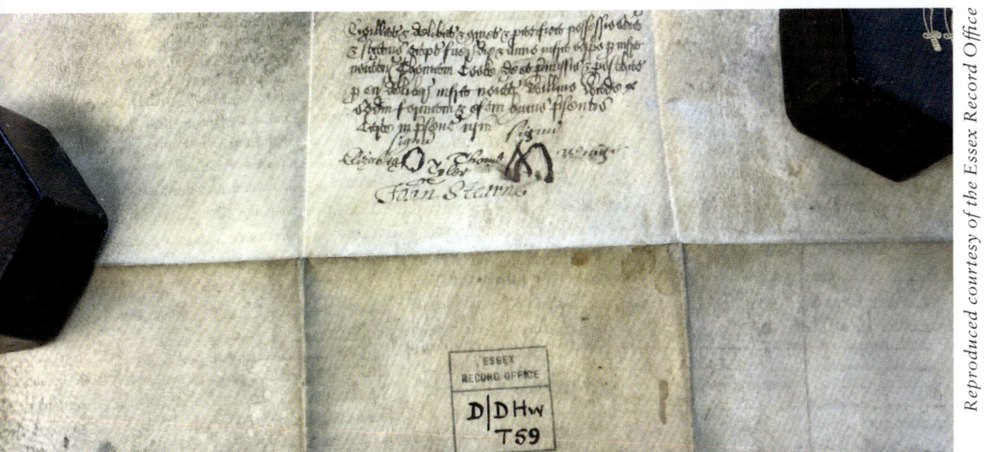

'itchfinder John Stearne's signature on a land transaction from Bradfield, Essex, where agistrate Harbottle Grimston was lord of the manor, accused 'witch' Bess Clarke was born, and where accuser Robert Taylor's father was rector. Ref: D/DHw T59.

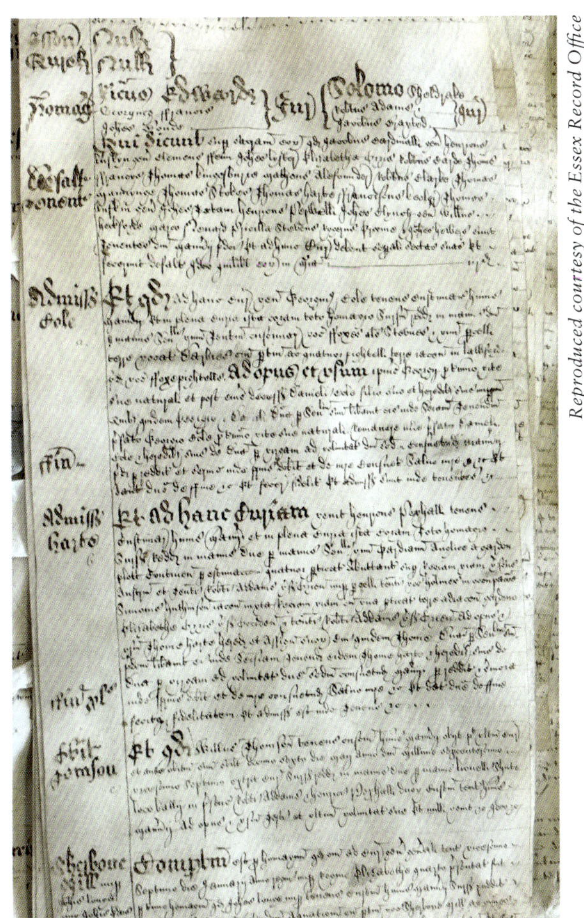

Lawford manor records showing land transactions by Thomas Hart and by Rector ohn Edes, who questioned suspected 'witches', with witch accusers George Francis and Manningtree's Richard Edwards serving as manorial court jurors. Ref: A14693 Box 1.

Courtesy of the author

Cottages in Framlingham, Suffolk.

Reproduced courtesy of Suffolk Archives and Reverend Ann Kember

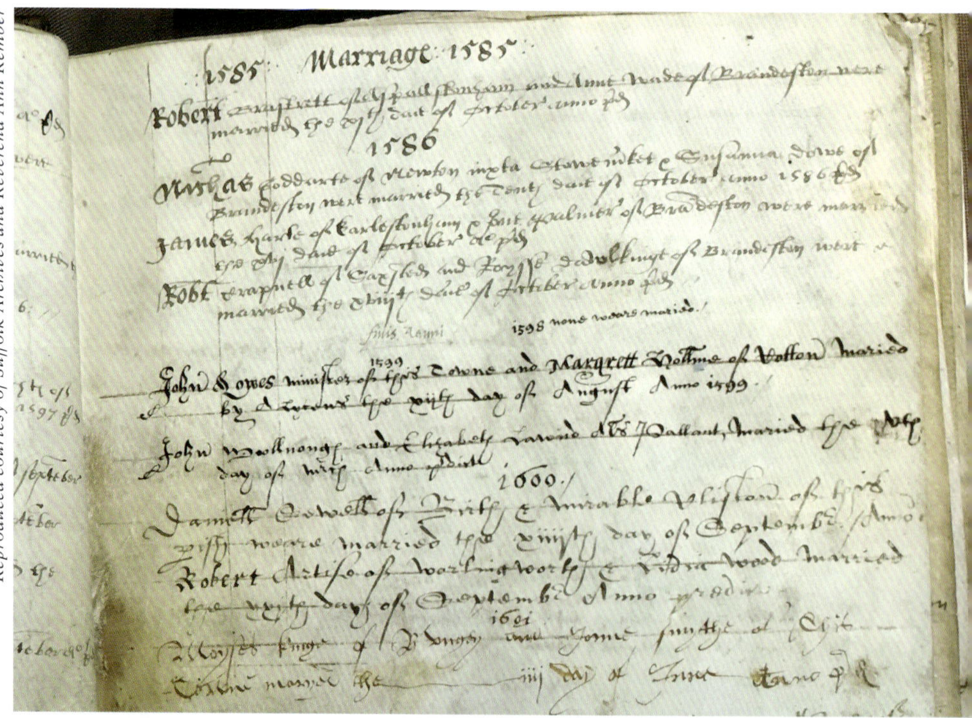

Record of the marriage of Vicar John Lowes, the accused 'witch', and Margaret Hollme, from the Brandeston parish register, Suffolk.

Courtesy of the author

Framlingham Castle, Suffolk

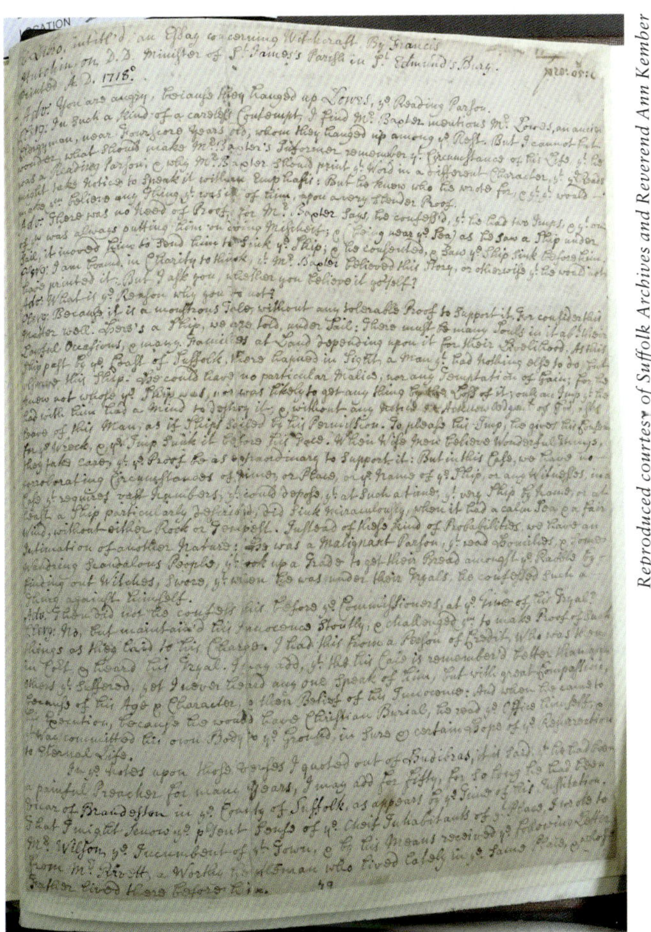

Reproduced courtesy of Suffolk Archives and Reverend Ann Kember

Note on Vicar John Lowes and witchcraft in Brandeston parish register, quoting Francis Hutchinson's eighteenth-century account of the case. Ref: FC105/D1.

Courtesy of the author

Norman gatehouse, the Abbey, Bury St Edmunds.

Courtesy of the author

The old prison at Moyses Hall, Bury St Edmunds, Suffolk, now a museum.

treating the war and witchcraft, two calamities that they knew were both afflicting eastern English communities around them, as if they were linked. They charged many of the women who were dependent on their parish charity with witchcraft. One was the last-named person on this list, Mary Scrutton. It's impossible to know who the first accused woman in Framlingham was, because what survives of the witch hunt there is a scrappy list of names and rich but undated confessions. Some names stand out, however, because we also see them in other town records. Mary Scrutton is one of these. By midsummer 1645, her name headed a long list of suspects: let's meet them one by one, since each has her own story.

Mary Scrutton

Mary was a youngish mother with a small child. Her husband was William Scrutton, a widower from a previous marriage and reasonably well-off. William and Mary lived with their blended family of children and stepchildren on the outskirts of Framlingham. At some point, they fell on hard times; we don't know why. We also don't know what witchcraft charges were made against her, but once she had been accused, Mary was arrested and watched for at least one night in exactly the same way as the Manningtree suspects had been. That might have been because Matthew Hopkins had arrived in town on his march north through Suffolk. He likely knew his way there, because his father James Hopkins had held property in Framlingham from the 1620s to his death in 1635, for which he paid twelve shillings' annual rent. James may have inherited the land, since it was fifty miles from his birthplace near Ely and thirty miles from Great Wenham, where he was rector – then he passed it on to Matthew and his brothers. Whatever the story, part of Framlingham might have felt like home to the witchfinder.

Arriving in Framlingham, Hopkins's first interrogation could have been Mary Scrutton's. When she was unable to resist any longer, her confession was witnessed by Edward Weeding, a visitor who had joined the witch hunt as it spread from Essex. Edward knew Framlingham well – better than Matthew Hopkins. In 1643, the town's officials paid Edward to collect a local maidservant from Ipswich magistrates' court and in 1645 he was given two shillings to serve legal documents on Framlingham's behalf. He was a trusted assistant to Framlingham's magistrates, just the sort of man to help document a witch hunt.[5] As Edward Weeding, and perhaps Matthew Hopkins, watched Mary Scrutton that night, three imps supposedly visited her to suckle. These imps, Mary admitted, had been with her for three or four months, drinking her blood two or three times a day, and squeaking for attention when they wanted to be fed. When Mary and William Scrutton heard them inside the plancher or eave of their house during the night, she told her watchers she had explained them away to her husband as house mice – which is likely what they were in reality. But her husband knew better, she told her questioners regretfully. William Scrutton did not like some of his wife's friends and he retorted to her that the creatures in the roof were not ordinary mice: 'you [keep] company with witches and you're plagued with some of their imps', he rebuked her, woundingly. She accepted his theory and, when questioned, expanded on her guilt: Satan had appeared to her himself, she said. He'd come once as a bear, once as a cat, once as a man. The devil spoke in a hollow voice, tempting her to kill her child – perhaps an indication of post-partum illness, depression or psychosis, or the despair of a woman unable to feed her family adequately.[6]

Margaret Wyard

Alongside Mary Scrutton, another poor welfare claimant was arrested for witchcraft. Margaret Wyard was supported through the 1640s with rent paid on her house in Back Lane. She was a widow whose husband had died in 1623, leaving her pregnant. After at least two nights watching and walking, she confessed that seven years ago the devil appeared to her as a calf. He also posed as her husband's ghost, before returning as a 'handsome young gentleman with yellow hair and black clothes', telling her 'some witches had gold rings on their fingers'.

Margaret's confession is eerily like that of Bess Clarke or Rebecca West, just as it would be if she were being forced to repeat fantasies those women had shared with Matthew Hopkins. Like Bess and Rebecca, Margaret confessed Satan often 'had the carnal use of her', made her deny God and Christ. He also forced her to sign a demonic pact. To do this, he 'brought writings' to her, drew blood and 'writ in the paper' himself, because she could not write.

Just like the Manningtree women, Margaret was searched for marks that would confirm her demonic covenant. Her searcher was Mary Tracy, wife of William Tracy. William often acted as one of the parish overseers, doling out charity to Mary Scrutton and Margaret Wyard. The Tracys were rich themselves: they held land in Framlingham and Hawfield, and William served on the manor court jury and was one of two town constables in 1639. By May 1645, he was 'agent of the Committee' of Parliamentarian Suffolk gentry, deputed by townsmen to ride to Woodbridge on business.[7] Like so many of the accusers we've met across Essex, he and his wife imagined they were reforming their Suffolk town by hunting for witches.

Chillingly, Margaret Wyard tells us about the fear the witch hunt's progress across Essex and Suffolk was causing women like her, even before the visiting witchfinders arrived. A month before she was accused, she said, the devil had told her 'that a man and a woman should come to search for witches'. Framlingham knew trouble was coming from the south. The woman Margaret Wyard had heard about might have been Mary Phillips or Frances Mills: as his witch-hunting journeys continued, Hopkins often took these searchers, his Manningtree neighbours, with him. But he could work with local women like Mary Tracy, too.

Apparently, Satan warned Margaret Wyard of this coming stripping and searching, but told her not to be afraid because 'she was his'. She must not reveal anything, he lectured. But of course she did, and as soon as she began to confess, 'the devil beat her down' in the form of a shadow. Presumably this meant she collapsed, falling down during her interrogation. Pitifully, Margaret thanked her torturers for their abuse, explaining desperately that 'she was now glad she had got time to confess'. Perhaps she believed her confession would save her soul, if not her life. She had seven imps, she fantasised, in the shapes of flies, bees, spiders, toads and mice. But she only had five teats on her body, so that 'when they came to suck they fight like pig[let]s with a sow'.

Margaret's imaginary devils had told her to kill little John Sheldrake, she said: he was the son of another ofttimes parish overseer, the tailor John Sheldrake and his wife Anne. The Sheldrakes lived on Framlingham's main road, known simply as The Street, where they rented a house and meadow. Little John had been born in October 1638, when his father was a constable working alongside the town's other constable, William Tracy. The two families' bond can only have been strengthened in March 1640, when their children died tragically within a week of each other. Two-month-old William Tracy was buried on 2 March and eighteen-month-old John Sheldrake on the 9th. Perhaps searcher Mary Tracy asked Margaret Wyard whether she'd hurt both the children. All Margaret would have had to do was say 'yes': she confessed she'd attacked John Sheldrake, adding that she'd worked with another witch, Margery Chimney, also known as Wyeth or With, to do it. Margaret Wyard had also helped one other witch, whom she named only as Mother Nevell, to 'blast' or blight corn belonging to the wealthy gentleman William Mase, a neighbour of the Sheldrakes' in The Street.[8]

Ellen Driver

Another widow, Margaret Wyard's Back Lane neighbour Ellen Driver, was also accused. Ellen was a clothworker, preparing hemp and flax fibres to make linen. She'd been the wife of Thomas Driver, whom, as Ellen Mosse, she'd married in October 1602. Thomas was poor and illiterate but trustworthy, witnessing the will of wealthy widow Margaret Capon in 1625. And as 'Driver's wife', it was Ellen who was chosen by parish overseers in 1623 to nurse her dying neighbour, Widow Harsham, and then prepare her for burial, the sort of work given to respectable townswomen. Ellen was paid twenty pence 'for watching, laying [the widow] forth and washing'. In 1630, she received eightpence to buy hemp, in 1633 a penny, then tenpence.

Thomas Driver had enlisted as a soldier in June 1631, and the parish bought him a shirt and stockings, also giving him a shilling and fivepence 'at his going away . . . for his supper and breakfast'. A neighbour was paid 'to deliver him to his captain' – the wording suggesting that, like many men, his enlistment might not have been entirely voluntary. Thomas probably died in 1641, since the parish account book refers to 'Goody Driver' ('goodwife') in January 1641 but 'Widow Driver' on 1 March.

After that, payments to Ellen multiply: fourpence on 1 March, tuppence on 8 March, fourpence on an unnumbered day, fourpence on 28 March and sevenpence in mid-April. In spring 1641, 'being sick', she was given sixpence and a shilling to buy hemp. During this difficult time, her name is linked with an Anne Usher in charitable payments, and it's possible the two women had moved in together. In 1643, Ellen was given four faggots of firewood. This dependence on parish funds meant that she was in the same vulnerable position as the other Framlingham women alongside whom she was arrested on suspicion of witchcraft.

During her imprisonment and watching, Ellen held out for a dreadful three days and two nights, despite questioning by Edward Weeding and one of her Framlingham neighbours, Robert Wayts or Wayth. Robert was a wealthy farmer living towards Baddingham, another parish overseer and a manor juror in the 1630s. In 1641, he was chosen as supervisor of the town's roads, responsible for fixing potholes. Unlike Ellen, he was literate enough to sign his own name on documents. And at last, worn out, she confessed to Robert that she had two suckling imps. The devil had appeared to her sixty years ago (in about 1585, which seems more likely to be when she was born) in the shape of a man, who told her to deny God and Christ and 'wooed her to marry him' – that story again! Ellen explained urgently to her interrogators that she had not had sex with Satan until they were married. Indeed, she said, it was only the sin of pride that made her succumb to his wooing. In her insistence on premarital chastity, Ellen sounds like a well-behaved Christian rather than a promiscuous witch. As she fantasised about wedding the devil, she even imagined they'd married in a parish church, although she didn't say which. Perhaps she thought it was St Michael's, Framlingham, the devil swaggering up the aisle to kiss her under the marble noses of earls, dukes and the lovechild of a king.

But her questioners didn't heed those pious details. Further interrogated, Ellen went on to tell them she'd had two children with Satan. Confusingly, she thought of these devil-children as changelings, infants supposedly left by fairies in place of human babies. Changelings were often sickly children, which was explained folklorically by their fairy blood. They usually died, distanced from their grieving parents by the belief they weren't really human. Perhaps that was what had happened to Ellen's boys. She'd had two sons early in her marriage: Thomas, born in 1604, and John in 1607. No more children are recorded, and no funerals appear in the parish register, but neither do weddings or grandchildren. Pitilessly, Ellen's interrogators were more interested in her babies' conception than their fate. Ellen told them Satan was a cloven-footed, cold lover – the supposed iciness of demonic semen was an obsession of some European witchfinders and the English questioners seem to have brought that idea to Framlingham. Although the devil lived with Ellen for two or three years – she wasn't sure which – he hid from the neighbours. And then, she concluded, 'he died as she thought', perhaps like her real husband, Thomas. The phrase 'as she thought' suggests her questioners were distancing themselves from an obvious theological error – as *they* thought, Satan was an immortal demon. But they accepted all the other parts of her story with satisfaction. Job done; another witch unmasked.

Anne Usher

Inevitably, Ellen Driver's friend Anne Usher was drawn into the witch hunt too. Anne was watched for two nights and confessed that about a year ago a thing like a small cat had walked over her legs and scratched them. After that she 'felt two things like butterflies in her secret parts'. They were both 'dancing and sucking'. She 'felt them with her hands and rubbed them and killed them'. In another context, Anne might have been reprimanded for masturbation, but this time her confession probably cost her her life.

She also told her questioners how a polecat leapt into her lap and spoke to her, asking her to reject God and Christ. If she did, the polecat offered, he would bring her food, 'but he never brought her anything after'. Anne knew what it felt like to be hungry when gifts of food weren't forthcoming from people or devils. Alongside Ellen Driver, she had been paid sevenpence from parish funds in 1641 and had received fourpence earlier that year. She said she had consented to the polecat-devil sucking two or three drops of blood from her hand – she wasn't sure if the blood had dripped onto a paper the animal had brought, or whether he had licked it up. Either way, it seemed an agreement had been made.[9]

Ann Palmer

Meanwhile, more people in witch-watcher Robert Wayts's household were coming forward with evidence against Ann Palmer, another poor widow. Ann lived in the suburbs and had been married to the farmer John Palmer. In the 1620s, the Palmers were paying at least three shillings and fourpence rent annually, including for their cottage, Madges, on the road to Framlingham Green. They were doing well.

But in the late 1630s, John gave up some of his land, and he died in 1638. Although his widow carried on at Madges with her three daughters, they were left poor. Ann received around eighteen shillings in parish charity in the first years of her widowhood, and although things improved after that, she still needed seven faggots of free firewood in 1643. By that time, she had lived under suspicion of witchcraft for at least five years.

Her accuser, Mary Gunnell, had worked as a servant in the house of Robert and Anne Wayts since the late 1630s, and she said that Ann Palmer had visited one day to ask for a mug of beer. Mary refused. Ann, she said, threatened her that 'she might want [lack] a cup of beer herself ere long'. Perhaps Ann was brooding on her own fall from security into want. But Mary did get a taste of deprivation: the Wayts' beer went bad. In Mary's mind, it was obvious what had happened. After her arrest, Ann Palmer was watched for at least one night, and confessed she had two unusual imps: Great Turkeycock and Little Turkeycock.[10]

Mary Edwards

Matthew Hopkins's witch hunt spread with crazy rapidity in Framlingham, far more eagerly pursued by townspeople than his previous hunt in Essex. The list of suspected women lengthened, and Mary Edwards, another widow, was accused of killing Elizabeth Smith, perhaps the daughter of blacksmith Edward Smith and his wife Elizabeth, born in 1633. Young Elizabeth died a fortnight after Mary gave her an apple, just like the witch in a folktale. Supposedly, in 1642, Mary also killed another child, Frances Wood, daughter of sexton Godfrey Wood, after a row over a hat.

Another charge against Mary was brought forward by the powerful Laund Pallant family, whose lands stretched across several local parishes, at Highfield and along the Woodbridge road. Edward Laund Pallant served regularly on manor court juries. Like the Wayts, the Laund Pallants employed servants, and one, twenty-three-year-old Margerie May, testified that Mary Edwards had come to the Laund Pallants' home in January 1645 asking for milk. Margerie knew Mary was poor and outcast: she'd had an illegitimate child in 1618 and received help from the parish from 1632 onwards.

So Margerie gave her some milk, but not as much as she

wanted. Mary shivered away into the winter cold, mumbling. Margerie feared Mary's muttering was actually cursing. The next day, her employer Edward Laund Pallant's son Robert, just twelve months old, began to 'shriek out fearfully' in his nurse's arms. Half his body became paralysed and tragically he died. He was buried on 13 January 1645, about the time his family should have been celebrating his first birthday. It was also the same day as the funeral of Frances Wood's father Godfrey. Grief was ripping through Framlingham, and weeping families compared notes. Several of them had upset Mary Edwards before tragedy struck. Searcher Mary Tracy added that when she had been examining Margaret Wyard, Margaret had told her it was common knowledge that Mary Edwards was the witch who killed Robert Laund Pallant.[11]

Elizabeth Warne

Other women were accused too, as the witch hunt reached a frenzied peak. Elizabeth Warne, a widow whose husband Charles had died in 1640, had tried to help her neighbour John Butteram. He had fallen out with someone else about a rent – perhaps for the house in The Street where he paid fivepence annually – and his son John had subsequently suffered cramps, leading him to fear that the boy might be bewitched. Elizabeth suggested 'an apple of a thistle' (a gall that appears on thistle stems) might help the child if pinned to his clothing. At first it seemed to be working, but soon his fits returned and suspicion turned on Elizabeth.

It's likely Elizabeth advertised herself as a magical practitioner – hence her suggested remedy – but whatever income she may have received from this, she was also described as 'being in want', and had received three pounds and two shillings from parish funds in 1642, as well as other gifts.

After her arrest, she was watched for three days and nights, until she despairingly cried out that 'pride and lustfulness had brought her to this, and desired she might be walked apace for she had the devil within'.

Ann Moats

Ann Moats, wife of Robert, who lived towards Dennington, confessed without such torture, although still under pressure of suspicion and hostile questioning, as well as body searching for demonic marks. She said the devil had come to her when she was cursing her husband and children. She'd covenanted with him and had two familiars. Mary Tracy searched Ann, and John Calver questioned her. He was another wealthy townsman, a manor juror with a house on Back Lane, land at Home Close and a cottage he rented out.

Margaret Bayts

Like Ann Moats, a further suspect, Margaret Bayts, confessed to Mary Tracy before any watching. Margaret said a thing like a mouse had sucked her; after two or three days' watching, she added that something nipped her 'secret parts', even in church. She was searched and 'marks' were found. We don't know any more about her, but she joined the ever-growing list of confessing 'witches'.[12]

Anne Nevell

So did Margaret Wyard's alleged co-conspirator Anne Nevell, whom Margaret had referred to in her confession as 'Mother Nevell'. Based on Margaret's evidence, Anne was suspected of bewitching corn in the fields of farmer William Mase. She was another poor widow, receiving help from the parish to pay her house rent.

Mary Becket

Then Anne's questioners moved on to Mary Becket, who lived towards Kettleburgh. Mary had been a widow since 1626 and – like Margaret Wyard – was pregnant when her husband died. She then had two illegitimate sons, in 1629 and 1634. Mary was watched for two nights, confessing that Satan appeared to her as a man. He told her 'her sins were so great there was no heaven for her'. Poor guilty Mary's familiars were unusual. They were bees – and she called them 'dors', dumbledors or bumblebees. When she became a witch, they flew over her bed, landed on her thigh and sucked blood. Her searchers confirmed two teats, presumably stings, remained.

Like most of her fellow accused, Mary had been in need for years. In 1631, she received four shillings and fourpence to buy hemp and a further gift of a shilling and sevenpence 'in her distress', with more gifts in 1632. Her landlord had to petition parish authorities to pay her rent in summer 1642. Meanwhile, Mary and one of her sons received around two pounds in charitable payments in 1640 with six shillings' worth of cloth to make a suit of clothes in 1642 and at least a shilling in 1644. In 1642, she was paid fourpence to nurse a sick neighbour. It was a hefty welfare bill, supporting Mary's whole family. Some neighbours must have resented her neediness, and of course she was also considered to be immoral because she was an unmarried mother. It was the classic profile of a witchcraft suspect, and she joined the crowd of imprisoned women.[13]

Margery Chimney Wyeth

Framlingham's witch hunt had so far shockingly ensnared eleven people, all female and almost all of them victims of the economic crisis that had beset the little town. However, as accusations spread, suspicion travelled up the social scale. Margery Chimney, also known as Wyeth or With, was accused by suspects Margaret Wyard and 'Widow' Man – perhaps Alice Man, who lived towards Baddingham. We know Matthew Hopkins questioned Margery Chimney himself, because he later gave evidence against her in court. Margery was accused of killing John Sheldrake, along with her fellow witch Margaret Wyard. But her motivation was unclear: not, apparently, charity refused or economic envy, since she was moderately well-off. In 1625, Margery Chimney Wyeth was left a cottage for life and ten pounds, a fourposter bed, two feather bolsters and a pillow by her father, the carpenter Nicholas Cole. Her children, Thomas, Grace and Ann Chimney (from her 1587 marriage to George Chimney) and Edward and Mary Wyeth (from her 1604 marriage to Thomas Wyeth), each received legacies too, as did Margery's mother Margaret. Robert Wayts, an accuser of other witches, witnessed Nicholas Cole's will and in 1645 he offered no complaint against Nicholas's daughter Margery Chimney. Evidently she still had friends in her community, unlike many of the other suspects.

However, at least one important man believed her to be a witch. Thomas Fisher was another longstanding official, a churchwarden and manor juror, part of the same social group as many of the other Framlingham accusers. He farmed parish land at Bellrope Meadow, paid large sums in tax and in 1642 was constable and supervisor of roads. Earlier in summer 1645, Thomas's unnamed child had suffered 'strange fits' after quarrelling with Margery. The child was covered in blue spots, boils or bruises, and the little body did not stiffen after death as expected, leading Thomas and his wife Mary to conclude it was bewitched. There is record of an unnamed son of Thomas and Mary Fisher being buried on 25 August 1645, likely this child. His father may have had to leave the funeral to ride directly to the Assizes and give evidence against the boy's supposed murderer, since the court was already in session by then.

Desperate to rebut the charge, Margery told her questioners the devil had tempted her to serve him, but she had refused. Then she said something revealing: John Lowes, 'Mr Lowis' as she called him, the vicar of the nearby village of Brandeston, had once instructed her 'never confess anything about witchcraft'. Matthew Hopkins's name appears directly after the reference to him in Margery's testimony, suggesting the appearance of the vicar in stories about Margery might have piqued his interest. But unfortunately, Margery couldn't follow John Lowes's advice. Although she fended off suspicions about the death of Thomas Fisher's child, she was bullied into confirming a tale circulating around herself and Margaret Wyard: that she had blasted farmer William Mase's corn along with her fellow witch Anne Nevell.[14]

As the witch hunters ran out of time to question their suspects before the Assize court met, all the Framlingham women whose stories you've read were sent to Bury St Edmunds, twelve miles away, to be tried. The Assize records are lost, so we don't know with certainty any of the outcomes of their trials. Certainly, many were hanged. But we do know something about how the Assize grand jury of twenty-four men perceived them. When the grand jury were tasked with vetting charges made against the accused, someone made notes recording their decisions. The jury approved the indictments of Mary Scrutton, Margaret Wyard, Ellen Driver, Anne Usher and Anne Moats, so all these suspects went to trial. However, they rejected the indictments of Ann Palmer, Margaret

Bayts and Mary Becket as insufficient. It's still, unfortunately, possible that these women were tried on other charges or returned to prison. But in 1646, a widow 'Pamer' and widow 'Becett' were recorded in Framlingham as receiving parish charity of three shillings and one shilling and sixpence respectively. Are they our Ann and Mary? We don't know – they could be. The grand jury did not approve either of Mary Edwards's first two indictments for killing the Smith and Wood children, but did approve a final indictment for killing Robert Laund Pallant, so she was tried for that. Perhaps she was acquitted, since a Mary Edwards is listed as receiving charity in Framlingham in April 1646, but it is a common name.

The grand jury accepted Elizabeth Warne's indictment for witchcraft but rejected her other indictment for hurting the Butterams' child. Likewise, they did not accept that Margery Chimney had killed the Sheldrake or Fisher boys but did decide she should be tried for using witchcraft. Finally, although we have no details of the crimes alleged against 'Widow' Man or a woman called Anne Sherwood, wife of William and mother of several children, the notes tell us the grand jury rejected Anne Sherwood's indictment.[15]

The confinement of the women at Bury was covered by the anonymous author of a news pamphlet, *A True Relation*, in September 1645, although only one of the women can be identified as part of the Framlingham group. The writer records one hundred and twenty nameless suspected witches being held in Bury, 'who had all their trial now'. This phrase could mean that the suspects had been tried already or were awaiting trial. Note the huge number: as Matthew Hopkins left Framlingham and moved on to other Suffolk communities, he became more and more successful in spreading his witch hunt across the county, as it escalated dramatically in scale. John Stearne was doing the same in adjacent Suffolk communities, the two men having split up to cover more ground. Many of these suspects' trials were held at Bury in late August. Then, however, the Assizes were adjourned for three weeks because a Royalist army was approaching. By then, the one hundred and twenty remanded people had neither been released nor hanged.

Ellen Driver was one of the many stranded in prison during the adjournment, and during that time the pamphlet's author heard her story: 'some [prisoners] have confessed they have had carnal copulation with the devil', he exclaimed, 'one of which said that she (before her husband died) conceived twice by him [Satan], but as soon as she was delivered of them they ran away in most horrid long and ugly shapes'. There's enough detail here to recall Ellen's two devil-fathered changeling children. We don't know whether she was tried after this date or had already been tried and acquitted or reprieved. But in 1646, 'the vido Driver' (vido meaning widow) is listed as receiving parish charity back in Framlingham – a penny.[16] Perhaps, just perhaps, Ellen was released? But 'vido Driver' may be someone else and, like so many of the hundred and twenty Suffolk suspects tried in August 1645, Ellen's story is preserved only in fragments that leave us guessing. Only one of the Suffolk 'witches' has a near-complete biography, and he is the subject of our next chapter.

CHAPTER 7

The World Turned Upside Down

John Lowes of Brandeston, Suffolk, 1645

During her last illness in September 1648, John Lowes's wife Margaret must have looked back with both pride and grief at her long life in public service. The vicar's wife in the tiny Suffolk village of Brandeston, she had arrived in her new community half a century before, in 1599. There she'd been expected to promote respectable living and good works, maintain helpful relationships with her husband's colleagues and parishioners and keep happy his patron, one of the Seckford family whose mansion dominated the nearby town of Woodbridge. Margaret managed social interactions with such gentry, gifts to the needy and polite exchanges with businessmen and farmers. She kept the vicarage running smoothly, marshalling servants to care for its larder and linen, fowls and firewood. She sat through hours of her husband's sermons, prayed for his health and success, talked – perhaps even argued – with him about matters of conscience and politics. It was an ordinary, pious life. Then Margaret's husband was accused of witchcraft, and he died in 1645 in traumatic circumstances. With John dead, her widowhood was lived out in a very different world from the welcoming one of 1599, and her memories traced a tragic four-decade fall: from security, respectability and grace into terror, ignominy and chaos.

Margaret's husband, John Lowes, was appointed vicar of Brandeston on 6 May 1596, although he was not yet a fully ordained priest. John was a deacon, a lesser ministerial role that was a step on the road to ordination, meaning he could perform some ceremonies – baptism, marriage – but not others. He might have been the son of a previous vicar and his wife, George and Alice Lowes, although that's not certain. John did possess, however, Bachelor and Master of Arts degrees from Cambridge University, where he'd studied in the 1590s. He'd attended St John's College, which tended to produce evangelical radicals and possibly began his ministry holding subversive views. In 1594, he was questioned by church officials at Ipswich about whether he conformed to the rites of the state church, a concern based on sermons he'd given at Bury St Edmunds. Bury was known for its Puritan preaching; every Monday up to thirty clergymen would assemble to lecture. During his career, John was described both as a 'painful preacher' – meaning painstaking, and often code for 'Puritan' – and merely a 'reading parson', someone content to trot out pre-printed sermons. One enemy said he changed his mind 'as the wind blows' while some Brandeston parishioners complained both that he constantly criticised their lifestyles – that sounds like a picky reformer – and that he taught 'strange points of doctrine not fit . . . to be repeated'. Others said he favoured Catholics and various dissenters who refused to attend church.[1]

But despite this lack of religious clarity, John must have appeared a good catch for his fiancée Margaret. He held land in Brandeston, in Cretingham about a mile west, and would later lease land at Framlingham, four miles east. For the latter he paid eight shillings a year – four shillings less than his fellow tenant

James Hopkins, father of Matthew, but a sizeable sum. John and Margaret Lowes were married on 12 August 1599. Margaret – then Margaret Hollme – was the widow of another clergyman from the village of Cotton, fifteen miles west of Brandeston.[2] That summer she wrote her name in Brandeston's parish register in a firm but unpractised hand alongside John's assured flourish and relocated to her new home, Brandeston's vicarage on leafy Cretingham Lane, a few minutes' walk from the church.

The old vicarage is a two-storey timber-framed house, built in the 1500s, comfortable and sturdy. It is now known as The Broadhurst, and when I visit, it has been painted pink and a Union Jack waves over its porch in the spring sunshine. In contrast, the Lowes' first winter was a harsh one, with icicles hanging from the porch jetty and John's congregation shivering in the unheated church. All Saints stood in an exposed spot beside Brandeston Hall, home of the lords of Brandeston Manor. In 1599, the lord was John Revett, and on his death in 1616 his forty-three-year-old son Nicholas succeeded him. The Revetts got on adequately with John Lowes, but they soon knew him to be 'a contentious man', who made enemies easily.

Like Richard Golty at Framlingham, John Lowes chased his parishioners for tithe payments, but his argumentativeness went deeper than that. Early on, he fell out with at least two important families: the Laund Pallants and the Pulhams. In 1606, he gave evidence in a church court against Mary Laund Pallant, who was accused of aborting an illegitimate baby at her father Thomas's home in Brandeston. Mary had been skipping church from September 1604 onwards and in December she had confessed to John this was because she was pregnant and had taken a 'poison' made from opium and juniper leaves to cause an abortion. In March 1605, John went to the church court to reveal this, badly damaging her reputation. By 1611, he was so much at odds with another family, the Pulhams, that some even whispered he'd poisoned their son. One day in late April of that year, George Pulham had been drinking with John and shortly after fell suddenly sick at Brandeston. He died on 29 April and was buried at Framlingham on the 30th. His grieving family took no action at the time, but shocking rumours continued to circulate that the vicar had murdered him.

There was a nasty story, too, about a 'poor tailor' whom John apparently hated for his 'sobriety and constancy' – virtues which he lacked himself and scorned in others, so they alleged. It was said that John had wanted to harass the tailor with vexatious lawsuits or charge him with some kind of sin in a church court, but because of the man's quiet, godly lifestyle, even his vicar could find no reasonable complaint against him. At last, or so the gossips said, he hit on an amusing plan. One Sunday morning, John had his servant summon the tailor to his bedside, where he asked him 'to mend his breeches presently [immediately], for he was to put them on'. The emergency repair was completed quickly and the tailor went home. But the day after, John denounced him to the church authorities for Sabbath-breaking. Did the tailor not know, he sneered, that 'it was not lawful to mend breeches on the sabbath day'? It was God's mandated day of rest, when work was forbidden. If the story was true, this was an ugly trick. But even if it wasn't, the gossip stuck.[3]

Soon, the Brandeston villagers openly disliked their vicar. Some believed he enjoyed taking his neighbours to court to 'plague' or annoy them. Some thought he had troubling knowledge of drugs and charms, that he read occult books and presented himself as a magically adept 'physician and surgeon', but that his incompetence caused 'hurt' to those who consulted him. Others resented his interference in their lives: he 'did taunt and check' them in church in unusually personal ways. He got very angry, very quickly and had a habit of telling people they would rue the day they'd crossed him. John's rages seemed strikingly unclerical to those who experienced them. Flinching from his wrath, they began to believe he was attacking them out of spite.

This came to a head in early 1614, when John became embroiled in another row, this time with twenty-one-year-old tailor Ellis Maye. The fact that Ellis was a tailor might mean that he or his father – also a tailor – was the hapless Sabbath breaker we heard about in the village's gossip. This time, however, the argument between vicar and tailor was well documented. It was about a pigsty Ellis had built against John's barn. As was his habit, John went to court to argue the matter out. Ellis was terrified: he was a poor, illiterate man who signed his name with a mark shaped like a pair of scissors, reflecting his profession. How could he match the vicar's lawyers? Then, in late March, Ellis's father, John, died. Ellis blamed the witchcraft of Ann Amison, a friend of John Lowes.

Ann was likely an older or single woman: there's no trace of her as a bride or mother in John's parish register. She may have lived outside Brandeston, since as well as Ellis Maye's allegations, she was accused of killing the cattle of farmer Toby Barrow at Hoo, two miles away. Toby and Ellis were disgusted that a vicar kept 'frequent and familiar company' with this 'vile and wicked witch' and planned to have her arrested. They approached a magistrate, Samuel Blennerhassett of Loudham, six miles from Brandeston, to do that. But when John heard, he threatened Ellis: he 'would undo him or make him run [from] the country'. Ellis panicked – he had 'but a poor cottage and one acre of land to maintain himself, his mother [Anne] and two poor fatherless children of his brother's' – but he persisted in demanding Ann Amison's arrest.

So, John offered his home to Ann as a shelter from the authorities. When Brandeston's constable, George Sterling, arrived with other men to seize her, John pretended she wasn't there. The constable insisted he wanted to talk and eventually Ann opened the vicarage window. Immediately she was dragged out. Outraged at the violation of his and Margaret's home, John swore 'by Jesus God' that if he'd spotted his neighbours' trick 'he would have shot bullets in their flesh'. He then pursued Ann to Loudham Hall and told the astonished magistrate Blennerhassett he would stand bail for her, 'body for body or soul for soul'. That meant he would pay a sum guaranteeing her appearance in court, so she wouldn't face remand. John's brother Nicholas Lowes paid the sum agreed and Ann went home.[4]

John also managed to get Ann's court appearance delayed so she was not summoned to the summer Assizes, but instead to the winter ones in early 1615. He spent the period between her arrest and trial threatening terrible consequences for any parishioners who dared give evidence against her. Under legal convention, if no one appeared at the Assizes to accuse a suspect, then their trial would be abandoned: they would be discharged by proclamation of the court, effectively the same as acquittal. So, John told Ellis Maye, Toby Barrow and others who had voiced suspicions about Ann that he would ruin them if they became prosecution witnesses. He even had one woman arrested for slander. He also threatened he would 'be revenged' more generally on Ann's accusers. That was an unfortunate phrase when everyone was edgy about poisoning and witchcraft. Ann's accusers hoped John meant he would fight them in court or criticise them in church – and he did both – but they also wondered if he meant something more. In late 1614, they took a stand against his verbal aggression and complained to their magistrate, so on 11 January 1615 at Woodbridge magistrates' court, John Lowes was charged with being a barrator – a compulsive quarreller and bringer of lawsuits – a disturber of the peace and a person of bad reputation.

By this point, one of his and Ann's enemies had come to believe that John could do harmful magic himself. The farmer Jonas Cooke, a business connection of Ellis Maye's, had become suspicious when his son Francis fell ill, his 'mouth and face most woefully drawn out of the right course'. When John Lowes saw the child, he put a good-luck charm, a golden chain, around the little boy's neck and Francis soon felt better. The two men's conversation warmed and drifted to horses – good luck in breeding, trading, perhaps racing. Then Jonas remembered a funny proverb. Recalling Margaret Lowes had been a clergyman's widow when she married John, he joked there was a saying about sex with clergymen's wives: 'he that would have good luck to horseflesh, he must lie with a parson's wife'. He expected a laugh, but – not particularly surprisingly – John was livid, seeing the remark as a slur on Margaret's reputation. Great harm followed from his immediate chivalrous impulse to defend her. 'In very angry manner', John spluttered he would make Jonas repent the joke and he stalked away. The farmer went home mortified. Then several of Jonas's horses and cattle fell sick and some died. *Dear Lord*, Jonas must have thought, *what have I done? I made a silly remark about his wife, and my vicar has cursed me! The world had turned upside down.* Suddenly the man of God at the vicarage looked very much like an agent of the devil.

Even as he put two and two together and made five, Jonas must have been perplexed by these implications of his suspicion. Clergymen did sometimes have magical interests: astrology or a claimed relationship with angels and spirits. John's good-luck charm suggested he was that sort of minister. Later, there was also a rumour he'd consulted a magician about finding silver spoons stolen from him. But it was very rare for pastors like John to be accused of witchcraft. There had been a couple of cases in France and Germany, and in England a few medieval monks had been mythologised as devil-raisers, such as the thirteenth-century Oxford lecturer Roger Bacon and his Suffolk-born colleague Thomas Bungay. These learned men were thought to be able to control demons by using holy rites. But the idea that a parish priest might curse his congregation and kill their livestock was a very different thing. Yet Jonas Cooke recalled that, in defending Ann Amison, John Lowes had said something significant. He stated that 'he was as much a witch as the said Ann Amison was'. Of course, John meant neither of them was a witch. But, looking back, Jonas now believed his vicar was taunting him with an admission of guilt hidden in plain sight, one that he must act upon before it was too late.

Unfortunately, Jonas's situation worsened fast. Around 3 May 1615, his daughter Mary Cooke began to grizzle with 'strange passion and in a strange manner'. Soon she was shrieking in pain and, tragically, the little girl died on 6 May. Her father was sure John Lowes was to blame. He made the vicar conduct Mary's burial service on 7 May, then went to a magistrate and accused John formally of murder by witchcraft. It all made sense now, Jonas felt. John Lowes was friends with a woman accused of witchcraft and had defended her against a constable. He had raged, blasphemed and sworn revenge. Then Jonas had insulted John's wife and tragedy had followed. He felt more certain about his accusation of John because Ann Amison herself was no longer a threat. True to her word to John and Nicholas Lowes, who had stood bail for her, she had presented herself at the Assizes at Bury St Edmunds on 9 February 1615. The jury had found her guilty and she had been hanged. This logically meant that any witchcraft practised in Brandeston after mid-February 1615 couldn't be at her hand. In the eyes of Jonas Cooke, that left John as chief suspect. Indeed, during Mary Cooke's illness, her now-bereaved father had had nightmares about the vicar. He told friends that

John had appeared to him surrounded by animal familiars. Imagine Jonas' horror when Toby Barrow, Ann's accuser at Hoo, confirmed he'd seen the same vision. Toby even reported that John's familiar spirits said 'come, let us kill him and then the rest will be quiet'.

Soon, Jonas and Toby were overheard saying in public, 'Mr Lowes is a witch and I will prove him so' and 'I have seen him and his imps or evil spirits appear to me', with Jonas adding: 'and he did bewitch a child of mine'. So, John sued Jonas and Toby for slander. The case was set to be heard in the court of King's Bench, London, in April or May 1615. But because Jonas had also accused John of witchcraft, instead both the slander suit and the charge of witchcraft were tried together at Bury St Edmunds Assizes on 19 July 1615. Since witchcraft was a felony, it had to be assessed by Assize judges – and if John was guilty, he would be hanged like Ann Amison. As well as being charged with the murder of Mary Cooke on 6 May 1615, he was also charged with being an abettor, or helper, of Ann in her crimes. The suspicion that John had murdered George Pulham was finally given its day in court too, with an indictment alleging John had given him 'a cup of poison' back in 1611. And lastly, a new charge surfaced: that John Lowes had attacked his parishioner John Scott in the churchyard at Brandeston, an assault with a cudgel that left the victim bleeding from his nose and with a wound on his skull. John Scott was a young father from Brandeston, but we don't know how he'd upset his vicar.[5] The outcome of some of the charges against John Lowes is unknown, but we do know that he was acquitted of witchcraft, while Jonas and Toby were found guilty of slander and fined. Jonas had to pay thirty pounds and Toby fourteen.

These were large sums. Indeed, several of John Lowes's accusers later said they'd been bankrupted and driven out of their homes after fighting him in court. One, Toby Wade, whose family farmed at Moores in Brandeston, and Millmount in Cretingham – where he neighboured the Laund Pallants – moved as far away as Essex. In September 1615, these multiple enemies attacked John again, and on 4 October he appeared at Woodbridge to answer renewed charges of barratry. No witnesses came forward, however, so he was discharged. In mid-October 1615, he complained to the Court of Star Chamber, London, about Jonas Cooke, Ellis Maye and Toby Wade, but there's no record of the outcome. In 1616, Jonas surprisingly brought a King's Bench lawsuit alleging John had slandered him, claiming: 'Jonas Cooke is a witch and I will prove him to be a witch and I will be bound to the king [for] one hundred pounds to give evidence against him for witchcraft and murder'. Maybe John did come to think Jonas had cursed him or maybe he was just making a point: could anyone prove they were *not* a witch? There's no further record of evidence in this case, and by 1617 the feud seems to have fizzled out. Jonas Cooke died in 1628, and perhaps the Brandeston community was calmer for a time: in 1630, John Lowes witnessed land documents for one of his neighbours in the normal way expected of a trusted clergyman. But he still had many enemies.[6]

In the mid-1630s and then again in 1641, he was summoned to the Assizes, accused of barratry and possibly witchcraft as well – the account is unclear. At the second trial he was convicted of barratry, according to a later report, although the court records are lost. In 1641, his enemies also petitioned the Archbishop of Canterbury, William Laud, to fire him (they were unlucky, as Archbishop Laud had just been imprisoned for treason). They also told John Lowes's story to a journalist – or, at least, their version of it. The result, a pamphlet titled *A Magazine of Scandal*, was published in 1642 in London. It told several tales about John's spiky personality and alleged witchcraft during a rant about the 'heap of wickedness of two infamous ministers'. The other pastor named was from Earl Soham, two miles from Brandeston, and had been convicted of manslaughter.

The anonymous journalist was careful not to repeat the directly slanderous statement that John Lowes was a witch, but suggestively noted 'many have so accused him upon their deaths'. 'It is most certain that he hath used the society and help of those that have been convicted and executed for witchcraft', the writer continued, meaning Ann Amison, and adding he 'hath the society and daily frequentation of diverse others that are vehemently suspected for witches'. Margery Chimney Wyeth and Anne Sherwood of Framlingham are the most likely people referred to here, since in 1645 both confirmed they knew John Lowes and Margery recounted his advice to her never to confess any witchcraft offence. John 'without doubt hath had the help of such [witches] to work his intended purposes', the journalist concluded back in 1642. It was an effective smear campaign.

In 1643, the year after the pamphlet's publication, the lord of Brandeston Manor, Nicholas Revett, died. Just as the loss of Thomas Witham's stabilising influence from Manningtree in the same year created opportunities for insurgent voices, so Nicholas's death left a power vacuum in Brandeston. His son John Revett was slow to establish himself as he wrestled with legacies and politics – he was a Royalist, spending time with the king at Oxford in 1644, and then one of his sons died so that his attention naturally focused on his own family's future rather than his vicar's. Meanwhile, a national campaign began to eject traditionalist ministers from their jobs, partly so their salaries and landholdings could be used to finance the ongoing civil war. Even the Bishop of Norwich, Joseph Hall, was removed.

Now famous thanks to the printed pamphlet, John Lowes was also targeted. Following an order of Parliament in March 1644 'for removing scandalous ministers', he was questioned by a panel of five local gentlemen, and a dossier of evidence was compiled based on complaints made by his parishioners. He was given fourteen days to answer. As was inevitable, he was judged to be a 'delinquent' and the Committee of Parliamentarian gentry for Suffolk ordered he be sacked and his assets seized. In autumn 1644, sequestrators moved into Brandeston, evicting him and Margaret from their home. They diverted John's tithe payments into repairing the dilapidated church, fencing and draining the vicarage lands, mowing and stacking his hay. Then they gave a large donation to 'the British army and the six [Parliamentarian] garrisons' out of the sequestration fund and paid themselves and their lawyers a daily rate for the time it took to strip John of his post.[7]

When Matthew Hopkins and John Stearne's witch hunt reached Suffolk, it was only a matter of time before the disgraced vicar John Lowes was denounced to the witchfinders. He was arrested and taken to Framlingham, where questioning by Hopkins was ongoing. There, horrifyingly, the now elderly former vicar was thrown into water – perhaps the castle moat – to see if he floated or sank. This was the witchcraft test John Stearne had proposed for Bess Clarke back in Manningtree: floating meant guilt. His proposal had been vetoed in Essex, but the Suffolk witchfinding volunteers had no such reservations.

John Lowes's hands and feet were probably tied, this being the usual practice during such a swimming experiment, and he was hustled into the water. His abusers tell us offhandedly that 'after his swimming at Framlingham he confessed'. It was actually quite easy for suspects to float, because of the air in their lungs and the natural buoyancy of a prone, clothed body, as was evidenced by the number of volunteers, people not under suspicion, who joined the vicar in the moat and attempted to sink – but they floated too. Later John reportedly told his interrogators, 'the water was enchanted by another witch', in the hope that he would be cleared of suspicion in the confusion over these unexpected test results. But regardless of the outcome, minds had been made up, and so he was watched, walked and searched – and supposed witch marks were found on his head and beneath his tongue.

Under this assault, the clergyman – once so pious and secure, a pillar of church and state – confessed he had seven spirits who sucked at these teats, called Tom, Flo, Bess, Mary and other names. The spirit Tom also served Anne Sherwood at Framlingham, he said. John and Tom had sunk ships together between Great Yarmouth and Winterton, Norfolk, and killed many cattle. John denied having made a contract with his spirits, however, although he said Tom sometimes spoke in 'a hollow voice', suggesting that he should.

Yet when Matthew Hopkins re-questioned John at Framlingham after his initial confession, the vicar contradicted his earlier assertion that he had made no pact with the devil. That was presumably because Hopkins bullied him into confession in his usual ways. John explained he'd agreed to the demonic contract because 'in pride of heart' he had wanted to be equal with, or above, God. It was a shocking moment: the venerable vicar humbling himself to the self-righteous youth, going further even than Rebecca West in his ambition to be equal with the Christian deity. We might wonder how Hopkins felt about interrogating a clergyman: a man holding the same office as his own father, James Hopkins, and stepfather, Thomas Witham. Who had the whip-hand now? Exhausted and wandering in his mind, the old minister told Hopkins how he'd sealed the covenant with his blood and received three spirits in exchange. He also added a new story about sinking a ship, further to his previous confession. Once, he said, he had been walking on the sea wall at Landguard Fort near Harwich, a place he'd visited to preach. He saw a fleet of ships and told his spirit to sink one, a new craft from Ipswich sailing in the middle of the fleet. This ship was wallowing amid frothing waves and soon sank with the loss of all fourteen crew and passengers. When Hopkins asked if he was not grieved to have caused such harm, John Lowes replied defiantly that he was delighted to have 'made fourteen widows in one quarter of an hour'. He even had a charm to save him from imprisonment and hanging, he said, although he could not explain why, if this were the case, he was now in custody.[8]

At this stage in the witch hunt, dozens of people were now being arrested and tortured by watching and walking, searching and swimming, across Suffolk. Suspects from eastern Suffolk were sent to Ipswich prison to await trial, while suspects from western Suffolk went to Bury St Edmunds. Unless they could pay for better treatment, they lived for months in filthy, crowded cells, sleeping on straw – and they were even expected to pay for that. Prisoners caught plagues, fevers and bacterial infections in summer, and influenza and tuberculosis in winter; many went hungry because they couldn't buy food. Ipswich jailer James Rigges had to petition magistrates for more public funding because 'very many persons of several parishes have been committed … for witchcraft', so there was 'very great and extraordinary charge'. Most of the prisoners were 'no way able to provide for themselves being very poor and impotent nor any way able to pay of themselves any fees'. In Bury, where there was a prison on Cornhill at Moyse's Hall, Bury's jailer Joseph Alexander petitioned magistrates to recover six pounds and ten shillings spent on bread specifically for these 'prisoners of the franchise of Bury committed for witchcraft'. There were so many that the Cornhill prison was full and a barn in the grounds of the former abbey had to be turned into an overflow jail. The sum the jailer requested to feed all these people is around £760 in today's money, and the 'franchise' covered only about a third of the county, so imagine how many suspected witches there must have been imprisoned across the whole of Suffolk! We know there were at least a hundred and forty of them (again, *one hundred and forty*), but there could well have been more. Eventually, in August 1645, all of them were taken to Bury for trial.[9]

At first the court was set to be a regular Assize session, with normal personnel and rules. But Parliament granted a special commission instead, believing this was justified by a state of emergency – that emergency being the sheer number of witches apparently roaming wartime Suffolk. Presiding over this special court would be a fully qualified judge, John Godbolt or Godbold, just as if the court were a regular one. But Godbolt would now be assisted by two reformist ministers: Samuel Fairclough, rector of Kedington, Suffolk, and Edmund Calamy, rector of Rochford, Essex. This was, of course, unprecedented: clergymen did not serve as Assize judges. Fairclough had already been involved in examining witches identified by John Stearne, who like Hopkins had been working his witchfinding way across Suffolk, the two working separately but in tandem. Meanwhile, Calamy served as a religious advisor to Parliament.

Both men had preached repeatedly about 'the sins of England' committed by 'enemies of God', those who were 'profane and impious', members of Satan's 'rout and company', and the punishment of 'oaths, blasphemies, beastly uncleanness [and] swinish excesses' by 'the heartcutting threatenings of the law'. Indeed, before the trial had even started Fairclough preached two sermons to the court. By the time this story was told to the Bury clergyman Francis Hutchinson in the later seventeenth century, Fairclough's exact words were lost, but Hutchinson was suspicious: 'what notions he laid before them [the court] to proceed upon', he wrote, 'we cannot now say; but the effect was that they went on to execute them [the convicted witches] in great numbers ... we may believe he recommended these prosecutions as a piece of piety and reformation, that showed the zeal of their time'. A more sympathetic account suggests Fairclough insisted no one should prosecute a suspected witch, much less condemn them, without 'plain convincing evidence', but admits he began his preaching with a rousing proof that 'there was such a sin as that of witchcraft ... and did then confute all those arguments ... produced to the contrary'.[10]

Fairclough, Calamy and Godbolt's blended state/church court met in Bury's Shire Hall, nestled against the wall of the former abbey's churchyard. Part of it had once been a chapel dedicated to St Margaret, while some was used as a schoolhouse until it was given to Bury's equivalent of a town council, the Guildhall Feoffees, as a courtroom and office. To this repurposed monastic building came John Lowes, the Framlingham women and their hundred-plus fellow suspects, exhausted, in chains and many surely in great distress.

When he was marched into the courtroom, John Lowes had recovered sufficiently from the torture inflicted on him to retract his confession and plead not guilty. But his defiance did not help his defence. Someone who attended the trial told Francis Hutchinson that Lowes 'maintained his innocence stoutly' in the face of his accusers 'and challenged them to make proof of such things as they laid to his charge', but the judges were not convinced. Only one of them, Godbolt, was used to enforcing legal standards of proof, while Fairclough and Calamy would have relied on faith, divine revelation and theological argument to make their decisions. While the trial records are lost, we know Matthew Hopkins and John Stearne both gave evidence against several suspects, including John Lowes, along with many other speakers over the course of the trial, which lasted several days. By now, both men were presenting themselves as expert witnesses, witchfinding professionals with wide experience in Essex and in over thirty Suffolk communities. Unfortunately, their words were more persuasive than John Lowes's fair demand for proof of his crimes, and he was found guilty of witchcraft.[11]

Vicar John Lowes was hanged on 27 August 1645 at Bury, along with seventeen other convicted people. The night before their execution they were kept in the old abbey barn, where they had bravely sworn to each other that none of them would confess at the gallows, perhaps hoping this final act of resistance might help stop the witch hunt. The sight of a former clergyman being killed for supposedly making a pact with Satan must certainly have sent ripples of amazement and confusion through the assembled crowds. Even more troublingly, this 'witch' not only refused to confess, but he recited the Christian burial service for himself, according to a witness who spoke years later with Francis Hutchinson. John 'committed his own body to the ground', Hutchinson related sadly, 'in sure and certain hope of the resurrection to eternal life'.[12]

After his execution and that of the seventeen unnamed people hanged alongside him, one hundred and twenty witchcraft suspects remained imprisoned in Bury during a three-week adjournment of the court. The witch trials then resumed, but their outcomes are unknown to history. Some reports suggest 'more than twenty', or sixty, or seventy, hangings in total, while one suggests a hundred. Some suspects died in prison during the adjournment, such as Henry Carre, a scholarly young man from Rattlesden who had confessed to John Stearne after supposed witch marks were found on him. Henry broke down, lamenting 'that he had forsaken God, and God him, and therefore [he] would be hanged'. Stearne was disturbed by the similarities between

Carre and John Lowes – both 'well educated' men of 'knowledge' who had perhaps read too many books trying 'to understand secret and hidden things'. Why, he mused, would these men – so unlike the usual ignorant, female witch – 'give themselves over to Satan'? Was it vanity, scholarly pride, 'over much curiosity'? Of course, the answer was that they had not.

When the court closed its session and the hangings were over, John Godbolt and one of his court officials were awarded the huge sum of one hundred and thirty pounds in expenses for their two return journeys from London to Bury for 'the trial of the witches and other malefactors'. For them, it had been time lucratively spent. The money came from the Parliamentary sequestration fund, which included the assets seized from John Lowes's home at Brandeston. The property and savings of convicted felons were confiscated by the state to pay for their imprisonment and processing and, of course, John and his wife Margaret had already lost their home to the government when he had been dismissed from his job. At least Margaret was not accused of witchcraft herself, and under the law she was able to claim some compensation to keep her from absolute destitution. Cash being in short supply during the war, part of her sequestration and widow's settlement was derisively paid in cheese. Margaret Lowes died in Brandeston three years after John's execution, stripped of her husband, her reputation and her financial security. How cruel it was that she and John were even forced to pay for his imprisonment, trial and execution and how sadly their lives had both ended because of witchcraft accusation.[13]

CHAPTER 8

The Devil and the Deep Blue Sea

Nazareth Fassett, Mark Pryme, Elizabeth Bradwell and the Great Yarmouth witches, Norfolk, 1645

On 13 September 1631, Nazareth Fassett, a labourer's wife from Great Yarmouth, Norfolk, was the last person to appear before that town's magistrates at the Sessions of Gaol Delivery held in the Tolhouse Hall. Before Nazareth was summoned to stand before the town's great men, they had adjudicated on several other cases: the theft of some pillowcases and a petticoat by a sailor and his widowed mother, illicit gambling with dice and cards at a house in the town, an argument about who was responsible for an unsafe bridge and funding for repairs to the church. Nazareth's case was no more serious than these, and less serious than some. While the pillowcase and petticoat thieves risked execution, Nazareth was only likely to be fined or required to make a public apology if she was found guilty. She was charged with slander, spreading – according to her indictment – great scandals and lies about her innocent neighbours to their lasting harm. We don't know the outcome, but the trial left her with a criminal record that we can still view today in the town's sessions book. Hearing the case against her were eight Justices of the Peace for Great Yarmouth. One, Miles Corbet, would meet her again fourteen years later, when Nazareth was charged with being a witch.[1]

The Tolhouse where she was on trial in 1631, and would be again in 1645, is a characterful two-storey building of grey flint. There are bricks inset where doors and windows have been re-built over the centuries, gothic arches competing with rectangular leaded lights. Once the Tolhouse was part of a medieval home but by the seventeenth century the upper half of the house's great hall had become the courtroom, divided from the lower-storey prison by a plank floor. Prisoners would scrabble up a narrow, steep, dark chute from their cell, scaling rickety wooden stairs, to emerge blinking into the daylight of the courtroom and face their trial. The Tolhouse was bombed in the Second World War, but was later rebuilt, and you can now stand in a reconstruction of the courtroom where Nazareth faced her judges.

It's easy to imagine her panic: she was trapped in the web of the town's government, thick walls cutting her off from the chatter and bustle of the streets below, the smell of the prison seeping up through the floorboards. The corporation or council of Great Yarmouth owned the whole complex, holding its civil, criminal and maritime courts in this upper room, then known as the Heighning Chamber. 'Heighning' tolls were taxes charged on herring caught by non-Yarmouth fishing boats and sold in the town. And the council's Tolhouse was, and still is, at the centre of Great Yarmouth's old borough, surrounded by fine gentry homes and churches built with the profits of the fishing industry.

Great Yarmouth tops a sandspit at the mouth of the River Yare, which flows through the watery Norfolk Broads eastwards into the North Sea. It's an isolated place, almost an island, with no sprawling suburbs or market towns nearby. Instead, even today, visitors must brave the Broads to reach it, trusting causewayed, reed-rimmed roads to lift them a few feet above the black-earthed marsh. Such roads as there were in the seventeenth century were hacked through willows and bulrushes and banked against erosion into the swamp. Great Yarmouth still feels a long way from everywhere, and in the seventeenth century it would have felt even further. Once you've arrived in the town, it's also clear its surrounding marshes are the lesser of two wet threats, the more potent being the North Sea. In the past the town often flooded during sea storms, when the tide surged into the Yare, bursting its banks and washing salty sand through the streets. Every few years the harbour required rebuilding after a storm or movement in the river's silts, and the town's population would be called out to dig and dredge, haul rubble and drive piles into the shifting ground. Between the river and the deep blue sea, Great Yarmouth was literally built on sand: a metaphor for optimistic obstinacy, or gnawing vulnerability, depending on how you look at it.

The town's life depended on its harbour, a long haven bending south behind the sandspit into which several rivers flow. Stone quays lined its eastern edge for about a mile south to north. Up to seven hundred vessels could be accommodated, sheltering behind the spit when there were storms at sea. As well as being fortified strongly against bad weather, the town was armed to resist Danish, Flemish, Spanish, Scottish and French raiders and any pirates who might fancy seizing people or goods from the coast or blockading the river. Great Yarmouth's twenty-three-foot-high walls, hulking behind the quays, stretched over two thousand yards. They were built of black and white flint and brick like the Tolhouse: the flint hard and shiny like glazed ceramic, the brick dark red and rough, some of it from the Roman era. There were sixteen towers and ten gates, almost all of them facing out over water, which made the town feel like a moated castle. The town's least defensible points were to the east and north, where the sandbank continued into swelling dunes. This hummocky grassland, called the Denes, was common land: townspeople grazed their cattle and dried their linen and fishing nets there. From time to time, sand that had blown off the dunes and into deep drifts along the walls, reducing their external height, was carted away so that no invader could easily climb them. Labourers like Nazareth Fassett's husband John were repeatedly called on for such work.

Great Yarmouth was under serious threat from invasion. It faced European nations' navies, which sailed from ports across the North Sea and whose commanders knew its harbour was a valuable strategic asset. The town was wealthy too, especially for its size: a fortune netted from fishing.

From medieval times to the seventeenth century, the herring fishery underpinned the town's economy. By 1619, over a thousand men in over two hundred boats were harvesting the fish. People caught and traded in herrings, pickled and dried them, salted and smoked them until they turned scarlet – making the smoked fish into 'red herrings' or kippers – pressed oil out of them, turned their guts into fertiliser, and feasted on them until the very air of their town reeked of herring. To secure all this activity, Great Yarmouth had a monopoly on herring sales across an area seven miles from its walls in each direction, meaning that fisherfolk had to land their catches at its wharves and vend them through the thriving fish market and annual herring, hake and mackerel fairs. Otherwise, they faced fines and sometimes harsher punishments, such as imprisonment in the Tolhouse. Fish processors, brokers and merchants grew rich and the town used heighning dues paid by fishers and traders to further fortify its walls and beautify its streets.[2]

It was an aspirational community, proud and striving constantly to raise its moral and cultural standards. Successive rectors reprimanded townspeople for drinking on Sundays, brawling in the streets, gambling and 'laughing at church'. That was why Nazareth Fassett was put on trial for slander and why, in 1638, her husband John would be prosecuted for swearing. Such matters were not private vices, according to the Puritan reformers who ran the town council. These dour men drew their wealth from the industries fed by fishing but, in contrast, the fisherfolk in their workforce were lively individualists – so much so that the term 'fishwife' came to mean a scolding, shouting woman who sold her products with noisy cries, haggled and argued with everyone.

Great Yarmouth's fishmarket stalls were almost all run by women, and their behaviour set the tone in the streets. The councillors who assembled in the Tolhouse often had to expend significant time and money projecting an alternative image for their town, one of respectability, order and piety. They suppressed the more anarchic alehouses, banned fishing on Sundays despite its centrality to the town's economy and rooted out anything they labelled as sin, but it was a struggle. The town was famously overcrowded, many streets no more than narrow paths, because space on the sandspit was limited, and that led to disorder and dispute.[3]

Nazareth and John Fassett lived among these constricted streets, known as the Rows – tight-packed, pebble-paved alleys linking the town's three north–south highways. There were over one hundred and fifty Rows, totalling seven and a half miles in length. One Row was just thirty inches wide. On an old map, the town looks appropriately like a fine-boned fish, with the Rows as ribs branching from a central spine. People lived crammed together among inns and hostels, chandleries and roperies, gutting and salting houses, smokeries and fish oil warehouses. Herring dominated the Rows just as it filled the quays and factories: indeed, a Norfolk satirist described the fish as a patron saint of the town: 'saint Patrick for Ireland, saint George for England, and the red herring for Yarmouth'. The immense canvas of the herring fleet's sails, he said, could cloud over a whole sky and every day five thousand pounds' worth of fishing nets – nearly £1 million today – lay drying in the sun on the Denes. This was Nazareth's world – and if she spread scandal about her neighbours, it might have been related to the financial corruption and cut-throat competition that inevitably followed this enormous natural resource. Her Christian name suggests she came from a godly family, and perhaps she had some salty views about the behaviour of others.[4]

But although fish made Great Yarmouth wealthy, it also made it vulnerable: like Framlingham in Suffolk, the town had only one large industry. Shoals of fish appeared off Norfolk in late summer – or not. From early September to mid-November, boats converged to catch them. Fishers and traders came from Northumbria, Devon and Cornwall, Scotland, Flanders, Holland, Denmark and France. And during Nazareth's time, there was trouble in the fishing industry. Changes in fish movements – most likely caused by the 'little Ice Age' that plagued the 1600s – had reduced the catch, and all the citizens of Great Yarmouth suffered as a result.

Then, in 1643, disaster struck: pirates attacked the herring fleet. They called themselves Royalist 'privateers', but what they did was theft and kidnapping. Marauding ships crossed the North Sea from the Netherlands, specifically Catholic ports under Spanish control which supported King Charles. Lookouts shinned up the rigging and scanned the horizon for the tiny dots of herring boats: the spike of a small mast, a flash of white sail. As soon as they spotted the fishers, they chased and boarded them at gunpoint. Herring boats were encumbered with nets over their sides and hauls of fish in their holds. They could not escape. Their captains and crew were seized, a ransom demand was sent and until it was paid, the men were held in foreign jails. Their boats were sailed to places like Ostend, in modern-day Belgium, and the catch sold there. Suddenly Great Yarmouth was missing hundreds of its fishermen and almost all its income. Given the existing strains of the civil war, the pirate attack must have felt like the last straw.[5] Surely enemies were at work within the town itself? So, drawing on the panic about witches that was growing in Suffolk, a witch hunt started to snowball in Norfolk too. Let's meet the accused people:

Mark Pryme

The first tidings of the Norfolk witch hunt came in early April 1645. They began with someone who had come under previous suspicion: the gardener Mark Pryme (Pryme is a surname of Flemish or Norman origin). Mark had first been accused of using 'diabolic arts and incantations ... charms and sorceries' back in 1638. He practised divination and astrology that, he said, helped him find lost goods and money. He'd done just that for a mason, John Ringer, who had lost a silver coin, and for the seaman John Sparke, who had lost a felt hat. Such superstitious practices were disapproved of in reformist Great Yarmouth. But, confusingly, Mark had also been paid by the town's corporation for healing work when he apparently cured a mentally ill man detained by the authorities. His position was unclear: favoured healer or magical nuisance?

He doesn't appear in records often enough for us to know much about his life – we know that in 1638 he lived in a house he rented from Matthew Brooks, the town's traditionalist minister, and held some land outside the town's north gate, and in 1643 he could afford to give two shillings and eightpence to a collection to support the war effort in Ireland. However, the satirist John Taylor, who knew him, joked in a printed poem that Mark constantly talked magical jargon and had a reputation for finding anything missing: 'cow, calf, horse or cart, or silver spoon, or bodkin, knife or ring, or millstone, windmill, cork or anything heavy or light'. John Taylor thought Mark was a 'cheat', but an impressive one.

One of the indictments against Mark relates to magical work he'd done in Suffolk, suggesting that as well as practising his art in Great Yarmouth, he'd travelled to do jobs elsewhere. It is likely that clients would also have travelled from further afield to consult him. Now, however, he was accused of serious crime. The goldsmith John Howlett said Mark had bewitched him and his son Robert on 12 April 1645, cursing them with a wasting disease.[6]

Elizabeth Bradwell

As well as the accusations made by John Howlett against Mark Pryme, two young women, Elizabeth and Susan Linstead, accused the widow Elizabeth Bradwell of bewitching them on 1 April 1645. Like the goldsmith Howlett, the Linsteads were wealthy. They were a populous Great Yarmouth family whose most high-profile member was William Linstead, a councillor and maker of craning equipment who lived near the church. Elizabeth and Susan may have been his daughters: there is record of an Elizabeth who was born in 1637 to William and his wife Ann, named after a sister who had tragically died as an infant the previous year, but Susan's birth doesn't seem to be recorded.

Once the Howletts and the Linstead girls had complained about witchcraft, other accusers soon came forward. Henry Moulton, another councillor and a hosier who manufactured knitted stockings, added to Elizabeth and Susan's accusations against Elizabeth Bradwell. Henry said she had bewitched his toddler son John in May 1645. John looks to be Henry's youngest child; there are records of a number of other children born in the 1630s and 1640s to his first wife Abigail and then second wife Bridget. As well as being a town councillor, Henry Moulton was a stalwart of Great

Yarmouth's St Nicholas's church, a frequent churchwarden and overseer of the poor. In 1644, he was chosen again as churchwarden, reflecting the congregation's approval. He was an ideal witch accuser of exactly the kind we saw at Manningtree and Framlingham: pious, experienced and trusted by his community.[7]

Barbara Wilkinson and Nazareth Fassett

With the witch hunt gathering pace, and attracting the accusations of prominent citizens, it was only a matter of time before people previously accused of other, unrelated misdemeanours came under fire. So, the supposed scandalmonger of the 1630s, Nazareth Fassett, was soon accused of keeping demonic spirits and charged along with a widow, Barbara Wilkinson. Both their offences were dated to 12 June 1645, suggesting they were suspected of working together.

As we know from the record of her slander trial, Nazareth was the wife of John Fassett, whom, as Nazareth Huggins, she'd married in June 1619. Her married name was variously spelled Fassett and Fossett and was probably pronounced Fawcett. A 'faucet' was a slang term for a server of ale. Maybe John's ancestors had worked at one of the town's inns: the Three Wrestlers on Church Plain, The George in George Row, The Angel in the marketplace, the Rose or Dolphin in Town Arms Row – there were plenty to choose from. The Fassetts had nine or ten children: George (born 1620), Margaret (born 1622), Lettice (born and died 1624), Rachel (born 1625, died 1626), Robert (born 1627), Francis (born 1630, died 1632), Daniel (born 1632), Elizabeth (born 1634) and Judith (born 1637) – and possibly a son called William (born 1629, died 1631), although records are unclear.

We know less about Nazareth's co-accused; she was an older woman who had married Clement Wilkinson in September 1603, as Barbara Brantingham. Like the Fassetts, Clement and Barbara had many children, in her case between 1606 and 1617, so they were now all adults. Both families attended the official, now-Presbyterian church of St Nicholas regularly.[8]

Mary Vervy

Meanwhile, the wealthy brewer, merchant and councillor Augustine Thrower had been concerned about witchcraft attacks on his family since at least autumn 1643. Augustine and his wife Anne were prominent in Great Yarmouth society. A Freeman since 1621, Augustine had served as a councillor and town official. But he had also made some court appearances on the wrong side of the law, since not everyone in the town approved of his religion, brewing or the proliferation of alehouses as his business boomed. Nevertheless, the Throwers were consistent attendees of St Nicholas until they joined a new, Congregational church.

The couple had a large family born between 1628 and 1643 and had them baptised one after another. By 1645, it was little Augustine junior whose health most concerned his father. Two previous children with this Christian name had died in 1641 and 1643 and now their namesake seemed sickly, languid and was failing to thrive. His father became convinced that Mary Vervy had bewitched the child on 7 September 1643. Mary might be the Mary Vervy born to Robert and Dorothy Vervy in 1617, if she remained unmarried, and her trial records do call her a spinster. Alongside Augustine Thrower's suspicion of her, sometime after 1 April 1645 the sailor John Holmes became convinced Mary had bewitched his daughter Elizabeth. Soon afterwards, the shoemaker James Lambert and his wife Lucy – who had been a Holmes before her 1636 marriage – accused Mary Vervy of bewitching their daughter, also named Lucy.

Across summer and early autumn 1645, further accusations were made against Mary. John Wade, a hosier like Henry Moulton, accused her of bewitching his wife Bridget. Bridget had become ill on 12 August. The Wades were a middle-aged couple with several children born between 1633 and March 1645 when little Bridget, named after her mother, had joined the family. Perhaps Bridget senior was ill after her birth, which would not have been uncommon.

~

By 12 August, at least ten different Great Yarmouth families, many of them wealthy and well connected, believed witchcraft was rife in their town. The council decided to act. Luckily for them, they had heard of the notorious witch hunt taking place further south and identified the man who had become its chief celebrity: Matthew Hopkins. So, in mid-August they agreed to send a letter to Hopkins, inviting him to Great Yarmouth. 'Mr Hopkins to be sent for', they recorded in the minutes of their meeting on 15 August, adding: 'it is agreed that the gentleman Mr Hopkins, employed in the country for discovering and finding out of witches, shall be sent for hither to come to town to make search for such wicked persons if any be here, and shall have his fee and such allowance for his pains and labour in that kind as he hath in other places in the country'.[9] Hopkins had travelled across Suffolk sparking witch hunts: now he was to visit Norfolk as well.

By the time he rode up to the Tolhouse prison to start his work, Matthew Hopkins had also visited the small town of Aldeburgh on the Norfolk coast, where he was paid two pounds in total for finding seven witches. That was the kind of payment he could expect at Great Yarmouth, where there were already at least five suspects. So – racing north from the summer Assizes at Bury St

Edmunds to Aldeburgh and on to Great Yarmouth – the witchfinder arrived on or about 9 September.

However, he was not given a free hand with the accused people: the town's corporation wanted to retain control of proceedings by having their own men supervise his work. They deputed two of Great Yarmouth's ministers, the Presbyterians John Brinsley and his curate Thomas Whitfield – whom they'd recently appointed themselves to serve at St Nicholas's church – to question the suspects with Hopkins's assistance. We don't have details of what the prisoners were asked or how they were pressured to confess because, unfortunately, most of the Great Yarmouth suspects' statements are lost. But we know their bodies were searched for demonic marks and there is a clear similarity between the one confession we know the ministers and Hopkins obtained and the stories the witchfinder and his friends had wrung out of their suspects in Essex and Suffolk. That makes it likely the accused people were watched, walked and asked the usual leading questions. We know what Elizabeth Bradwell confessed because the son of one of the ministers, Thomas Whitfield, preserved her words and later gave a transcript of them to the East Anglian jurist Matthew Hale, who published them.

Elizabeth's confession relates to her relationship with Henry Moulton, whose son she was accused of bewitching. Henry had once employed Elizabeth: her job had been to work from home knitting stockings for his hosiery business. It was a type of precarious self-employment known as 'out work' or 'piece work', paid per finished piece of knitting, and it was often given to poor people to keep them from dependence on parish welfare payments. A skilled knitter working with double-ended needles could finish a couple of pairs of fancy stockings a week, using yarn supplied by the hosier, and she would then be paid for her time. While highly skilled knitters who crafted the best stockings out of worsted or jersey could earn several shillings for a pair, most were paid just a few pennies for standard wool socks. This was not very much, and one day Elizabeth walked to her employer's home to ask if she could take on more jobs. Perhaps this was shortly after she was widowed – we don't know exactly when her husband John died, but the couple had a son baptised at St Nicholas in 1641, so it will have been just a few years before her trial. Henry Moulton was out when Elizabeth called, and his servants told Elizabeth they could not authorise any extra hours. Elizabeth was 'exasperated'. She went home and to bed, perhaps hungry and certainly worried.

That night someone knocked at her door. She may have thought that it was one of Henry Moulton's agents offering her work after all. Elizabeth got up and looked out of her window, or so she told Matthew Hopkins, John Brinsley and Thomas Whitfield. She saw below her in the moonlit street 'a tall black man'. 'What will you have?' she shouted sleepily, meaning 'what do you want?' The visitor clearly wasn't bringing a commission to knit more stockings. But it turned out he did have something to offer Elizabeth. He'd heard, he called up to her window, that she could get no more work. But he had a suggestion: 'he would put her into a way that she should never want either work or anything else'. It was an alluring prospect for a poor knitter, and so Elizabeth let the man in. 'What do you have to say to me?' she asked, and suddenly the man took her hand, scratched it with something like a pen knife, pulled a pen and book out of his pocket and told her to sign her name in the book with blood from the scratch on her hand. Like so many of the other witchcraft suspects who confessed similar things, Elizabeth had not been taught to write, but the man guided her hand and so she signed his book, she said. Of course, that was what her questioners wanted to hear: a confession of making a pact with a devil, sealed in the witch's blood. Elizabeth was persuaded to agree that this was what she had done and said that afterwards the devil appeared to her and provided her with a familiar spirit in the form of a blackbird.

Elizabeth's new friend promised her revenge on her employer Henry Moulton for his failure to offer her enough work. More importantly, he gave her some money. Satisfied, she went back to bed. But when the devil came the next night, he had bad news: 'he could do nothing against the man [Henry Moulton], for he went constantly to church to hear Whitfield and Brinsley and said his prayers morning and evening'. What a coup for Elizabeth's questioners: Satan himself had identified their preaching as a godly protection against witchcraft! The protection also extended to Henry Moulton's maid, who went to church with her employer. But the devil had a suggestion: 'there was a young child in the house, which was more easy to be dealt with'. The next time he visited, the devil brought with him a wax image of a child with a nail driven into its head, saying that it represented young John Moulton, whom he'd already caused to feel great pain and would now attempt to kill. If they buried the image in the churchyard, he said, as it decayed the child would waste away. Elizabeth and the devil crept through the deserted streets of Great Yarmouth to St Nicholas's churchyard by the Tolhouse and there, using a spade the devil provided, they buried the wax image. The boy was sick for eighteen months, at which point Elizabeth was arrested and questioned.

Delighted by Elizabeth's confession, the ministers John Brinsley and Thomas Whitfield, helped by Matthew Hopkins, wrote everything down and sent a messenger to deliver it to the town's magistrates. The magistrates had probably questioned Elizabeth already, if she had been arrested after being accused in the spring, but Hopkins's arrival seems to have secured a confession just in time for her trial to begin the next day.

Elizabeth's confession had also sparked another idea, and the magistrates released her from the Tolhouse prison so she could be marched over to Henry Moulton's house, 'where the child [John Moulton] lay almost dead'. Surrounded by insistent ministers and angry, frightened witnesses, Elizabeth was forced to repeat her admission of guilt in the child's bedroom. Suddenly the little boy, who 'was thought to be dead or dying, laughed and began to stir'. He tried to sit up 'and from that instant began to recover'. By then it was night, and too late to dig in the churchyard for the wax image, but the next morning Elizabeth was hustled out again from the Tolhouse, through the marketplace to St Nicholas's graveyard, accompanied by Hopkins, Whitfield, who lived next to the church, and a number of other questioners. There she was forced to identify the spot where she said the wax figure was buried. 'But though they dug and sought for it as well as they could', the account of her confession ends, 'they could find nothing'. Perhaps the devil had taken it, the frustrated searchers concluded, unable to accept that it had probably never existed at all.[10]

The religious politics of St Nicholas's church played a key part in Great Yarmouth's witch trial: hence the starring roles of its ministers John Brinsley and Thomas Whitfield and its churchyard. Brinsley, Whitfield and their council backers needed to stamp their authority on the hunt because by 1645 their town was full of competing sects. Its people were well informed about European Protestant reform and there was even a Dutch chapel in the town, setting an example to its rival, St Nicholas. While St Nicholas was the town's official religious centre, flexing towards Presbyterian as the state church evolved, its dominance was under threat. It was only recently, too, that the council had gained the unchallenged right to choose St Nicholas's ministers.

Previously, the Diocese of Norwich had a veto, and Norwich's bishops were religious conservatives. So, when townsmen installed John Brinsley as minister in the 1620s, the Bishop of Norwich dismissed him as too radical a reformist. Defiantly, he preached at the Dutch church instead and at two out-of-town congregations, one of which met in a barn. Meanwhile, St Nicholas's new minister, the traditionalist Matthew Brooks, was attacked and intimidated. Lawyer and politician Miles Corbet – later a magistrate at both Nazareth Fassett's trials – fought a legal battle over the right to criticise him. In 1631, Brinsley regained his role at St Nicholas, once agreement was reached with the Bishop of Norwich. But he was removed again after Corbet and others had Brooks arrested – it was ruled they had gone too far. A new preacher was recommended by the corporation to work alongside Brooks, but he was removed by the bishop and at that point relations broke down with the Diocese. The conservatives had won – Brinsley was out – and their control of St Nicholas lasted for a decade. During that time, the victorious Brooks rented out a house to the magician Mark Pryme, and his later targeting by witch hunters, which sparked the Great Yarmouth hunt, might be related to that.[11]

However, as had happened elsewhere, the civil wars reversed Brooks's position and radicals took over. After 1642, the council could choose the town's ministers unopposed. Brinsley replaced Brooks at St Nicholas and the corporation appointed a new curate, the other witch-questioner Thomas Whitfield. But since several councillors, including Miles Corbet, now wanted to join a Congregationalist church, they also announced they would allow multiple sects to operate in Great Yarmouth, subject to corporation approval. Eventually St Nicholas was divided: Brinsley's Presbyterians would use the nave and the Congregationalists the chancel. Soon Anabaptists, Baptists and mystics who rejected all authority joined the crowd of competing ministries, and although the corporation refused to license them, it was clear the Presbyterian ministers, Brinsley and Whitfield, had lost their monopoly.

Of course, they were desperate to regain their power, sparking intersectarian conflict, and the whirl of religious confusion fed townspeople's fears about the devil working among them. By 1645, there had been years of contradictory preaching about Satanic threat, accompanied by further fortifying of the town, the arrival of a Parliamentarian garrison, increased concern about keeping a constant Watch patrol and the beginning of pirate attacks. It was unsurprising that townspeople started to seek out agents of evil: people who broke the Sabbath or drank too much, people like Nazareth and John Fassett who already had a reputation for scandalmongering and swearing.[12]

Naturally, Brinsley and Whitfield were keen to lead this moral crusade. Brinsley had made a name for himself preaching against sin, remarking crisply that it should be rewarded by 'the curse of the law ... woe and misery, temporal, spiritual and eternal' and devoting four 1643 sermons to the concept of 'purging' Great Yarmouth's church of the ungodly, wicked, corrupt and erroneous. Likewise, Whitfield would go on to publish several attacks on the 'licentious tenets' of other sects. By waging war on sinners and misbelievers at the 1645 witch trial, both men hoped to make St Nicholas's church the centre of Great Yarmouth's reformation. They did everything they could to assert their superiority over other, more radical, churches whose influence was growing.[13] Elizabeth Bradwell's statement that Henry Moulton and his maidservant had been protected from demonic attack by their attendance at Brinsley and Whitfield's sermons was a gift to their claim that Presbyterianism was the true way forward. It's hard to imagine Elizabeth invented that claim without knowing exactly what her questioners would want to hear. Interestingly, her confession contains no story of sexual intimacy with the devil, something that Matthew Hopkins often extracted from those he interrogated. The absence of such a tale suggests he had more limited influence over what the Great Yarmouth suspects confessed than he did in other places, and that more of Elizabeth's story was determined by Brinsley and Whitfield. Because Hopkins had been delayed by his work in Bury and Aldeburgh, there was probably little time for lengthy watching and walking or questioning by him before the Great Yarmouth court session began on 10 September, although we do know the suspects were searched for demonic marks, which was one of Hopkins's favoured methods.

By the time the court met on the day of the trial, there were specific allegations of harm against three people: Mark Pryme, Elizabeth Bradwell and Mary Vervy. Their supposed victims had been named, and accusers were ready to give evidence against them. In addition, there were vague but dangerous accusations of spirit keeping against Nazareth Fassett, Barbara Wilkinson and five other women. These accusations range across 1643 to 1645, suggesting that some were made as part of a general trawl for suspects. This might have taken place on 9 September as Hopkins roamed about looking for trouble and getting suspects committed for trial, or it might already have been going on when he arrived.

Charged alongside Nazareth and Barbara were two spinsters, Alice Clipwell and Bridget Howard, and three widows, Mary Blackborne, perhaps widow of Robert Blackborne, Joan Lacey, widow of Zachary Lacey, and Elizabeth Dudgeon, widow of Thomas Dudgeon. Mary and Robert Blackborne had a child in 1619; Joan Roberts had married Zachary Lacey in 1602 and they had at least one child (born 1605); and Elizabeth Johnson had married Thomas Dudgeon in 1596 and had at least one child (born 1599) – making her perhaps the oldest suspect. Beyond this, there is very little traceable information about these five women in the town's court book or elsewhere, beyond the nonspecific charges recorded against them. We don't know who they are supposed to have attacked, if anyone, or how.[14]

There may also have been more than the ten suspects we can identify. Matthew Hale, commenting on the confession of Elizabeth Bradwell, which he wrote up in the 1660s, recalled that up to sixteen people had been accused in Great Yarmouth, although some of those might have been at a later trial held in 1646. Whatever the case, in mid-September 1645 the witch trial of Nazareth Fassett and her co-accused was held at the Borough Sessions in the Tolhouse, with the town's magistrates meeting to judge the accused people in the Heighning Chamber. These were not special meetings of the court, but instead a regular twice-yearly 'delivery' of all the prisoners housed in the jail below the courtroom, whatever their alleged crime. Great Yarmouth's court structure was unusual: under its medieval borough charters it had the right to hold its own Assize-style trials which could deal with felonies and condemn convicted people to death. It was usual elsewhere for trained and experienced judges to make the life-or-death decisions of an Assize, but – just as in the 1645 witch trials across Essex and Suffolk, where the civil wars forced changes in procedure – in Great Yarmouth things were done differently, in this case as they had been for centuries. The judges were eight of the local magistrates, officers of the corporation. Some, like Miles Corbet, were lawyers or Members of Parliament, but others had a less learned background in business or local administration.

That crisp September morning, the assembled magistrates and the town's clerks sat together on the dais in the Heighning Chamber, shuffling papers, comparing notes and reading through the statements from the accusers. When they were ready to begin, each prisoner was shoved up from the cells below by the jailer Richard Wright and his officers to face the fine gentlefolk and rich merchants of their town, men whom most of them would recognise only because they had seen them praying and preening in church or riding by in the street. Mark Pryme was the only suspect who had experience of working with the corporation, and Nazareth Fassett had of course appeared before some of the magistrates when she was charged with slander in 1631. The officials were an intimidating group: eight magistrates, two coroners, eight constables and fifteen men chosen as potential jurors (twelve were needed to judge each case, with three reserves).[15] Evidence was also presented in an unusually aggressive manner by the town's Recorder or keeper of records, the magistrate Miles Corbet, who had done so much to remove the conservative clergyman Matthew Brooks from St Nicholas's church.

During the witch trials, the proactive Corbet took on a role more like that of a prosecutor than a judge, suggesting he had been instrumental in promoting the hunt. This was particularly the case at Mark Pryme's trial, where Miles Corbet brought into the courtroom books owned by Mark, which he brandished and reviled, suggesting that Mark had used the texts in his magical work. It was at least an attempt to provide physical, legal evidence of witchcraft, though of a very partisan kind. Mark Pryme owned theological, historical and philosophical books and an almanac, a handbook that typically contained a calendar, information about dates and the seasons, phases of the moon, the stars and planets and random facts, jokes or proverbs. 'This is the book the knave doth conjure by!' exclaimed Miles Corbet, proposing that Mark used the book to cast horoscopes and consult demons about future events. He displayed it to the jury, saying, 'this book is damnable and dangerous' and alleging it contained the names of devils such as Lucifer and Mephistopheles. It wasn't the first time he had acted unjustly in court, at least according to John Taylor, who wrote a report on Mark Pryme's trial. In a scathing denunciation, *A Brief Relation of the Gleanings of the Idiotisms and Absurdities of Miles Corbet*, he described how Corbet routinely presumed defendants were guilty, was a 'grim judge' and 'no lover of poor folk'.[16]

The court did at least allow a witness to speak up for Mark Pryme. This was the forceful minister Thomas Cheshire, a traditionalist and Royalist, formerly of Brasenose College, University of Oxford. He'd assisted the conservative minister Matthew Brooks at St Nicholas, though he'd been forced out in the late 1630s by the intimidation of radicals whom he said interrupted his sermons, jeered and accosted him in the street. A lover of poetry, history and classical learning, Cheshire initially regarded many reformers as ignorant fanatics, but by 1641 his criticisms had escalated and he was warning they were practically Satanic: 'pulpits in many places do ring of doctrines of devils', he mourned in reference to reformers inciting attacks on bishops, ancient church decorations and rites. He was especially offended when 'cobblers and weavers and feltmongers and tailors . . . take upon them to interpret God's word', making statements such as 'the Old Testament is now of no more use than an old almanac'. Yet, ironically, he agreed with reformers that old almanacs were not useful – and was keen to demonstrate they were not demonic either. Accordingly, returning to Great Yarmouth to take on his enemies at their witch trial, Thomas Cheshire challenged Miles Corbet's description of Mark Pryme's almanac, contemptuously explaining that it was a text of no importance and he was misrepresenting it anyway. An almanac was not a magical artefact and it could not be used for conjuring. Miles Corbet's prize physical evidence was accordingly discounted and, thanks to Thomas Cheshire's intervention, Mark Pryme was acquitted by the jury.[17]

This gave hope for the other suspects. Whatever Matthew Hopkins and his associates had been allowed to do, whatever confessions they had procured, not everyone would be found guilty. There were other hopeful indications too, chiefly that accusers were not permitted to act as jurors. One reserve juror was Henry Moulton, but he recused himself from any case where he had a personal interest: the woman he'd charged, Elizabeth Bradwell, was assessed by his neighbours. Sadly, she was convicted despite Henry's absence on the jury bench, and was sentenced to hanging, along with Alice Clipwell, Bridget Howard, Mary Blackborne, Elizabeth Dudgeon and Joan Lacey. Joan was temporarily reprieved, perhaps because she had claimed pregnancy or more evidence was sought, but her stay of execution was cancelled. All the women were marched to the gallows on the North Denes sandhills on 29 September, and turned off the ladder into the salt wind. They were buried in the churchyard by the sexton William Matchet and labelled in the parish register as 'executed for witchcraft'.

Mary Vervy, Barbara Wilkinson and twice-tried Nazareth Fassett were acquitted, however. We don't have a detailed description of their trials but we do know that, once freed, they could go home: Barbara to her solitary fireside and Nazareth to her husband and those children still living with her, the youngest of whom was just eight. Perhaps it helped their cases that Barbara and Nazareth were longtime attendees at St Nicholas. We don't know when Barbara died, but Nazareth continued as a parishioner after her acquittal: her husband John was buried in St Nicholas's graveyard in August 1647, and when Nazareth herself died in winter 1657, so was she. Her funeral was on 14 November.[18] And as her widowed life seems to have continued to a more peaceful end than her enemies had intended, that suggests that opinion about witches was changing around her, perhaps in part because of her acquittal and those of Mark Pryme, Mary Vervy and Barbara Wilkinson. Despite Hopkins's attempts to proliferate trials in Norfolk, when there were further accusations at Great Yarmouth in 1646, all the suspects were acquitted, marking a significant shift in attitudes.

This might be because Hopkins spent too long witchfinding in East Anglia in 1645 and 1646, making enemies and costing communities large sums of money with no apparent result. By late 1646, many of the suspects he had accused at King's Lynn and Ely had been acquitted, as well as the Great Yarmouth survivors. In 1647, Hopkins would even be questioned at Norfolk Assizes – where once he'd heaped scorn on Hempnall's baker Henry Maggs – by an unnamed critic of his witchfinding techniques. Infuriated, Hopkins reported this man had accused him of 'unlawful courses of torture to make [suspects] say anything for ease or quiet', walking them 'till their feet were blistered' and using 'abominable, inhumane and unmerciful trial of these poor creatures by tying them and heaving them into the water'. This bold and humane sceptic added, revealingly, that Hopkins lied to suspects, telling them that if they confessed they would be freed. He also questioned the witchfinder's ability to distinguish demonic teats from ordinary bodily marks. Finally, he remarked cuttingly that 'all that the witchfinder doth is to fleece the country of their money', voicing the suspicion that Norfolk's towns were wasting taxpayers' money on a scam.[19] Hopkins refuted these allegations, but they must have made an impression. Additionally, in 1646, a Huntingdonshire vicar, John Gaule of the village of Great Staughton, about eighty miles west of Norwich, had published *Select Cases of Conscience Touching Witches and Witchcraft*, which attacked the witchfinders' interrogation methods in similar ways. In the communities south of the Wash, the tide was turning against Matthew Hopkins.

Ironically, Gaule agreed with almost everything Hopkins, Stearne and the other witch hunters believed about witches – he thought they were anti-Christians with animal familiars that harmed their neighbours, that they had made pacts with Satan, and so on. But, importantly, he rejected the practice of watching and walking and the swimming test, questioning the reliability of confessions obtained by these 'lawless' means. Gaule included in his book a copy of a letter from Matthew Hopkins in which the witchfinder haughtily demanded the right to examine suspects 'without control, but with thanks and recompense' in Gaule's home village: Hopkins's arrogance and pointed focus on payment were thus displayed to the public very clearly in his own words. As the perception grew that he was carrying on what Gaule called a 'trade' of witchfinding for money, Hopkins's reputation began to falter and he was forced to publish a self-justification in the form of his 1647 book, *The Discovery of Witches*.[20] It was a step towards the end of Hopkins's witch-hunting career, but his friend John Stearne – less well known, but equally fanatical – was still busily questioning suspects in neighbouring counties as Hopkins struggled with his opponents in Norfolk. For Stearne, at least, the witch hunt would continue undiminished into 1646 and 1647.

CHAPTER 9

Give Me Your Poor

John Winwick and John Chirrey of Thrapston, Northamptonshire, 1646

The journey from Great Yarmouth in Norfolk to Thrapston in Northamptonshire is about a hundred miles, along a more or less straight road west through the city of Peterborough. You can see Peterborough's cathedral for miles, its towers spiking the huge sky above the flat fens like a great stone crown. In the 1640s, a five- or six-day journey on horseback would have brought travellers comfortably from the Norfolk sea coast to the midland county town of Northampton and then on to Thrapston. But the witch hunt didn't travel directly between those two places: there was too much work to be done along the way.

Having left the 1645 Norfolk Assizes, the witchfinders lingered in the counties between Norfolk and Northamptonshire, earning money in expenses and fees, setting up watching and walking groups, pointing fingers and spreading fear. Through 1645 and 1646, they sporadically examined witchcraft suspects across the fen counties, circling back towards the coast. In spring 1646, however, John Stearne moved on west again, apparently by himself.

Perhaps Hopkins was ill or preoccupied with his East Anglian or fenland cases – certainly he was in northern Norfolk later that year. Either way, John Stearne continued inland towards the English Midlands, which brought him into Northamptonshire.

He might have been drawn to the little town of Thrapston specifically, although he visited other Northamptonshire communities too. But Thrapston had a lot to offer a witch hunter, and by now Stearne may have been planning the book he wanted to write documenting his hunt, *A Confirmation and Discovery of Witchcraft*, which would join Hopkins's book in print in 1648. He might have targeted Thrapston to confirm his theories and discover further witches because a suspect Stearne had interrogated during his travels in Huntingdonshire had mentioned it as a devilish location. This man, John Winnick or Winwick, told Stearne and the Huntingdonshire magistrates Robert Bernard and Nicholas Pedley a gripping story about an encounter with Satan in Thrapston, where he had lived and worked at the time, that had apparently caused the accused to become a witch. Further to this, the Thrapston area had a long history of witch trials dating back at least to the 1590s. The Pickering family, who lived in the hamlet of Titchmarsh just two miles east and held lands in Thrapston, were early puritanical reformers, and in 1593 their investigations into witchcraft had got a family of three hanged for the crime: a father, mother and daughter. They'd proudly published an account of the case that ran to over a hundred pages, documenting the witches' attacks on five children and including day-by-day accounts of symptoms, behaviour and the tests to which the accused people had been subjected. That was just Stearne's kind of book, and it became something of a model for his own.

Stearne also may have read about Thrapston in a pamphlet of 1612, the alluringly titled *The Witches of Northamptonshire*, presented as a sort of county guide to evil. The pamphlet's cover was adorned with a striking woodcut print showing three witches riding on the back of a sow, which may have been one of the witch's familiars, or intended as a representation of the devil. This punchy little text described how, among other Northamptonshire witches, in Thrapston Helen Jenkenson had been searched for demonic marks after her neighbours had begun to suspect her of killing a child and cattle belonging to local farmers. An insensible spot had been found on her body – one that was immune to pain when pricked or pinched – and then one of the women who'd searched Helen had discovered terrifying blotches on the linen hanging out to dry on her washing line. The blotches were, she thought, shaped like toads, snakes 'and other ugly creatures' that reminded her of 'hobgoblins', as she put it, or familiar spirits. When the searcher threatened Helen, the marks mysteriously disappeared. Helen Jenkenson was tried for her supposed crimes and executed, pitifully crying out, 'woe is me!' and protesting her innocence even as she went to her death.[1] In Stearne's eyes, this was a good outcome.

In spring 1646, as the last civil war battles between King and Parliament were fought in Devonshire, Gloucestershire and Oxfordshire and the king lost the last strongholds of his kingdom, Stearne hoped to commence a third Northamptonshire witch hunt. He came to Thrapston armed with the story he'd dragged out of his previous suspect, John Winwick, in Huntingdonshire.[2] When John had lived in Thrapston nearly thirty years earlier, he'd worked for the Bateman family as a servant. The Batemans were prominent employers in Thrapston because of their wealth, property holdings and the sheer number of their relations. Thomas Bateman senior and Thomas Bateman junior both had at least eight children with their respective wives, Joan and Helen. With each generation, their grip on local affairs tightened across village, church and state. Margaret, daughter of Thomas the elder, married Michael Westfield, rector of the nearby village of Raunds, in 1611, and her sister Joan married John Dalby, later a steward of the Hundred court which ran a group of local villages, in 1617. Their brother Thomas Bateman was a churchwarden as well as holding a farm, several shops and the George Inn in the centre of Thrapston. The Bateman property dominated the High Street – it still does, although now its buildings have Victorian and Georgian facades, behind which estate agents, charity shops and a café carry on their business.

In the seventeenth century, this area of Thrapston was known as the Drapery, because in addition to their other activities the Batemans were mercers – textile merchants – who sold cloth there. They'd made such a fortune in that business that on his death in 1614 Thomas the elder left nearly seven hundred pounds to his four elder daughters and son, a house and lands in Titchmarsh and land at nearby Ringstead, as well as all his houses and three shops in Thrapston. It was in this retail and hospitality complex around the George Inn, on the corner of High Street and Chancery Lane, that John Winwick probably lived and worked for Thomas Bateman the younger. John was a farm and stable labourer, caring for his employer's crops and animals. In 1617, the year of Joan Bateman's wedding, John was often at work in the Batemans' barn, where the family's hay and grain were stored, handily close to the stables of the Inn, which faced onto the marketplace and St James's church. There were medieval warehouses, tenements and dealers in corn and farm produce all around, a livestock market and bull ring. It was a busy working environment, bustling with creaking carts and whinnying horses and all the shouting of the market held every Tuesday. John laboured among the shops and stalls, the fine houses of gentry and merchants, but he had little money himself.

Then one Friday, while he was binding hay into bundles for

the Batemans' horses, John realised with horror that he'd mislaid what few coins he had; he'd lost his wallet. In panic, he began 'swearing, cursing, raging and wishing to himself that some wise body ... would help him to his purse and money again'. Where had he dropped it? Had it been stolen? But when he wished for a 'wise body' to help him, John Winwick wasn't just hoping for a helpful neighbour or street trader who might happen upon his purse. He was wishing, he confessed, specifically for 'a wizard', someone who could find the purse by divination. Such a wizard might consult spirits or books, mutter charms or promise to pray for the discovery of John's lost money. This was exactly the kind of magical work that Mark Pryme did in Great Yarmouth when he found that silver coin his client John Ringer had lost, and charm-using women like Agnes Bishop and Margaret Thomsone of Mid Calder might have performed similar feats. Poor John Winwick wanted a wizard like Mark Pryme in his own village, and he could hardly wait to finish work and go to look for one. We don't know whether he found such a person, but we do know that he found the purse in the barn the next day, with all its seven shillings' worth of precious coins still present. He was overjoyed.[3]

In April 1646, however, John Winwick told John Stearne and the Huntingdonshire magistrates – Member of Parliament and lawyer Robert Bernard and Bernard's lawyer son-in-law Nicholas Pedley – a very different story about what had happened the day he lost his money in 1617. Stearne helped a group of local watchers to extract the tale from Winwick, whose body he had already examined and possibly pricked, searching for witch marks; Bernard and Pedley were the magistrates to whom he then took his evidence of Winwick's supposed guilt. They both had contacts and business interests in Molesworth, where John was living in the 1640s, and may have known him before he was accused of witchcraft.[4] As poor John obliged the gentlemen by recalling the events of 1617, under the twin pressures of fear and exhaustion, he soon confessed what Stearne expected to hear. Harking back, he imagined he was once again standing in the barn on Thrapston High Street that Friday morning, discovering he'd lost his purse. He remembered wringing his hands, fretting in impotent rage and misery. And suddenly, facing Stearne's interrogation, he knew what to say next. As he wished that day for a wizard to help him find his money, he improvised, 'there appeared unto him a spirit, black and shaggy, and having paws like a bear, but in bulk not fully so big as a coney' or rabbit. And after this sharp break with reality, poor John Winwick started to tell John Stearne, and then the magistrates Bernard and Pedley, how he had become a witch.

First, he told them that this rabbit-sized bear could speak. It asked John what was wrong and encouraged him to tell it why he was so sorrowful. John explained to the creature that he had lost his purse and had no idea how to get it back. The spirit had a suggestion, and it was – of course – the suggestion so often made by a demonic familiar upon its first appearance to a human in trouble: 'if you will forsake God and Christ, and fall down and worship me for your God, I will help you to your purse and money again'. Desperate, John Winwick told the witchfinding team he'd dropped to his knees and held up his hands in supplication, joining the anti-Christian church described by Rebecca West, Ellen Driver, Elizabeth Bradwell and so many others. The spirit was satisfied with its new recruit. 'Tomorrow', it said, 'about this time of day, you shall find your purse upon the floor where you are now'. This would be no lucky accident, however. The spirit explained that it would bring the purse back to John and place it where he would be able to find it. Now, in this version of his story, John had no need to go and find a wizard: his purse would be returned by a supernatural friend, whom – of course – the witchfinders identified as a demon.

Courtesy of the author

The town walls, Great Yarmouth, Norfolk.

Courtesy of the author

The Tolhouse, Great Yarmouth, where Nazareth Fassett, Mark Pryme, Elizabeth Bradwell and the other accused 'witches' were imprisoned and tried.

The stairs leading up to the courtroom from the prison, the Tolhouse, Great Yarmouth.

Reproduced courtesy of Norfolk Record Office

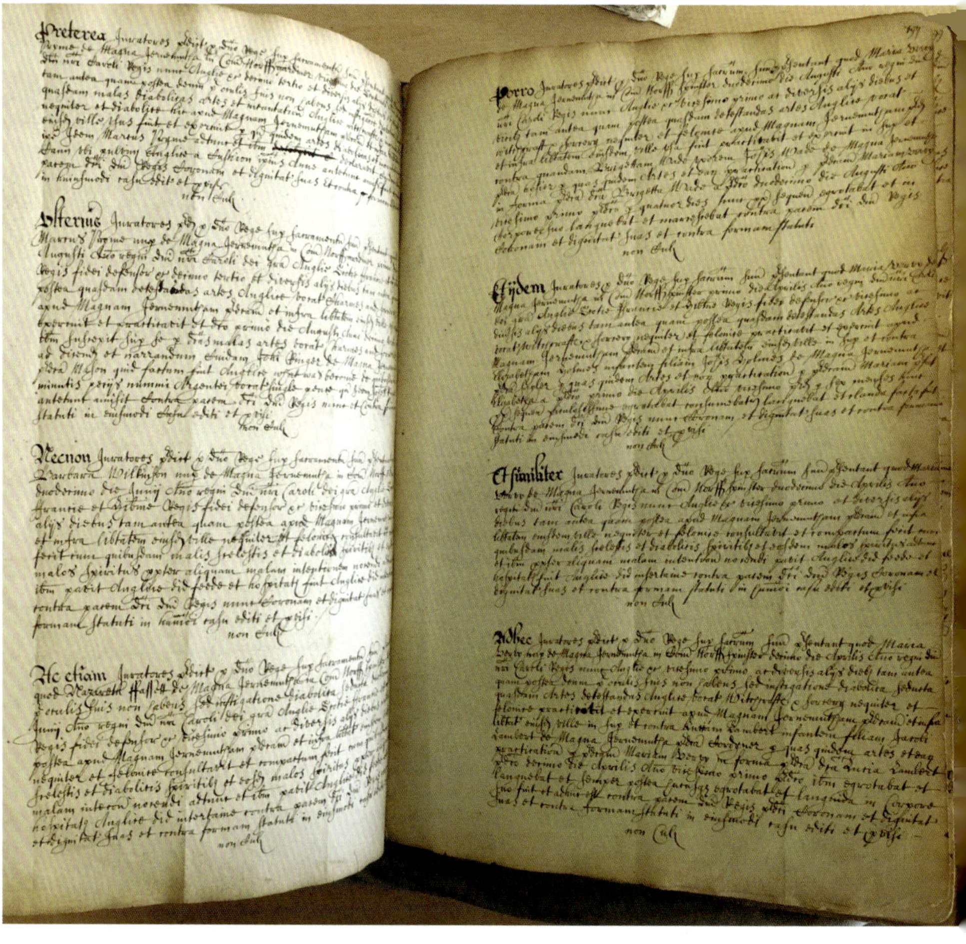

Trial records of the accused 'witches', Great Yarmouth.

Reproduced courtesy of Huntingdonshire Archives and Tabitha Stanmore

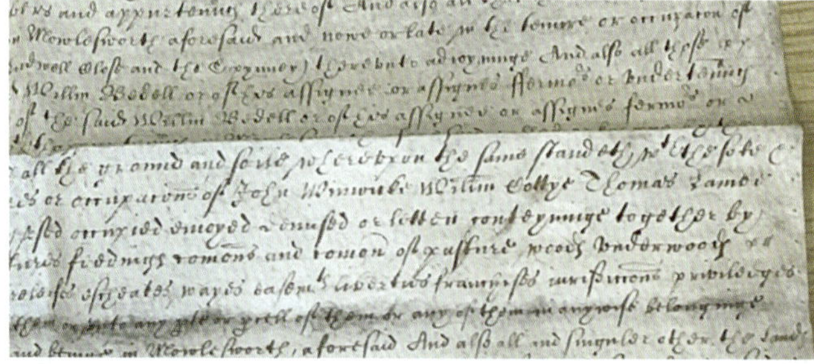

Document referring to accused 'witch' John Winwick's cottage on the Says' land, Molesworth, Huntingdonshire. Ref: KCON 3.9.5.

John Morrison/ Alamy stock photo

Cottages in Thrapston, Northamptonshire, where John Winwick and John Chirrey lived.

Marshall Hall/ Alamy stock photo

Thrapston bridge, over which accused 'witch' John Chirrey dreamt he was walking shortly before his death.

Janusz Konarski/ Alamy stock photo

Cottages in St Teath, Cornwall, where accused 'witch' Ann Jefferies lived.

Rebecca Griggs/ Alamy stock photo

St Teath church, where Ann Jefferies and her employers, the Pitt family, including her biographer Moses Pitt, were worshippers.

Courtesy of the author

Lanhydrock House, Cornwall, where magistrate John Tregeagle worked as steward of the lands of the Robartes.

Courtesy of the author

St Breock church, Cornwall, where John Tregeagle is buried.

Courtesy of the author

Seventeenth-century merchants' houses on Sandhill, Newcastle upon Tyne, where the witch-pricking took place.

Courtesy of the author

Castle Stairs, Newcastle, on the path from the Guildhall to the Town Moor gallows

Courtesy of the author

t Andrew's churchyard, Newcastle, where the executed 'witches' of 1650 are buried.

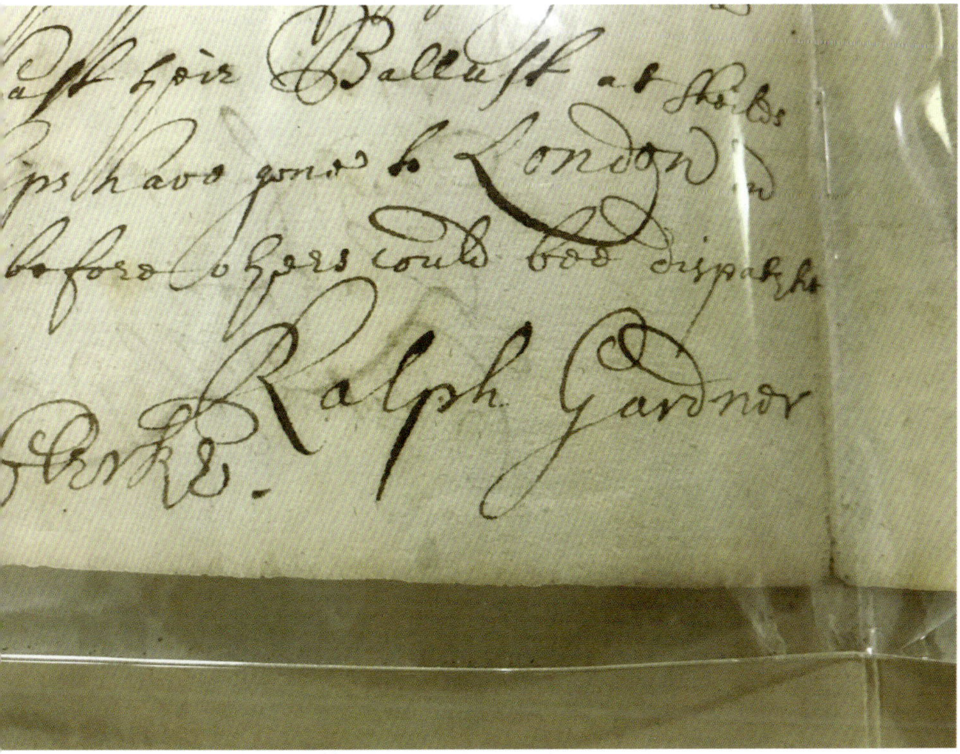

Reproduced courtesy of Tyne and Wear Archives, North East Museums

Signature of witch-defender Ralph Gardner. Ref: MD.NC/D/4/5/8-26.

Courtesy of the author, with kind permission of Shelley Ings

Memorial street art by Shelley Ings, in Chelmsford, on the road taken by condemned 'witches' to the gallows.

The next day, John recounted, on returning to the Batemans' barn, he did indeed find his purse. It was lying on the barn floor among the heaps of hay. He counted the money and found all seven shillings were still there. But now, in his recollection in 1646, the bear spirit reappeared with two others: a white cat and a grey rabbit. John told his interrogators how he knelt in gratitude, saying to the bear, 'my Lord and God, I thank you!' Most likely, he had in actuality thanked the Christian God, or perhaps the trinity of Father, Son and Holy Spirit, which many Christians believed to be the nature of their deity. But in his fantasy of 1646, John morphed these orthodox thoughts into heretical devil worship, which was exactly what his questioners wanted. It was just the sort of story Stearne and Hopkins had heard before, and were now spreading across the Midlands through the help of leading questions: perhaps something like 'and these devils – did you thank them for their help? Did you worship them? How did you pray to them?' To his confession that he did thank them, John Winwick therefore added that the bear spirit had explained to him that the two other familiars, the cat and the rabbit, were deities like the bear himself. They were just as important as him and so the bear mandated that John 'must worship these two spirits as you worship me and take them for your gods also'. And John did – or so he told his questioners.

There was more demonic doctrine to come. The bear spirit added that John must allow these three 'gods' to suck his blood and when he died he must give them his soul. Wretchedly, John told his interrogators he'd agreed and he was soon part of a devil-worshipping sect with over twenty members. In any witchfinders' judgement, that constituted a witchcraft offence and meant the magistrates Bernard and Pedley were duty-bound to commit John Winwick for trial at the Assizes, which they did. Both men were godly reformers – and Bernard remained interested in witchcraft his whole life, attending further trials right into the 1660s – so they would have been inclined to believe their suspect might be guilty.

Since John Winwick now lived in Huntingdonshire rather than Northamptonshire, his court hearing would be held in the county town of Huntingdon rather than Northampton, although his only recorded offence had been committed in Thrapston. Stearne promised that he'd attend the Huntingdon Assizes, where he would present evidence of finding three demonic marks on John Winwick's body. It seemed obvious to him that Winwick was a witch, since he fitted all Stearne's criteria: he was a foul-mouthed swearer, an ungodly peasant so upset by the loss of seven shillings that he sold his soul to Satan to get them back. When he wrote contemptuously about Winwick in his book two years later, Stearne argued that 'upon the least displeasure, with bitter bannings and cursings', the 'malicious' labourer had demonstrated 'preparedness for the devil' and so drawn to himself the evil spirits that ensnared him.[5]

Although the witchfinder had prompted John Winwick's confession by torture and from this inferred that he was 'full of revenge' and 'swollen with rancour', he was right that John was a poverty-stricken, unskilled worker who could not afford to lose seven shillings. No one had taught him to write – he signed his confession with a mark – and during the thirty years we glimpse him in the historical record he must have scraped a living from hard physical work, like so many people in agricultural communities. His story of the Batemans' barn shows that the apparent loss of this sum (about fifty pounds today) was a disaster to him, remembered vividly three decades after it nearly happened. Additionally, as he elaborated on his wish-fulfilment fantasy of recovering the money, John told his questioners that the three spirits promised he 'should never want victuals', meaning he would never go hungry. Hunger was a real possibility to him – back in 1617 and likely in 1646 too. Perhaps the Batemans didn't pay their workers a good wage or only employed John casually or seasonally – and it's very likely that by 1646 he'd been out of work frequently. Agricultural labourers were routinely forced to seek new jobs as yearly subcontracts and contracts ended, and would put themselves up for employment at hiring or 'statute' fairs after each harvest. Thrapston held a statute fair each September. While the fair itself was fun, with stalls and games, it had a starker side, thronged as it was with hopeful attendees working in a gig economy with no guarantee of employment, no minimum wage, no commitment to housing, safety or welfare. No wonder John Winwick longed for someone to tell him he wouldn't starve to death between jobs.[6]

John probably left Thrapston to find work, which was how he ended up in Molesworth, Huntingdonshire. There he had a daughter, Mary, in 1622, although there's no record of her mother's name; Mary married William Chaundeler at St Peter's church in Molesworth in 1642. Like Thrapston, Molesworth was a small community, one of a group of interconnected settlements in Navisford and Leightonstone Hundreds surrounded by flat, fertile arable and pasture fields. By the 1640s, such places had been slipping into economic crisis for several decades. In sheep farming and cloth-processing areas, wool prices were falling, and with grain values similarly affected, even areas where farming was mixed between livestock and arable were poorer than they had been. John's former home, Thrapston, which lies in an area known now as the Northamptonshire Vales – the valleys of the River Nene and River Ise – was this sort of place. As well as wider changes in prices and costs for farmers and their labourers (people like John Winwick), the landscape around them was evolving. The strip fields of medieval times, with each tiny acreage farmed by a separate tenant of a manor, were gradually being replaced by bigger fields owned by a single farmer. People might be taken on as agricultural labourers for such a landowner, but equally they might not, and in the meantime they'd lost the few acres where they once kept cows or pigs or grew a little corn. Areas of common land, fen and heath beyond the strip fields were being enclosed – taken from the ordinary people of each community without compensation and fenced in – so they could no longer graze animals there or gather wild food or firewood. To such people, seven shillings was a fortune.[7]

But John Winwick's unsympathetic questioners wanted more from him than a story about spirits helping agricultural labourers to survive hard times, so they pushed him for further confession. An admission of causing harm to a neighbour was what they were expecting and, at last, John obliged. Vaguely and unconvincingly, he said that his cat spirit had promised him it would hurt any cattle whose owners he wished to attack and his rabbit spirit had added it would hurt people he hated. He offered no specifics – apparently John did not hate anyone in particular or wish to hurt their cattle. But he had now conceded both that he had sealed a covenant with his three spirits and that, if requested, they would harm people or animals for him. Yet, despite this admission, John was tough enough to refuse to admit to anything he considered to be a definable witchcraft crime. He had not, he said, ever actually used the spirits' proffered services. He had not instructed them to hurt cattle or people. Once, he said, returning to the theme of poverty that preoccupied him, he had sent the bear spirit to beg from a maidservant working in the house of 'Mr Say' of Molesworth – his new home village in Huntingdonshire, where by 1632 he rented a cottage from the Says as lords of Molesworth Manor. The maid was, apparently, persuaded into doing so.

There were two Mr Says, Francis and Alexander, in the village at the time, with Francis Say the more prominent. John's aim was to 'provoke' or tempt one of their maids to steal food from her employer's larder to give to him. Since she did, perhaps she got into trouble for it. John's story sounds like an attempt to spare her from punishment – after all, if a devil had caused her to take the food and donate it to a poor man on the doorstep, then she could not so easily be blamed. But other than encouraging theft, John concluded, he had not hurt her or anyone in the Say household in any magical way – so there was nothing further to discuss. Presumably someone had alleged he had harmed them, but we can't be sure who it was. It might have been someone within the Say family: it's noteworthy that a 'Mistress Say' was buried on 14 April 1645, according to Molesworth's parish register. She must have been Francis Say's wife Elizabeth, since Alexander's wife (also called Elizabeth) gave birth to a son the following January. Possibly the elder Elizabeth Say's death was thought to have been caused by witchcraft. But if so, John Winwick resolutely refused to take responsibility for it. He might have hoped that his brave stand against confession would keep him safe, and so he signed his statement for the magistrate. But he was then imprisoned in Huntingdon where he would stand trial, likely facing an indictment charging him with having contact with evil spirits back in 1617. Maybe there was also a charge of harming the Say family or their maidservant, but all that we know relates to the historic events at Thrapston.[8]

When John Stearne arrived at Thrapston, therefore, he already knew from John Winwick's detailed story of the devil in the barn that this corner of Northamptonshire had a lurid reputation for witchcraft. If one agricultural labourer had covenanted with Satan right in the centre of Thrapston, surely there must be other witches there too. And indeed, soon Stearne and his fellow witch hunters found another suspect to question. He was an elderly man nicknamed 'Old Cherrie' by his neighbours, and we don't know his Christian name for certain because Stearne did not bother to record it. But the accused person may have been John Chirrey, who appears in Thrapston's parish register just once and is the only male Chirrey, Chirrie or Cherrie mentioned there. In 1596, the register tells us, John Chirrey came to St James's church with his unnamed wife to attend the baptism of his daughter. It was probably the Rector Edmund Massie who conducted the baptismal ceremony on 11 December. The group would have clustered around the fourteenth-century font in the chilly church, likely hoping the baby did not cry too loudly when the icy water touched her. The little girl was named Elizabeth. In addition to this one record of John Chirrey's life, in 1623 a Millicent Chirrey – his wife, perhaps, or daughter – was buried and in 1628 Joan Chirrey, perhaps another daughter, married John Carter at the church. This is everything the parish register tells us about the Chirrey family.

But we can learn a good deal about their world. In particular, we can imagine how, at Elizabeth's baptism and during other visits to the church, the Chirreys would have noticed monuments to the Washington family. The Washingtons lived in Chancery Lane in Thrapston – in fact, their front door was less than a hundred yards from the George Inn, where John Winwick supposedly chatted with Satan. One branch of the Washingtons owned a large manor house at Sulgrave on the other side of Northampton, and their cousin Sir John Washington lived at the house in Chancery Lane, now known as Montagu House after a later inhabitant. On the family tombs, the Washingtons' arms were displayed in Thrapston church, then as now, on a stone shield. Across the top shone three red stars against a white background, and below them lay three horizontal stripes in red and white. It's not an accident that the name Washington, and these 'stars' and 'stripes', appear together both at Thrapston and in American history, since Sir John

Washington was the great-great-great-uncle of the first President of the United States, George Washington. The Washington family crest appears to have been incorporated into the flag of the new nation, although precisely how that happened is unclear.[9]

Sir John Washington's brother, Lawrence, was the President's great-great-grandfather. Lawrence's story, like that of Sir John, is linked to the British witch hunt of the 1640s as well as to the future history of the United States. Lawrence Washington was a lecturer at Oxford University until, in 1632, he was appointed rector of Purleigh in Essex, by the traditionalist churchman Archbishop Laud – the man who consecrated the new chapel at Manningtree for Rector Thomas Witham and was petitioned to remove Vicar John Lowes from Brandeston – and he retained his conservative stance on religion throughout his career. In 1643, eighteen months before Laud's execution, Washington was fired for opposing church reform. He lost his home and income and his son, John, emigrated to Virginia in the 1650s, tired of the turmoil and radicalism he'd left behind in England.[10] Virginia was one of the more religiously conservative and tolerant American colonies and better suited Lawrence Washington's son than Puritan England. Both he and John Chirrey seem – ironically, as we'll soon see – to have been victims of the new hard line on religious purity in Britain in the 1640s and 1650s. John Stearne would have liked neither of them. Yet both ended up in his stories of witchcraft.

In 1646, three years after Lawrence Washington's dismissal, Stearne began to question 'Old Chirrey' looking for just such stories. He described his suspect as 'a very aged man' but was uninterested in other details of his life. When he wrote up their encounter, he remarked offhandedly that he did 'not now well remember' the story he'd dragged out of the accused witch. He had tortured the poor old man, then forgotten what he said.

Stearne did recall that one of Chirrey's neighbours had fallen out with him over cattle that had been chased away from their field by a dog – but he couldn't remember whether the cattle or dog belonged to Chirrey or his accuser. Either way, he wrote, the two men 'fell at odds and worded', exchanging threats and insults. Unfortunately, soon afterwards, Chirrey's antagonist died with his tongue hanging out of his mouth. Tongue protrusion is a common feature of suffocation or drowning, but in this case the symptom was perceived as strange by those who observed it. The man's tongue remained attached 'only by the roots thereof', as Stearne put it, and his death was discussed all over Thrapston. 'Many of the townsmen', Stearne wrote later, commented upon it. So when he was questioning Chirrey sometime after the event, the protruding tongue would no doubt have been mentioned.

Under pressure, the exhausted old man confessed that during their argument about the cows he had 'wished that his [neighbour's] tongue might rot out of his head'. That conveniently explained the symptom, or at least it explained it to the satisfaction of the witchfinder. The victim 'died with his tongue out', Stearne exclaimed triumphantly, and 'in a manner it rotted'. Glossing over the uncertainty of the phrase 'in a manner', he continued to a resounding conclusion: 'a fearful thing to be thought of, what a miserable condition the poor man died in!' Typically, although he claimed to care about the supposed victims, John Stearne didn't care enough to record any detail of their demise beyond that which further apportioned blame. Instead, he briefly noted that Chirrey 'likewise confessed the death of two more' unnamed people 'through his wicked cursing' and that he had made a covenant with the devil and agreed to reject Christianity with the promise of revenge on his enemies and immunity from hell's torments. By this point, Stearne was on page thirty-five of his account of witch hunting and felt he had listed enough evidence of Chirrey's guilt. He noted this suspect's similarity with John Winwick, however: both Thrapston men were, he tutted, 'given to cursing and banning'.

A final victim of Chirrey's supposed malevolence was more worth Stearne's time, however. During his interrogation, Chirrey was asked 'whether he did not do Sir John Washington, a knight which lived in the same town, any harm in his cattle or otherwise'. Whatever he thought of Sir John's religion and politics, Stearne knew that recently the knight 'had suffered strange losses'. His phrasing of the question to Chirrey seems to refer to the deaths of cattle in Sir John's herd, but the knight had also lost two children during the 1630s: Elizabeth, buried in 1632, and William, in 1639. Chirrey confessed he had caused 'the death of much cattle ... so many of his [Washington's], that he could not reckon them all'. His interrogators were disgusted by what appeared to them to be Chirrey's ingratitude to Sir John. 'Why', they asked, would Chirrey so afflict a gentleman 'who had been so loving to him in affording him relief constantly?' 'Relief' meant charity; like John Winwick and many of the other witchcraft suspects across Essex, Suffolk and Norfolk, John Chirrey lived in poverty. The old man did not rebut the accusation of ingratitude. Instead he fantasised, explaining that 'the more he [Sir John] gave him, the more power he [Chirrey] had over him to do him mischief'. His spirits tormented him with requests to be allowed to do evil. So he kept them busy attacking Sir John's cattle.[11]

Once the witchfinders had extracted the story they wanted, Chirrey was remanded in custody and sent to Northampton prison, on the Abington road next to the town hall. But the poor old man was desperate, perhaps ruminating on what he'd confessed and believing he would certainly be hanged. A few days before his trial, his jailers found him in peril of his life with his mouth stuffed full and a cord wrapped around his neck. Perhaps he had tried to choke himself, using fabric from his coat, which was reportedly torn 'right down on the back'. Or perhaps someone had attacked him, believing him to be a dangerous witch instead of a vulnerable cellmate. The jail's employees cleared out his mouth, and Chirrey then told them of what seemed to be a vision he'd had, that 'he had been at a bridge going into Thrapston' – presumably the long, multi-arched bridge over the River Nene across which lay Chirrey's way into town. Pitifully, he was dreaming of going home. But on the day of his trial, as the grand jury were considering his (now lost) indictments and deciding to forward them for trial, Chirrey was discovered dead, most likely having committed suicide. Prison suicide was rare, because prisoners didn't have individual cells and fatal self-harm – which was considered self-murder and an attempt to cheat justice – could be prevented by jailers and other inmates. But Chirrey must have succeeded and would therefore be expected to be damned. 'A just judgement of God', Stearne summed up sourly, denied the satisfaction of seeing Chirrey killed by the executioner.[12]

Stearne had attended the trial of John Winwick at Huntingdon in May, however, and so was able to repeat his tale of demonic marks there. Like several other witch trials of 1645 and 1646, this one was held before local magistrates, without Assize judges, because of the ongoing disruption of the civil wars. The court met on the upper floor of Huntingdon's town hall on Market Street, the courtroom sited above a busy market in the open-sided arcade below, like the one at Chelmsford. Street cries and gossip drifted upstairs as witnesses were called forward. John Stearne was a key informant. By this time, he was something of a celebrity, and people were pushing forward to hear him speak. He laid out his evidence that demonic spirits had sucked John Winwick's blood, leaving three marks that 'I found on him'. Everyone wanted to see. So John Winwick shuffled towards the magistrates and the twelve-man jury, his fetters clinking. He might have been in the town's jail for up to three months by then, and would have been hungry (as so often in his life), dirty and thin. Parting his clothes, he displayed three marks, two on his body and one on his head. Perhaps they were birthmarks or injury scars, maybe a mole, wart or skin tag. Baring them to the court, however, poor John capitulated completely to the witchfinders' interpretation of the marks. On his head, he explained to the hushed courtroom, the rabbit-sized bear spirit had sucked his blood – although by now he was claiming it had transformed into a rat: perhaps he'd just forgotten the original nonsense he'd told the witchfinders. If they noticed, no one challenged the inconsistency in his account. The jury found him guilty.

Later that day, a crowd of local people waited for John Winwick outside Huntingdon's prison. He was probably held in the tiny lock-up in Gaol Lane, now Orchard Lane, to the west of Huntingdon Castle. The castle had been the town's prison until it fell into such ruin that other accommodation for remanded suspects and convicts had to be found. John would have shared his imprisonment in the new, inadequate and overcrowded, facility with at least seven other local witchcraft suspects: Elizabeth Weed and Frances Moore of Great Catworth, Elizabeth Chandler, John Clarke and Jane Wallis of Keyston, Ellen or Eleanor Shepherd of Molesworth and Anne Desborough of Bythorn. This was a smaller number of suspects than the witchfinders had accused further south, perhaps a sign of the increasing scepticism Hopkins had encountered in Norfolk.

However, that was no comfort to the people in Huntingdon prison. All had now been found guilty at the magistrates' sessions and condemned to death, which meant imprisonment in a special 'condemned cell' known as The Hole. It was only ten feet by four feet with a ceiling just six feet high – a terrible place to spend your last day. The prisoners might have shared prayers and bitter stories of their interrogations. John Stearne had personally questioned some of the other suspects, as well as John Winwick. The poor Keyston woman Jane Wallis knew the names of two of the witches' familiars from Manningtree – the very distinctive 'Grizzel' and 'Greedigut' – and claimed they had brought her money, and it's possible Stearne, with his knowledge of the Manningtree case, had suggested them to her during her interrogation.[13]

Eventually the seven condemned prisoners found guilty of witchcraft, together with others convicted of serious crimes, walked or were carted out of Gaol Lane into the High Street. To their right lay medieval cottages, but opposite is Castle Hill Lane, and the prisoners would have been hurried past luckier fellow citizens across a crowded street bustling with life, and along this narrow alley. It was then known, horribly, as Hangman's Lane. Ahead of them to the left, they could see the low green mounds of the ruined castle, demolished in the Middle Ages and overgrown by brambles and scrub. Beyond, the River Ouse widens and wanders through meadows, but the convicts were heading upstream towards Mill Common, where townspeople grazed their animals, gathered wood and played games on spring evenings like this one. Some of the Common is still open countryside today – flat, tussocky fields, surrounded by woods. But in 1646, Mill Common's most striking feature was a gallows. There, like so many accused witches in the last two years, John Winwick climbed the ladder and felt the rope noose settle around his neck. He confessed again to the untruths the witchfinders had fed him and, alongside his fellow convicts, was hanged.[14]

~

Ten years after that grim evening, Lawrence Washington's descendant – the one named John after his uncle Sir John Washington of Thrapston – arrived in Virginia. There he became a tobacco planter and merchant. But echoes of the Thrapston witches pursued young John Washington to the New World. In 1659, he lodged a complaint with the Provincial Court of Maryland alleging that Edward Prescott, a ship's captain with whom he had an ongoing dispute, had executed a woman as a witch on board his ship on its way to America in 1658. Indeed, Elizabeth Richardson had been hanged on board the ship *Sarah Artch*. Captain Prescott did not deny she had been killed, but he contended it was not his fault. Instead, he told the court that he had protested against Elizabeth's execution, but had seen no other option but to allow it to go ahead because his ship's master and crew were so convinced of her guilt that they threatened to mutiny. When Prescott reluctantly agreed, the master John Greene had organised the killing and had it carried out, the captain stated.

Partly because of the lack of clarity as to where responsibility for her death lay, the captain was acquitted. But of more weight was the fact that no witnesses came to court to give evidence against him. Prescott's chief accuser John Washington was given only five days' notice to travel the sixty miles from his Virginia home to the Maryland court, and he did not present himself. Before the hearing, he wrote to the court explaining that on the date appointed for the hearing he was due to attend his son Lawrence's baptism – guests had been invited and the date could not be changed. Additionally, he would have to gather those who had witnessed the hanging and transport them to Maryland at very short notice, something he did not believe he could do. Perhaps the court could change its schedule and postpone Prescott's trial to its next sitting, he suggested, since 'in this short time witnesses cannot be got to come over'. But the court did not agree and proceeded with the trial in the absence of any of Washington's witnesses. After Prescott's acquittal, no one was held to account for the killing of Elizabeth Richardson.[15] Lawrence junior, President George Washington's grandfather, whose baptism had clashed fatally with the date of Prescott's trial, grew up to become a Justice of the Peace, Burgess, Sheriff and Coroner for Westmoreland County, Virginia.

Twice in the ancestry of George Washington, his ancestors failed to intervene effectively in a witch trial, but in neither case can they realistically be blamed for their lack of action. Sir John Washington does not seem to have been directly involved in the accusation of John Chirrey and was probably absent from Thrapston at the time of his arrest and trial: most conservatives like him were keeping their heads down and sought safety in Royalist areas as witch trials tore through their reformist hometowns. Thirteen years later and three thousand miles away, his nephew John did what he could to hold to account the murderers of Elizabeth Richardson after her execution as a witch. That both of them failed in their endeavours demonstrates the pervasive belief in witches that spanned the Anglophone world in the 1640s and 1650s and the intercontinental power of the ongoing seventeenth-century witch hunt.

PART 5

Fighting Back: Cornwall and Tyneside

CHAPTER 10

Fairyland

Ann Jefferies of St Teath, Cornwall, 1646–47

If anywhere was safest from witchfinding in the mid-seventeenth century, it was the western parts of Britain where reformism and Parliamentarianism were, on the whole, weaker than in the east. Civil war still raged, with battles at Plymouth, Bovey Tracey, Exeter and Torrington in Devonshire, Stratton and Lostwithiel in Cornwall, Bath in Somerset and Stow on the Wold in Gloucestershire in 1642–46. But – initially at least – Royalists often won these battles with local support.

Most western people favoured decorated churches with elaborate services, Catholic-style prayer books, holy wells, and a spirit world of piskies, mermaids and fairies. During the fifteenth and mid-sixteenth century they'd rebelled twice to protect their traditional religious and cultural identity.[1] It's likely they held fewer witch trials too, although we can't be completely sure because they also kept fewer records: all the Assize indictments for Britain's southwestern counties before 1670 are lost, as are many records of magistrates' and town courts. Yet, even with these gaps, it would be hard to hide a witch hunt on the scale of what was going on in the east; the more tolerant west was showing the way to a future where witchfinders had to struggle to secure convictions. Nevertheless, there were some witch trials in the west.

One began to unfold in autumn 1646, just after John Stearne finished his Northamptonshire investigation. The final Royalist positions in west Cornwall, near Falmouth, fell to Parliament that August, effectively ending this first phase of the civil wars with Parliamentarian victory. As the national drama played out, twenty-year-old Ann Jefferies of St Teath, forty miles from Falmouth, was claiming that she'd been having visions of fairies for many months. Soon she stood accused of witchcraft.

Fifty years later, as a bankrupt publisher called Moses Pitt looked back on his career, he remembered Ann and that hot, strange summer, which had seen tornadoes and violent thunderstorms across Britain – omens, some said, of the defeat of the king in Cornwall. Moses had left St Teath (pronounced 'teth' and named after St Tetha, a Cornish saint) many years before he began his reminiscences in the 1690s. Since 1654, he had lived in London. Initially he was apprenticed to a haberdasher, a dealer in small items for the clothing industry, but Moses did not settle into selling buttons and braid and in the 1660s he set up a publishing house. He used his earnings to finance building projects as London was reconstructed after the Great Fire of 1666, but in the late 1680s he and his wife Mary went bust and Moses spent around seven years in a debtors' prison.

By the mid-1690s, he was free, however, and his thoughts returned to profitable publishing ideas. He remembered an evening some twenty years earlier, when he and his cousin Will Tom had dined with the Bishop of Gloucester Edward Fowler – back in the 1670s when Moses was wealthy and Will was a city councillor in Plymouth. That evening, Moses had told the bishop a story from his old hometown: the tale of Ann Jefferies and her visions. The bishop was 'pleased to take me by the hand and would not let me go, till I had promised ... to publish to the world [the] narrative of and concerning Ann Jefferies', he recalled. In 1696, Moses made good his promise.[2]

~

In the late 1630s or early 1640s, the prosperous St Teath farmers John and Joan Pitt – Moses' parents – had taken in Ann Jefferies, the daughter of a poor family in their parish. It was common for the children of large, needy families like the Jefferies to work as servants in wealthier local homes, where they were bound legally to their employers for a set term of years; Ann Jefferies's position may have been similar to the one taken by Rebecca West at Rivenhall in Essex several years before. We can't be sure of the details in either case, but by the 1640s Ann was certainly living with the Pitts, working as a maid and child-minder, and it was fixed that she would stay until she was twenty-one. The Pitts had several children in the 1630s and 1640s who needed a nanny. We know of at least three: Gregory (born 1634), Moses (1639) and Mary (1642). Ann was a bright, playful carer, 'a girl of a bold, daring spirit', as Moses called her. She 'would venture at those difficulties and dangers that no boy would attempt', he recalled. Ann was unwilling to be confined by her gender or social status to a dull life of modest, silent drudgery.[3] Soon she'd established herself as a lively, capable character in the Pitts' home.

Despite her self-confident front, however, Ann's position was delicate – it was not freely chosen waged employment, nor unpaid labour, nor fostering either. She was an employee, a dependent and part of the family all at once. Children and young people in Ann's position could find themselves abused and exploited or, conversely, nurtured and trained for independent life. They were better housed and fed than they would have been in their birth family and were given a chance to advance socially. The expectation was that the most successful young women would marry well – perhaps a skilled artisan – at the end of their residence with their hosts. But such girls could not direct their own futures: they might fail to find a husband or be forced into an unsuitable match. Meanwhile, they lived in a complex web of obligations and constraints. Many came to regard their employers as guardians rather than or as well as custodians or bosses. Ann seems to have been relatively lucky in this way, and was apparently beloved by John and Joan Pitt. Their son Moses recalled that she was always treated 'gently, lovingly and kindly' by them – although those were his words rather than hers – and she may have regarded the Pitts' farmhouse, garden and fields as a safe, protective space.

Ann valued the Pitt family too. When he was a toddler, Moses remembered, she would kiss and cuddle him joyfully. She joined them at meals on festival days and sat with the family in the evenings around the fire as they wound down after a day of shared work. But despite this apparent cosiness, Ann would have been unsure of her status. She was not the Pitts' social equal; she had to work, and her employers, kind as they were, did not teach her the skills they gave their own children, notably reading. Initially, Ann may also have spoken a different language from her host family, since in the seventeenth century working people sometimes spoke Cornish, or at least used Cornish phrases, while higher-status families like the Pitts communicated primarily in English. As her term of service, which was due to expire in 1647, crept towards its end, conversations must have begun concerning what she would do next. Would she have to leave her new family just as she left her birth parents – and for what future? By 1645, Ann's world as she knew it was nearing its end. It was around this time that she apparently experienced a convulsive fit while she was knitting in the garden of the Pitts' farm. She was found unconscious, carried inside and put to bed. When she awoke, Ann cried out something peculiar: 'they are just gone out of the window, they are just gone out of the window! Do you not see them?'[4]

Over the next few weeks she remained bedridden, unable to stand unaided or work, confused and mopey, sometimes unconscious. When she did eventually get out of bed, she held onto the furniture and spread her legs wide apart for balance, gradually learning to walk confidently again. But despite her recovery, she continued to make odd statements, repeating phrases over and over again. The Pitt family put her condition down to her being 'light-headed', but her symptoms varied and it was noted that fits would return 'if anything vex'd her'. When she came out of such a bout of insensibility, she would begin to pray earnestly. She would also call out for Moses, who was now six. Ann questioned the little boy insistently, showing great concern: had anyone annoyed, hurt or abused him? Was he alright without her presence? She came to refer to Moses as if he were her own son, calling him 'my child'. Ann likely didn't want to leave her loving home and the children she'd helped to raise, and perhaps that influenced her behaviour, causing fainting fits, migraines or dizzy hallucinations, feeding anxiety attacks and hysteria. But in the Pitts' eyes, Ann had gone 'silly' – a word that meant a range of different things in the seventeenth century, from innocent or foolish, to mentally ill or deluded.[5]

In summer 1646, Ann's ongoing fits took a surprising turn – one unexpected by the Pitts, at least. The first person to hear of Ann's new claims was Joan Pitt, Moses' mother. Over the years, Joan had built a close relationship with her, trusting the forceful, charismatic girl to mind and entertain her children. Ann also milked cows and acted as a general house servant. But now, instead of being able to rely on Ann's help, the girl was a constant source of worry for Joan. Challenging jobs and upsetting events had to be withheld from Ann, to the extent that in April 1646 Joan and her husband John Pitt had even kept secret the death of John's mother, Florence, in case the news triggered one of Ann's fits. This protectiveness shows how much the Pitt family liked her – many employers would have rid themselves of such a sickly servant if they could wriggle out of their contract, but instead Ann's needs dominated everyone's life. Yet Joan also feared the threat of a convulsing, hallucinating employee in her home. She 'dare not trust' Ann unsupervised, she told Moses later. What if she injured herself or – a particular fear of Joan's – 'set the house on fire' in her delusional state? Ann's odd behaviour and inability to work were causing problems and damaging the family business.[6]

Although she led a comfortable life, Joan Pitt was not idle. She took an active part in household management alongside her farmer husband John. One hot afternoon during the corn harvest of 1646, she and Ann were the only people in the farmhouse when Joan realised there was a supply problem. An order of flour she'd placed wouldn't arrive in time to make bread for the harvesters. Except for Ann, all the household's servants, male and female, and all available Pitt family members were out scything corn and binding it into sheaves, which were loaded into teetering piles and carted home to the farm's barns. The air rang with shouts and the clatter of heavy horseshoes on cobbles. But Joan knew that at dusk the reapers would trudge into the Pitts' big hall from the barnyard, aching and hungry, and there wouldn't be enough loaves in the larder. Joan had sent her manservants to carry two bushels of wheat to the mill that morning so her maidservants could bake bread in time for supper, but it was now late afternoon and no sacks of flour had come trundling back up the lane.

Joan decided she would have to walk to the mill, a quarter of a mile away on the River Allen, to hurry the miller along herself.

Ann appeared very weak and troubled that day, and so Joan hustled her outside, locking her out of the house – not a kindly act, despite Moses' later recollection that his mother and Ann had shared a loving understanding with each other. Although Ann resisted, Joan persuaded her to walk in the garden and orchard for a while. Off Joan went down the hill. She spoke to the miller, explained the need for haste, and set off home. But as she hurried, Joan suddenly slipped and fell, hurting her leg. The road had looked firm and clear, she said later, and she could not tell how she managed to fall over. The pain was so sharp she was unable to get up, and it wasn't until a neighbour found her and heaved her onto his horse that she returned home. Her family and servants were called in from the fields and it was decided to send for a chirugeon or surgeon from the town of Bodmin, eight miles away. Surgeons were the emergency responders of their day for ordinary villagers and lesser gentry, summoned to treat acute problems such as wounds, suspected fractures or dislocations when a physician was too expensive or too distant to call.

Meanwhile, Ann was alarmed at being locked out of the house. Perhaps, she might have thought, Joan Pitt was losing patience with her? Surely her expulsion from home that day foreshadowed permanent eviction when she was twenty-one and her contract was over? So when Ann realised a crisis was unfolding, she thought it time to reveal a secret – one that not only explained her behaviour, but made it useful.

Just as a horse was being saddled to call the Bodmin surgeon, Ann rushed in demanding to see Joan. How sorry she was to hear about the accident and where it had happened, she exclaimed. She begged to see the hurt leg. Nonsense, Joan snapped, pained and irritated – why should she show the injury to Ann, 'so poor and silly a creature as she was? For she could do her no good'. Ann persisted, though, and Joan was unwilling to risk upsetting her 'for fear of her falling into her fits'. So Ann was allowed to see and touch the leg, and sat down, cradling it in her lap and stroking the muscle. This rubbing reduced the pain and Ann asked Joan to confirm 'if she did not find ease by her stroking of it?' When Joan agreed, Ann asked her not to send for the surgeon, announcing that 'she would, by the blessing of God, cure her leg'. It was a bold claim by this daring young woman. But although Joan had her doubts about Ann's sanity, she was grateful for her help, and trusted her enough to tell her manservant not to fetch the surgeon.[7]

As Ann continued to rub the injured leg, Joan recalled a significant detail from their earlier conversation. How, she asked, had Ann known exactly where the accident happened? Oh, said Ann airily, 'half a dozen persons told her of it'. But, Joan replied, 'that could not be, for there was none came by' except the neighbour who rescued her. This was Ann's moment. 'Now', she said, 'I will tell you the truth of all matters and things that have befallen me'. On the day of her first fit back in 1645, Ann explained, when she was knitting in the Pitts' garden, 'there came over the garden hedge of a sudden six small people, all in green clothes'. They were fairies! Ann was so frightened she fell into the first of the unconscious states that had afflicted her ever since. And, she continued, the fairies were still visiting her. Just a few hours earlier, when Joan had forced her out of the house, they had returned. One of them had asked Ann if 'you [meaning Joan] had put me out of the house against my will'. It was true, Ann replied, so 'I told them I was unwilling to come out of the house'. Shockingly, the fairy responded with a threat to Joan. It said, Ann reported, 'you should not fare the better for it', meaning that Joan would fare worse, would suffer. 'And at that time', Ann concluded, 'in a fair pathway you fell and hurt your leg'. Joan's injury was the result of a fairy attack. Now she herself would cure the hurt leg, Ann explained. And indeed, Joan soon recovered.[8]

Today, we often imagine fairies as friendly creatures: cute, angelic, sparkly. But seventeenth-century people thought of them in a more traditional way, as kin to elves and goblins, a tricky, often malevolent presence across the folktales of northern Europe. Elves would curse you as soon as look at you if you angered them. They were thought to be armed with invisible bows and arrows, sharp-tipped projectiles that pierced unseen through human skin, causing otherwise inexplicable disease and death. Victims of this type of sickness were known as 'elf-shotten'. Sometimes it was thought that goblins could be helpful instead of deadly – but you had to treat them right, feeding and propitiating them, or be a lucky, specially gifted or blessed person. Fairies, as Ellen Driver of Framlingham knew, could steal human children and replace them with sickly changelings, although they could also heal or reveal secrets to those who befriended them. As in the rest of Britain, many Cornish people believed firmly in such fairy and fairy-like creatures, also known by the local name of piskies or pixies. Ann's claims that she could see them, that they defended her and bestowed magical powers upon her, was therefore plausible. And this was no bad thing; such supernatural powers were prized, and fairy-inspired magical healing or divination could be rewarded with material gifts, favours or payment from satisfied customers.

It was no surprise, then, that according to her, Ann's fairies continued their visits to her throughout 1646, arriving in parties of between two and eight and bringing new wisdom each time. They always came in even numbers – the fairy world was thought to have many such rules emphasising its potent magic – and they helped not just Joan Pitt but an increasing number of visitors who came after hearing Ann's story. People wanted to believe her, no matter what she claimed was happening. One day, the Pitts' neighbour Francis Heathman came over – the Heathmans farmed land at Suffenton Hill, a mile west of St Teath – and was told Ann was in her room. But when he went in, calling, he could not see her. Francis thought she might be hiding, so he felt up and down the room for her, hands outstretched – but there was nothing there. Yet as soon as he'd returned to the Pitts, who were sat at dinner, Ann appeared, exclaiming self-righteously that she'd been in her room the whole time but invisible. Francis was impressed, as she must have hoped he would be, and Moses Pitt later remembered the great excitement he'd felt that day, sure that his nurse was a miracle worker. One day, he added, he had even seen her frolicking in the orchard and she had told him that she was dancing with her fairies.[9]

Moses had one great cause of regret, however. He was wistfully jealous of his little sister Mary, because in 1646, when Mary was about four years old, she had seen Ann's fairies for herself. 'I never did see them', wrote Moses sadly, many years later. The fairies had also brought Mary a silver cup, he said, which she had tried to give to her mother, explaining that it was a fairy gift. But instead of being pleased, Joan Pitt was alarmed: fairy items were thought potentially corrupting or deadly. It was widely believed that fairies could bring or reveal treasure to their human friends – gold and silver coins, cups and plates, jewels and brooches that were probably in fact archaeological artefacts from the burial mounds where fairies were thought to live – but often such loot proved to be cursed, or withered away into dead leaves or thin air. Mothers who credited such fairy lore also worried that fairies deployed such snares in order to spirit their children away to their pisky realm – indeed, that might be where the Pitts and Heathmans thought Ann was when she was apparently invisible. Joan hastily told her little girl to give the cup back, and Mary toddled off with it, after which it was not seen again. Presumably she or Ann put it back wherever they had found it.[10]

One of the gifts fairies were thought to offer most freely was food. It was usually unwise to accept it because, like Mary's cup, it might be a portal to another world or cause illness and insanity. But from the time that Ann began to claim healing abilities, she also said that henceforth she would be fed by the fairies. She stopped eating the Pitts' meals at harvest 1646 and did not eat with them again until Christmas Day, when she allowed herself some roast beef. In the interim, she sometimes ate fairy food in her room – she told Francis Heathman that was what she'd been doing in her invisible state – and sometimes ate nothing at all. Nobody was able to discover how she sustained herself. Sceptics might argue that it is possible to fake lengthy fasting, particularly if Ann had an accomplice, or that some free food was available in hedgerows or could be filched from kitchens. But that was not enough to keep anyone fit and well, as any poor person like Mary Edwards or John Winwick could have told you. Mystics of the kind Ann claimed to be did often fast, weakening themselves to the point of visionary raptures or even death; some were diagnosed with demonic possession, while others were lauded as saints. Perhaps Ann believed such fasting made her holy. Or perhaps she was faking holiness in an attempt to secure her position with the Pitts. Maybe, instead or as well, she was experiencing an eating disorder and felt unable to consume anything, particularly in public.

A story told by Moses supports the suggestion of concealed eating, although it doesn't reveal Ann's state of mind or motives. One day the little boy went to Ann's room and naughtily banged and kicked on the closed door. Ann replied, 'my child, have a little patience and I will let you in immediately'. Unable to wait, Moses peeked through the keyhole and saw Ann eating a piece of bread. When she finished, she prayed to God and bowed to something – as he reported years later – before letting Moses in. Then she gave him a leftover piece of bread, which he believed was fairy food. 'I think', he reminisced in the 1690s, 'it was the most delicious bread that ever I did eat'. Moses was a bit of a dreamer and he wanted to be delighted by the fairies' magic gift. His story suggests Ann was eating in secret but also confirms that the Pitt family accepted her claim that she was a holy seer living without regular nourishment, whatever evidence was presented to the contrary. Despite their qualms about elves and piskies, they had also come to believe Ann's claim that her fairies were aligned with Christianity and that the healing gifts given to her demonstrated their inherent goodness. Although the fairies had harmed Joan when she upset Ann, they were basically God's creatures, dispensing divine wisdom and power. Many of their neighbours and visitors agreed with the Pitts that this interpretation of events must be true.[11]

As gossip about Ann's gifts spread by word of mouth and letter, ill, war-weary and distressed people walked across the moors from east and west Cornwall to seek Ann's healing touch, which was said to cure the lymph gland infection scrofula, fevers and even mend broken limbs. It was especially significant that she could cure scrofula because that disease was known as 'the king's evil'. Monarchs could cure it by touch, people believed, and that healing gift was proof of their divine right to rule. By late 1646, to claim the same abilities as the now-defeated King Charles I – skills demonstrating the holiness and legitimacy of monarchy – could not have been more controversial. Ann was wandering into dangerous territory as Royalist Cornwall, and Royalist Britain, fell apart around her.

As her visions continued and her reputation grew, it was inevitable she would attract attention from newly powerful Parliamentarians. In particular, the godly magistrate John Tregeagle of Trevorder, eleven miles west of St Teath, began to see Ann as a threat. It's not clear how he heard about her: most likely he picked up the same gossip as everyone else during 1646 and, as the war ended that autumn, he decided to act upon it. Tregeagle was Steward of the estates of John, Lord Robartes of Lanhydrock – the Cornish nobleman who'd fought in the Earl of Essex's army at the 1643 Battle of Newbury – and it's possible that the puritanical Robartes ordered him to investigate Ann. Whatever instigated his interest, Tregeagle began to look into Ann's claims, and that winter, along with several other local magistrates and ministers, he rode out to John Pitt's home to question her.

For all her daring and presence of mind, Ann was very naïve in what she told her visitors. After all, she was just twenty, illiterate and living in a small, rural, traditionalist community where she was valued and respected. She must have imagined her new audience would share her understanding of the supernatural, in which God and the fairies lived in innocent harmony. Unfortunately, her questioners, men like John Tregeagle, were lawyers and theologians well used to hair-splitting points of legality or dogma. Tregeagle in particular was a harsh, sophisticated man of the world. Ann could barely have imagined any aspect of his life: his manors stretched from Hartland in Devon to St Columb in west Cornwall and Lanlivery in the south, he had a house in London and at his death in 1655 he left over two thousand pounds to his children. He and his employer favoured Presbyterian religion and Parliamentary government. So when he heard Ann tell the story of the fairies' threat against Mistress Pitt, Tregeagle and his colleagues interpreted it in the same way as Hew Kennedie, Matthew Hopkins or John Stearne would have done: not as a happy account of God's healing gift, but as a story of witchcraft.[12]

To them, it was the classic narrative of Satan's temptation of a witch. As you'll have noticed, such stories follow a predictable pattern. First, a vulnerable woman suffers difficulty. In this case, Ann was forcibly ejected from her home. Then, as the victim of the difficulty becomes sad or angry, otherworldly creatures appear, promising revenge. In this case, they told Ann that Joan, her antagonist, would be harmed. Then the creatures enact that harm magically: in this case, Joan inexplicably fell and injured her leg. If Ann had authorised this magical assault by her supernatural visitors, that would make her a witch. Admittedly, she'd healed the injury that Joan had experienced, and she thought her visitors were fairies, not animal familiars, but that made no difference. Horrified, the clergymen who visited St Teath informed Ann that her creatures were 'evil spirits' who had successfully tempted her to hurt Joan. Further, her visions and healing gifts were merely 'the delusion of the devil', designed to entrap her into sin. Ann was, understandably, 'not a little troubled and concerned' by this interpretation of her gift, as Moses reported. Surely, she must have fretted, she hadn't unwittingly confessed to witchcraft? All she'd wanted was to be of use to her employer and show she could help other people too, with her holy marvels. She was a determined young woman, however, and her commitment to her story didn't wane.

On the dark winter evening when the ministers and magistrates rode away from St Teath, as Ann sat by the roaring fire in John Pitt's hall, she suddenly spoke to him. 'Now they call!' she said urgently, meaning she heard fairy voices summoning her. The Pitt family, spooked by the ministers' sobering conclusions, urged her not to respond. But minutes later, Ann repeated that the fairies were calling her. Finally she exclaimed, 'Now they call a third time' and she went to her room to commune with them. After a while, Ann returned carrying a Bible and reported an important conversation. When she'd met the fairies in her room, they had said, 'What, has there been some magistrates and ministers with you and dissuaded you from coming any more to us, saying we are evil spirits, and that it was all the delusion of the devil?' Of course, the fairies were correct. 'Pray', they continued, 'desire them [the magistrates and ministers] to read that place of scripture in the first epistle of St John, chapter four, verse one'. When John Pitt looked at the verse, he saw that it read, 'Dearly beloved, believe not every spirit, but try the spirits, whether they are of God'. For John's convenience, Ann's fairies had even turned down the corner of the page containing that advisory verse. Since Ann could not read, the astonished Pitt family reasoned, how could she have done that herself? The fairies must have handled the holy book – surely proof that they were not Satanic, or wouldn't it have injured them? They'd also used their intimate knowledge of God's word to offer guidance: such fairies must indeed be angelic creatures, better understanding the mysteries of religion than the puritanical clergymen who had doubted Ann.[13]

Magistrate Tregeagle, however, was unconvinced. Despite Ann's steadfastness and her continued claims that her fairies were not demons – or perhaps because of it, since he was not a man to be defied – he issued a warrant for her arrest and had her imprisoned in the nearest big town, Bodmin. It must have been a terrifying shock. But, before her eight-mile journey to Bodmin started, Ann seems to have embraced imprisonment and interrogation as an opportunity for vindication or perhaps even martyrdom. When St Teath's constable, the Pitts' neighbour Giles Bawden, came to deliver the warrant and take Ann away, she explained that her fairies had visited her that morning as she was milking the cows. The constable would come for her today, they prophesied, and she would be sent to jail. Ann asked them if she should run away and hide, but the fairies reassured and strengthened her. She should go with the constable, they instructed, and she should not be afraid. And so Ann submitted to being restrained and marched away, to fame and acclaim – or more likely to death. Soon Giles would be back for further members of the Pitt family.[14]

Ann remained imprisoned at Bodmin for at least two months,

spending part of that time in the town's jail, part under guard in Tregeagle's own house. John Tregeagle instructed her jailers that she should not be fed at all. If she claimed the fairies were feeding her, let her prove it, he insisted – or break down and confess. There's no evidence that Ann was deprived of sleep, or watched and walked, though she might have been and, even if not, she must have come close to starvation. Presumably visitors sustained her, or she would have died – the community, it seems, supported their local 'witch'. They were not going to join the fanatics who, in the past two years, had bloodied the east with their miscarriages of justice.

Times had changed, and Ann's resistance became the talk of the already divided town, which had been fought over in both 1644 and 1645 and retained strong Royalist sympathies despite Parliamentarian occupation. In March 1647 came the meeting of the magistrates' quarterly sessions. Cornwall's justice system retained its pre-war structures, so the magistrates were expected to forward any felonies that came to their court onward to the next Assize to be assessed by professional judges there. But they were permitted to hold preliminary hearings themselves and ask a grand jury to approve felony indictments for the Assizes. So, to their spring session, probably in Bodmin, the magistrates summoned the Pitt family to question them about Ann. First to be examined was Joan Pitt. We don't know what she was asked because our informant, Moses, wasn't in the room with his mother. But when Joan was allowed to leave, Moses was ushered in.

As Ann's special charge, the little boy could be an important witness against his nurse. Children were regularly questioned during the preliminary hearings of witch trials, and it was thought by some magistrates that the best evidence came from those around Moses' age: six to ten. Such young people were thought to be innocently unable to lie, and likely to reveal details of the familiar spirits kept by witches. Those questioning them seldom considered that they were intimidating vulnerable children, who would probably agree with anything put to them and add their own fantasies about talking animals, based on folklore, imagination and poorly understood adult gossip. Moses' evidence could easily incriminate Ann and lead to her execution if that was what the magistrates wanted – and if this had been the case, it would no doubt have left him with lifelong guilt and confusion about the dramatic effect of his words. It had already been a big day for the small boy: later, he recalled the long horseback journey to Bodmin as his first memory of riding. Now, tired and far from home, he stood before the committee of powerful men and noticed that his words were to be written down by a scribe.

The first question was not about witchcraft, however. 'My pretty little child', said one of the gentlemen, 'what have you got in your pockets?' Moses was puzzled but answered, 'nothing, sir, but my cuffs'. Cuffs were decorative sleeve protectors or a kind of fingerless glove, and Moses pulled them out to show his interrogators. Their interest became clear with their next question: did he have 'any victuals in my pocket for my maid Ann?' *Aha*, they must have thought, *was this how the prisoner was fed?* But Moses did not have any food, and he said so forthrightly. Such was his innocent outrage that some of the magistrates laughed. At this, Moses was shown out, and he and Joan were told to go home: the slightness of the questioning was further indication of the magistrates' reluctance to pursue a witch hunt. Tregeagle had started the judicial process, however, so Ann remained under guard, awaiting the Assizes.

The kindly laughter of the magistrates led to one good outcome: Ann was removed from the home of her accuser, John Tregeagle, and re-housed with Bodmin's mayor, Richard Webber.[15] This more comfortable imprisonment hardened her resolve. With crazy bravery, she began to utter prophecies based on fairy information, defending herself against accusations of witchcraft with even more ambitious claims to be a holy seer. Like the Pitts and their neighbours, the fairies were Royalists and, through Ann, they explained that God's chosen ruler Charles I would soon be victorious once again. 'She foretells the king's restoration', wrote one correspondent reporting news of Ann. Another said she had 'been before the committee [of local Parliamentarian gentry] and bids them be good in their office, for it will not last long'. Whether she had in fact said this or not, local gossips *wanted* her to have said it. Such defiance meant traditional forms of religion might yet triumph over new puritanism, God's work was still being done through his old world of spirits and wonders, and all would be well. That was joyful news in many parts of Cornwall: the Pitts and their neighbours hoped Ann was right.[16]

Finally, Ann was sent to the Assizes, most likely the court held at Launceston on 5 April 1647. This court was presided over by Judge Henry Rolle. Rolle was a Somerset Presbyterian, lawyer and former MP, who until 29 March had been trying cases across the western circuit with none other than John Godbolt, one of the judges of the accused Suffolk witches back in 1645. But again Ann was lucky: Godbolt left the western circuit directly after the Exeter Assizes, so that Rolle went on to Launceston alone. We don't know exactly what happened at the Assize trial, because its records are lost. One possibility is that Ann was indicted for witchcraft, but the grand jury of twenty-four men, who examined indictments to check whether they should go forward to trial, rejected the charges against her. If so, she would have been freed, so long as someone was prepared to pay her prison fees, which the Pitts and her other supporters likely were. Alternatively, the grand jury might have forwarded her indictment to trial, and there the petty jury of twelve men might have acquitted her. Either way,

Ann was extremely fortunate. Her self-defence was believed, and she was not judged to be a witch. Instead of condemning and executing her, Judge Henry Rolle let her go, and the half-hearted attempt at this witch trial of 1647 was over, thanks in part to the steadfastness of the suspect.[17] Ann had saved herself.

Rolle left the Cornish magistrates to decide what to do with Ann. To them it was clear that, despite her innocence, things could not go on as they had been, with fairy healing and unsettling prophecies. They issued an order removing Ann from the Pitt family, probably because they blamed her employers for encouraging her activities. However, there was apparently no wish to humiliate the Pitts, and agreement was reached that Ann would be placed with the Tom family, headed by John Pitt's widowed sister, Frances Tom. Ann lived quietly there for several years, alongside Moses' cousin Will Tom, who was later asked by Moses to confirm everything he had written about Ann. Will agreed – tersely but absolutely – that what his 'Cous[in] Pitt' had narrated 'is very true'.

After leaving the Toms, Ann went to live with her brother. Then she married William Warden, a hind – a farm worker managing other servants for a wealthy employer.[18] Initially, William worked for the London physician Dr Richard Lower, probably at Lower's estate in St Tudy, three miles from St Teath. We know this because Moses Pitt had some of his family seek Ann out in both 1691 and 1693 to ask her questions about her fairy experiences fifty years before, and he recorded certain details of her life after she had left the Pitts. In his published account of her fairy visions, the young boy grown up into a writer recorded these 1690s visits: detailing the last one, he said that 'she is still living, 1696, being now in the 70th year of her age'. Ann's husband William, he said, 'now lives as hind to Sir Andrew Slanning of Devon', whose main western residence was at Maristow, near Plymouth. Presumably, by 1696, Ann lived with him there.[19]

Ann Jefferies Warden had survived her witch trial – and the civil war, interregnum, the 1660 restoration of the monarchy (which she of course had predicted back in 1646), the reign of Charles II and his successors, James II, William III and Mary II. But despite the triumph of her long life, as an old woman Ann wisely refused to discuss her fairies. When Moses Pitt's emissaries – his sister Mary's husband Humphrey Martyn and her son – visited her to interview her for his book project, Ann clammed up. Frustrated, Humphrey Martyn asked her why. Although Ann was proud of Moses' achievements in publishing, she said presciently that she was frightened that if she told him about her fairy visions, he 'would make either books or ballads' out of her story. She did not want 'her name spread about the country', she said. Looking back fifty years, she spoke firmly about her supposed witchcraft: 'she had been questioned before justices, and at the sessions, and in prison, and also before the judges at the Assizes, and she doth believe that if she should discover [reveal] such things now, she should be questioned again for it'.[20] Even in the calmer west, and even in the mid-1690s, Ann, smart woman that she was, believed it was still dangerous to be imagined a witch. Such was the fearful legacy of witch hunting across Britain.

CHAPTER 11

Borderland

The Newcastle witches and their defenders,
Newcastle upon Tyne, 1649–50

In the southwest of Britain, witch trials appeared to be losing momentum, as suspects and their communities stood together against external witch hunters and their agitations. Something similar was taking place at the other end of the country, near the Scottish border, just a hundred or so miles south of where the witch hunt had sprung to life in Mid Calder six years earlier.

In the 1650s, the town of Newcastle upon Tyne was known for one thing: coal. Situated on the northeast shore of England, it was a large town for the seventeenth century, with ten to twelve thousand inhabitants, a similar size to York or Bristol at the same time. Sprawling up steep steps and down dark, narrow alleys, its homes and businesses stacked the sides of a gorge on the River Tyne like seabirds' nests. Townspeople grew rich on fees from their cloth, meat and grain markets, tolls from their stone bridge lined with fine shops, and profits from their coal mines and coal shipping.[1]

But in 1649 and 1650, Newcastle also gained a reputation for another reason: witches. The Newcastle witch trial of 1650 would be almost lost to history if it wasn't, surprisingly, mentioned in a list of coal trade malpractices blamed on Newcastle's town council. The council was being criticised because many of its officeholders were members of the Hostmen's Company, a traditional guild of brokers that controlled northeast England's coal trade. The Hostmen 'hosted' visiting coal merchants, negotiating coal deals exclusive to guild members. This networking made them rich and – as with all cartels or oligarchies – they were suspected of corruption. It wasn't just the Hostmen who held disproportionate wealth and power in Newcastle, though: other oligarch guilds included the companies of shipwrights, bakers and brewers, butchers, hatters, feltmakers and so on. Traders trying to operate businesses outside these exclusive clubs were denied what seemed to them basic legal and market rights. By the late 1640s, they were seething with resentment.

One of them, Ralph Gardner, a young businessman from North Shields, seven miles downriver from Newcastle, began a lawsuit against the Newcastle council – also known as the corporation – and its guilds. In putting forward his case, he tells us about the town's witch trial. Ralph was the son of a former master at Newcastle's Grammar School, Devereux Gardner, and his wife Joan, who had fallen into poverty after Devereux was dismissed by the corporation in 1632. Their son Ralph, baptised at Tynemouth in August 1625, was just seven. It is likely that from that date forward he regarded the town's authorities with suspicion: certainly he alleged multiple instances of malpractice and injustice when he wrote about them in the 1650s. He saw the witch trial of 1649 to 1650 as a particularly shocking example of reckless authoritarianism. For him, it symbolised the corporation's approach to everything from coal retail to women's rights. Rarely has a dispute about fossil-fuel logistics yielded such an interesting story.[2] Yet the protest group who ended up as the defenders of the accused witches were not initially interested in such matters. They were mostly shippers: the owners of coal vessels (known as colliers), captains, master mariners, merchants and their families. These trade lobbyists came together to allege that council and guild officials were mismanaging town affairs and industries, were corrupt and violent monopolists, and had overstepped their legal authority in all areas of town life.

The coal dispute was part of a wider breakdown in Newcastle and neighbouring Tyneside communities, partly caused by the civil wars, just like the wool, refugee, fishing and agricultural crises further south – but the fighting had special ferocity and an international dimension in this part of northern England. In 1640, Scottish forces had come over the border, captured Newcastle and occupied it, forcing the then-Royalist, English council to pay for the billeting of Scottish troops in their subjugated town. The Scots had left in 1641, but in 1644 they returned with greater vigour. Scottish troops besieged the town and ships blockaded the Tyne. Since most of the coal from the surrounding area – Newcastle, Northumberland and Durham – was shipped downriver and along the east coast to Hull, Great Yarmouth and London, the river blockade was disastrous. The siege of Newcastle lasted for eight months, injuring and killing troops and civilians as the town was bombarded, bankrupting businesses and starving people inside the town walls into illness or death. In October, the Scottish army had overcome the exhausted defenders and captured Newcastle again, sacking it in revenge for their long wait. Homes and business premises were seized or burned, defences demolished, and prominent citizens arrested. Royalist corporation members and Hostmen were thrown out of office. Many fled from the town with their families and whatever wealth they could carry with them.[3] These officials were replaced by Parliamentarians. But when they took control of the town's trade, they simply resumed the oligarchic practices of their predecessors, despite simultaneously agitating for the punishment of those councillors.

Charging high fees for trade made sense to both political factions, building wealth for the town. But those outside the new ruling group felt that the renewed restrictions only worsened wartime economic damage. Ralph Gardner documented their complaints. Firstly, under corporation rules, the loading of coal into ships or unloading other goods was forbidden outside Newcastle's walls. If you wanted to import cabbages or cloth, you had to unload at the designated quay. If you wanted to ship coal to Ipswich, Manningtree or Aldeburgh, you had to load in the permitted place and pay dues. It would have been easier to ship coal from North or South Shields, near the Tyne's mouth, but that was illegal, so shippers were forced upriver to use Newcastle's facilities. Secondly, before a compulsory docking to load coal, incoming ships had to unload ballast – sand piled into hulls to stabilise empty ships at sea – and dump it on the shore at designated places, again for a fee. Having charged for the dumping, the guilds then used this sand for glassmaking, so it paid for itself twice over. Then, thirdly, there were restrictions on trading once a ship had docked: only accredited Freemen of Newcastle were permitted to buy or sell coal. 'Free' status was controlled by the guilds and reserved for native Newcastle men who were in favour with them. Freemen became compulsory middlemen in any coal deal, and they took a cut. These three interlinked rules created an unfair advantage for some traders, Gardner's protest group argued.

But they had two further, more serious, concerns connected by a single belief: that council rules were killing people. It was a seven-mile voyage upriver from Shields to Newcastle to load coal within the oligarchs' rules, and many ships sank on this journey. Overuse of ballast dumps had worsened existing silting, as ballast slumped into the river, so ships with twelve feet of hull below the waterline could no longer sail safely upstream, and parts of the Tyne even froze during winter. The corporation had damaged the river by their greed for ballast dumping fees and products, Gardner's lobbyists concluded as their fourth complaint. Finally, there was a fifth concern: if a ship was sinking anywhere on the Tyne between Newcastle and Shields, only Newcastle-based salvers were permitted to rescue her. That meant crews racing miles to the stricken ship, often arriving too late. Meanwhile, if the crew disembarked and unloaded the ship to save her, themselves, their goods and passengers, they would be prosecuted, since it was illegal to unload outside the town. If they asked local carpenters, not Newcastle men, to make emergency repairs, then that was illegal too. Some mariners had been jailed for these 'crimes' and people who assisted wreck survivors had been attacked by the town's officials, Ralph asserted. One woman had died after being beaten. The protestors told heartrending stories of the loss of the *Adventure*, the *Refuge*, the *Henrietta Maria*, the *Ann Speedwell*, and compiled a list of those who had drowned in what they believed to be unnecessary wrecks. It made a compelling case against the council and its guild allies.

The authorities countered with claims that Ralph Gardner was a youthful upstart attacking trading tradition to create opportunity for himself. Every port in history has seen such tensions over restrictive taxes and shipping customs: the herring trade at Great Yarmouth was just the same. But the lobbyists of seventeenth-century Newcastle did have a point: their oligarchs held local life in a chokehold.[4] Gardner believed they disregarded legal rights and human lives as they wielded their power, using violence to legitimise injustice, and this insight drew his attention to the witch trial they organised in December 1649.

He believed the trial demonstrated the authorities' law-bending and violence – and it's hard to disagree. One key error was made by the council in summer 1649. It was then that the town of Berwick, sixty miles north, decided it had a witch problem. Berwick's authorities called in a Scottish witchfinder, whose name isn't recorded but who accused around thirty women and obtained confessions from some of them. His work caught the attention of Newcastle's corporation, which was at the time fretting about challengers like Gardner and other enemies within, and, tragically, they decided to follow Berwick's example. No doubt they believed they were acting responsibly, since in late March 1649 they had received a petition 'concerning witches' in their town. The council minutes do not record the petition's content or authors, but at Berwick it had been one of the town's guilds that had presented a similar petition, and it may be that in Newcastle it was similarly a guild that raised the concern.

It was inevitable that many Newcastle people would fear witches and consider adopting anti-witch strategies from any community that could offer a precedent. As well as looking to Berwick for help, Newcastle's authorities would certainly have heard about the witch trials of the mid-1640s across Essex, Suffolk, East Anglia and the Midlands. By 1649, these had been widely reported in multiple printed books, including those by the witchfinders Hopkins and Stearne, raised in Parliament and debated by church ministers like John Gaule. Gossip about the trials would also have been reported in Newcastle by the mariners who sailed up and down the east coast in ships carrying coal and other cargoes. No doubt the trials were discussed by crewmen on the *Sarah* or *Endeavor* of Great Yarmouth or the *Blessing* or *Abraham* of Manningtree, all of which regularly visited Newcastle. Indeed, the *Abraham*'s skipper was one of the Woolvett family who had accused their Manningtree neighbour Sara Bright of witchcraft back in 1645. Given these close connections between coastal communities, it would be entirely explicable that some Newcastle people shared the Woolvetts' beliefs that witchcraft was rife across Britain and that something should be done about it. Just as beliefs about witch conspiracies, and practical advice about methods of finding and interrogating witchcraft suspects, had spread south from Scotland in the mid-1640s, now knowledge of the southern trials would have filtered back to the north.

Whoever Newcastle's anti-witch petitioners were, the town's council was receptive to their concerns, ordering 'thanks be returned to the petitioners'. On 26 March 1649, councillors promised to 'contribute their best assistance' to combat witchcraft. So, later in the year, they summoned Berwick's witchfinder to their town. Two council officers travelled into Scotland to 'agree with' him, contracting him to find witches in Newcastle just as Great Yarmouth's council had agreed terms with Matthew Hopkins. However, the payment scheme said to have been agreed at Newcastle, and based on the practice in Berwick, sounds horribly, obviously flawed: as well as travel expenses, the witchfinder would apparently be paid twenty shillings for each witch found, rather than a flat fee for his work whatever its outcome. In December 1649, he came to Newcastle, unsurprisingly drawn by this incentive.[5]

Mayor William Dawson and his fellow councillors took charge of staging the witch test, likely in co-operation with St Nicholas's vicar and councilman Dr Robert Jenison and Richard Prideaux, preacher at All Saints, in whose parish William Dawson was an elder. Dawson was a reformist draper, whose family formed a powerful clique in town affairs. Jenison was the radical son of a former mayor. Expelled from his church in the 1630s for too-radical reformism, he fled to Danzig (Gdansk, Poland), from where Newcastle's council recalled him in 1645: his views matched theirs. Jenison believed that 'heresies are abroad uncontrolled', that people should be 'mortifying such sins as reign in us' (rebellion, pridefulness in women, Sabbath-breaking) and that 'magistrates ... must both enquire into offences and punish the same ... keeping off or removing [God's] wrath'. In 1647, he'd investigated the 'torments' of Northumberland teenager Margaret Muschamp and signed a witness statement supporting claims that she was bewitched. Prideaux had been appointed as a Presbyterian minister at Newcastle in 1646, initially roaming between parishes to provide sermons but soon settling at All Saints. These leaders all wanted to purify their hometown.[6]

With such a crusade in mind, the council sent for their town crier, Thomas Huntergroome, an official who would normally make announcements of the dates of forthcoming events and news affecting townspeople. Also known as the 'bell man', he would ring a handbell to attract attention to his speeches. Now he was to issue an invitation to accuse witches – specifically women, at least as recalled by John Wheeler, a London man, Eleanor Loumsdale and Bartholomew Hodshon, local witnesses to the events that followed.[7]

Thomas was ordered to go through the streets, ringing his bell and shouting that 'all people that would bring in any complaint against any woman for a witch, they should be sent for, and tried'. The accused would initially be examined by the witchfinder, residents were told, then tried in a manner to be determined by the council. The Scottish witch expert did not use all the same methods as John Stearne and Matthew Hopkins. Instead, his sole technique was to prick the bodies of accused people with a needle or bodkin. If they flinched in pain and bled, they were judged innocent. If they did not, the witchfinder would claim to have found an insensible mark made by the devil. Witch pricking was unusual in England, although it was used from time to time, including by Stearne. By the 1640s, however, it had become common in Scotland.

Unlike the suspects of Mid Calder, Manningtree, Framlingham and others across the years 1645–46, the accused witches of Newcastle upon Tyne would not be imprisoned and beaten or watched and walked – at least not initially: their test would be instantaneous. That meant they could be examined publicly in a one-off event, which would involve a quick physical assault in front of their fellow citizens. Newcastle's councillors seemed comfortable with this ugly plan, and their bell man Thomas Huntergroome duly announced that the test would be held under their authority. But because the town was also a garrison, effectively under military control, its deputy governor, Lieutenant-Colonel Paul Hobson, would also be present. This would turn out to be important – at least for one of the suspects.

Hobson was a compelling Baptist preacher and probably a barber surgeon. He'd served the army across England: London, Leicester, Bristol, Hertfordshire, Exeter, East Anglia. He was in Great Yarmouth in 1644 and 1645 and must have witnessed the growth of witchcraft suspicions there, and in the past he'd debated church policy with Edmund Calamy, one of the witch trial judges at Bury St Edmunds. Now quartered in Newcastle with his family – one of his children, Sara, was buried there in March 1650 and possibly another, Silas, in May 1650 – where he had been made a Burgess (a privileged official citizen) of the town in January 1649, he was about to see a very different type of witch trial from the sessions in the Great Yarmouth Tolhouse or Bury's Shire Hall. Initially, the powerful deputy governor may have approved, even helped to facilitate the witch pricking, but soon he would become suspicious of the witchfinder the town council had chosen.[8]

By the time the pricker rode into Newcastle, around thirty people had already been accused – roughly the same number as at Berwick earlier that year, building to a similar spectacle of a mass testing. The bell man's work had encouraged people to point the finger at their neighbours, who were then imprisoned in Newcastle's Newgate jail, an old gatehouse in the town's northern wall. So many were suspected that they cost up to twenty-nine shillings and sixpence per week to imprison. We don't know who half of these people were, because the records of their names and supposed offences are lost, but likely initial suspects include Margaret Maddison, Ann Watson, Eleanor Henderson, Eleanor Rogerson, Elizabeth Dobson, Elizabeth Anderson, Jane Hunter, Jane Koupling (perhaps Copeland), Isabel Brown (the wife of Robert Brown), Margaret Brown, Margaret Muffit (widow), Katherine Welsh, Alice Hume, Mary Potts or Pootes (the wife of William Potts), Katherine Coultor, Alice Read (widow), Elizabeth Horsely (widow) and Mary Dunn (widow), all of whom were certainly accused of witchcraft in either 1649 or 1650. They are impossible to trace confidently in Newcastle's records because their names were shared by lots of fellow residents across the four parishes of this large urban area. Other suspects might have included the smith Matthew Bowmer and Margaret Carr, who were both accused of witchcraft later in 1650, but they may not have been part of this initial group. We simply can't be sure.[9]

On the day of the pricking, the accused people were assembled at Sandhill, next to the town's medieval Guildhall, its clocktower chiming regularly above the gate. Here the mayor and civic officers of Newcastle met three times a year to debate and rule on problems raised by the guilds. The Guildhall complex also housed the Town Court: each Monday morning the mayor, William Dawson, ruled on business and property matters there, while his River Court, regulating Tyne trade, met in the afternoon. Sheriff and merchant Samuel Rawling held his court there on Wednesdays and Fridays. Everyone knew the Guildhall: they visited not just for legal cases, but also to have their trading weights and measures checked for accuracy, to pay coal trade, shipping and ballast dues, and settle other debts to the corporation. Many visited Sandhill weekly for the Tuesday or Saturday Market: 'such a concourse of people out of the country . . . that every Saturday's Market is like a fair'. There was likely a similar crowd for the witchfinding, another exciting civic pageant. Sandhill smelt of fish, vegetables, meat, coal dust and river mud from the quays, kittiwakes and gulls argued over refuse on the river, but it was still Newcastle's finest district. The accused witches stood waiting for their trial outside the fancy shops and elegant merchants' houses that stretched along the quays from Sandhill into the Close. Some were five storeys high, walled with carved beams and glass windows: the corporate skyscrapers of their day. How powerless the suspects must have felt.[10]

Expectantly, their fellow townspeople gathered to watch the witch pricker carry out his test. Despite its official sanction, it was an eye-popping event, pushing seventeenth-century boundaries of legality and public decency to their limit. Each of the accused was partially stripped, and in this vulnerable state they 'openly had pins thrust into their bodies'. The witch pricker chose the thigh or lower body as his target, perhaps because witches' marks were sometimes thought to hide within the genitals. Surely also, however, he chose these body parts because they created the most titillating display. His show was certainly an unusual and shaming display of public nakedness, shocking for beholders but even more so for the accused witches. As he carried out his test, twenty-seven of the thirty or so appalled, outraged suspects did not appear to feel the pin. Also, the witchfinder claimed, they did not bleed: so he judged them to be guilty.[11] But some among the crowd became gradually suspicious of the way the witchfinder obscured the very quick entry and exit of the pin, despite his claim of openness. Was the pricker really jabbing a pin into the half-naked suspects' flesh?

It was surprising how many of them did not cry out or bleed, as would be expected from at least some. Onlookers could not see clearly whether or not blood flowed from the stabbed spot, distracted as they were by the witch pricker's patter and flashes of body parts not normally seen in public.

Deputy Governor Lieutenant-Colonel Paul Hobson was particularly restive. His religion was founded on what he called 'the tenderness of God's affection' for humanity, and he saw none of that here. He disliked holier-than-thou people who 'have attained to a high discovery of light and enjoyments of love yet cannot ... manifest any endeared affection to poor groaning spirits who are not come up to that light and love'. Such a vision of 'melting mercy' to less fortunate souls did not sit comfortably with the witch pricker's cruel theatre. And when Paul Hobson thought something, being a passionate man, he spoke out. He had what he himself called 'a natural boldness ... being of a resolute, bold, hardy temper of spirit', and he believed 'God will vindicate his truth and ... make all opposers and slanderers ashamed'. So, troubled and suspicious, he and others started to ask awkward questions of the witchfinder. How did the pricker know for certain those whom he judged guilty were witches? The pricker explained that 'he knew women whether they were witches or no, by their looks'. That was a different claim to expertise from the one he was being employed for. Hobson can't have been reassured. So, witches *looked* different from other people? How? Uglier? More malicious? That was the stereotype of witchlike appearance, but was it enough to secure a fair conviction? Surely not.

Hobson had himself suffered what he considered unjust trial, imprisonment and abuse by people who regarded him as wicked, because he didn't share precisely the same sectarian opinions as them. He'd been arrested in Buckinghamshire in 1645 for preaching supposedly forbidden doctrine and then accused of blasphemy by fellow reformers. Why, he wondered, as he reflected back on these experiences years later, was there so much 'opposition and strange censorious dealings' between people who were all striving to be better Christians? No one had a monopoly on godliness, and there could be truth on both sides of an argument, he thought, rather progressively. 'Without all question', he wrote later, 'there are very precious hearts dear to God amongst the Presbyterians, and Independents . . . [and] Anabaptists and many others', so why did some of them regard each other as near-demonic enemies? Perhaps he saw the same self-righteous certainty in Newcastle's witch pricker, an echo of the fanaticism of Hopkins and Stearne and their ilk back in the mid-1640s. In 1645, Paul Hobson had been saved from punishment as a heretical rebel only by the intervention of superior army officers. Now that he held high military rank himself, he determined to do the same for at least some of the accused witches who were being paraded before him. Pointing to 'a personable and good-like woman' – a pretty, modest-looking person who did not appear to him to be a plausible witch – he spoke sharply to the witchfinder: 'surely this woman is none [not a witch] and need not be tried?'

The pricker decided to brazen it out and get the crowd on his side: 'she was' a witch, he retorted, 'for the town said she was'. Her neighbours had accused her and, shockingly, that seemed to be enough for him: a revealing insight into the rigour of his practices. 'Therefore he would try her', he continued, and immediately, 'in sight of all the people', he 'laid her body naked to the waist, with her clothes over her head'. Imagine the woman's horror – 'her fright and shame', as witness John Wheeler put it. As she reeled from his assault, the pricker 'ran a pin into her thigh', reported Wheeler, 'and then suddenly let her coats fall'. Then he questioned her, demanding lasciviously 'whether she had nothing of his in her body, but did not bleed'. He made his question sound sexual, like a test of virginity, and – not surprisingly – the woman was dumbstruck and did not know what to say. 'She, being amazed, replied little', Wheeler reported, at which point the witchfinder 'put his hand up her coats' – again, an outrage against seventeenth-century modesty – 'and pulled out the pin'. Brandishing it, he demonstrated to the crowd that the woman had not felt pain, had not known there was a pin in her leg, and that she had not bled. Therefore, she had a demonic insensible mark, and he 'set her aside as a guilty person, and child of the devil', as he put it.[12]

Lieutenant-Colonel Hobson was having none of this defiance. He may have thought the pricker's method looked like sleight of hand, and he also had a biological explanation for what might be going on, explaining the numbness of the woman's flesh. One account of his life suggests he had experience as a barber surgeon before the civil war and a military surgeon during it, and if so, he would have known something of the anatomical theories of his time. So he wondered whether the movement of blood in the woman's body might explain the apparent result of the test. The suspect had blushed scarlet when suddenly stripped. Perhaps, since 'all her blood [had] contracted into one part of her body' – her face – her leg had been unable to bleed? Now, Paul Hobson stated, 'her blood [was] settling into the right parts', so the test should be repeated. Also, some onlookers thought, the accused woman's shock and confusion at her arrest and public shaming might have distracted her from feeling any pain as the pin pierced her leg. So Deputy Governor Hobson forced the witchfinder to recall the suspect.

This time, he closely supervised the witch pricker to minimise the assault on the woman's modesty, in case that should make a difference to the result. Instead of exposing her completely, the witchfinder was instructed to draw up her skirts only 'to her thigh' rather than throwing them over her head, and he was to hold them up so that everyone could see her thigh with the pin in it. This time the test would be checked by impartial observers. In went the pin and the wound 'gushed out of blood', reported the witness John Wheeler. Truth was indeed vindicated, thanks to Paul Hobson's intervention. Cheated of the twenty shillings he'd been promised for each guilty witch and denied further sexual gratification, the witchfinder sulkily 'cleared her, and said, she was not a child of the devil'.[13] Unfortunately, however, the test does not seem to have been repeated with the other accused people, or if it was, no one recorded the outcomes. Perhaps there was an argument over jurisdiction or practice, or it seemed as if a riot might be brewing or people chose to reserve their doubts for the courtroom – we don't know what happened, but it appears that only one woman was re-tested and freed. Paul Hobson was able to save her, but he couldn't or didn't save all the suspects, even if he had thought them all innocent. And it's likely that he did believe some or all of the others to be guilty, hence his willingness to supervise their ordeal.[14]

After their testing, the accused witches returned to Newgate jail to wait for the Assizes to be held that summer, when they would be tried formally by London-trained judges and a jury of the town's Burgesses. Although their trial was to take this broadly conventional Assize form, determining guilt would be a perplexing task: after all, the witch pricker had already claimed he knew the suspects were guilty. Perhaps they were also watched and walked in jail and confessions were wrung from them; we just don't know. Documents setting up the witch trial were registered for some of them at the town's Quarter Sessions in January 1650: Margaret Brown, Mary Potts, Eleanor Rogerson, Isabel Brown, Margaret Muffit, Alice Read, Mary Dunn and Elizabeth Horsely. Other suspects were probably charged before January, but these records are lost. In January, Mary Potts, Margaret Muffit, Alice Read, Mary Dunn and Elizabeth Horsely were bailed: freed from prison temporarily after paying to guarantee their later court appearance, suggesting they had some wealthy supporters. During these proceedings, it was noted that most of the witchcraft indictments – the formal charge papers – were being held by Mayor William Dawson himself, suggesting he played a key role in the witch hunt. In April 1650, two more witchcraft suspects emerged at the Quarter Sessions, a court presided over by the mayor in his role as magistrate. Matthew Bowmer was a smith who had become involved in a dispute with his neighbour, Henry Simson. On 1 April, Henry was bound over to keep the peace against Matthew, meaning that he swore a binding oath not to quarrel with or attack him. Then, on 2 April, Matthew was charged by William Bullock and Elizabeth Man with an unspecified offence that, judging from subsequent events, may have been witchcraft. On the 4th, Margaret Carr was charged with witchcraft by Barbara Stevenson. Both Matthew and Margaret were bailed.[15]

Both seem likely to have lived in All Saints parish, which contained the workshops and tenements spilling down the hill to the Tyne quays in the east of the town. There were Bowmers, Simsons, Bullocks, Mans, Carrs and Stevensons there, among the sailmakers and pulleymakers, shipwrights, mariners, skippers, keelmen, wherrymen, watermen, brewers, tanners, fitters, smiths and glaziers. All Saints parish register has gaps and illegible entries and doesn't usually note the names of children's mothers in a record of their baptism or burial – sometimes not their fathers either. Such was the relative anonymity of a large town.

The parish register does, however, record the birth of an illegitimate boy named Matthew Bowmer in late February 1612 and his sad death: he was buried on 4 March. He is referred to only as 'bastard' at his christening and 'infant' at his burial and neither of his parents is named, but since illegitimate babies were often given the name of their father, he might be the son of the witchcraft suspect Matthew Bowmer. If so, Matthew may have had a reputation for a disorderly life. In the meantime, All Saints parish register records the deaths of Margaret, daughter of Henry Simson, in 1637, Richard, son of William Bullock, in 1647, and Elizabeth, daughter of William Bullock, in 1648. Perhaps Matthew Bowmer was thought to have caused these deaths in the families of his courtroom opponents; this would fit the pattern we have seen repeated throughout the witch trials. Alongside Matthew, a miller's wife from Chatton in Northumbria joined the list of witchcraft suspects: Jane Martin. Eventually she would be tried alongside Newcastle's prisoners.[16] All would have to wait, however, until the Assize judges rode north from Durham in mid-August to begin their work. In the meantime, Eleanor Loumsdale – later one of Ralph Gardner's informants about the witch pricking – was censured by the Quarter Sessions on 8 August for 'dissuading Mary Milbourne to give in any evidence or information [accusation] against [the suspect] Margaret Brown'.[17]

No details of the Assizes have survived, so we don't know who Mary Milbourne was or what her accusation might have been. But the witch trial took place in the Guildhall between 14 and 20 August. Of the twenty-seven people identified as guilty by the witchfinder in December 1649 and the others who had joined them as suspects in early 1650, fifteen were convicted. On 21 August, Matthew Bowmer, Margaret Maddison, Ann Watson, Eleanor Henderson, Eleanor Rogerson, Elizabeth Dobson, Elizabeth Anderson, Jane Hunter, Jane Koupling, Isabel Brown, Margaret Brown, Margaret Muffit, Katherine Welsh, Alice Hume and Mary Potts were all executed – along with Jane Martin of Chatton. The condemned people were marched from the Guildhall to Gallowgate, a twenty-minute uphill walk through Sandhill, up

Castle Stairs or the alley known as Side, through the Groat and Bigg Markets where oats and barley were sold, past Blackfriars and out through the town wall, which was still being repaired after the northern gates had been bombarded during the 1644 siege. Beyond Gallowgate, a path led onto Town Moor, an open heath where refuse and ballast were dumped: here the gallows stood, near the site of Newcastle United football stadium today.

One horrifying story survives from the Town Moor executions, collected by Gardner. As Margaret Brown climbed the ladder to the noose, she 'beseeched God that some remarkable sign might be seen at the time of their execution, to evidence their innocency'. When she was pushed from the ladder, 'her blood gushed out upon the people', perhaps from her nose or mouth. The witch-finder had said witches did not bleed – but Margaret bled now. Many spectators must have gone home troubled. Margaret and her fellow fifteen dead were buried at St Andrew's church, near the gallows, and their names entered in the parish register on a list of those killed 'for [as] witches'. Katherine Coultor may also have been hanged: Gardner says she was, but she doesn't appear on the parish register's burial list.[18]

A number of people must also have escaped execution, since several witchcraft suspects remained in Newgate jail until at least autumn 1650. They might have been acquitted or reprieved, but either way they were forced to remain in jail until they had paid fees covering their keep – often a hopeless task for poorer prisoners. These prisoners presumably included Alice Read, Elizabeth Horsely, Mary Dunn and Margaret Carr – none of whom were on the list of hanged convicts – and maybe Katherine Coultor too. There must, however, have been many more who survived the witch trial, because they cost the town a sizeable sum in the weeks after the hangings.

During their pre-trial imprisonment, we know Newgate's jailer claimed up to twenty-nine shillings and sixpence per week for the whole group of suspects. Then, in the third week of September, Sheriff Samuel Rawling claimed from the council's treasurers ten pounds, nineteen shillings and tuppence 'for the witches for two weeks ending the 23rd of August', two days after the hangings, including, grimly, 'charges for executing the prisoners'. With twenty shillings in a pound, that must have covered food, bedding and cell charges for some twenty-seven people plus expenses, which might have included the executioner's wages, transport and security charges, perhaps the building of an enlarged gallows, additional ladders and rope, and finally burial fees. But after the interments, Newgate's jailer continued to receive up to nine shillings and fourpence per week for keeping 'the witches' from the end of August until the last week of October. That might have covered, say, ten or eleven prisoners. Troublingly, they are referred to as 'witches' whether they had been judged guilty or not. But at least they had survived until 31 October 1650 – at which date the records, frustratingly, end.[19]

When he came to write about the witch trial as part of his attack on Newcastle's corporation, Ralph Gardner did not mention that any 'witches' remained in jail or that there had been any second witch trial. Nor did he challenge the Assize trial's legitimacy. But he did ask pointed questions about the witch pricker, ones that summed up the changing mood of the late 1640s with regard to witch trials and illustrated the importance of activists' rejection of witchfinding. 'By what law', Gardner queried, could Newcastle's council 'send into another nation, for a mercenary person to try women for witches, and a bell man to cry for them to be brought in, and twenty shillings apiece given to him to condemn them?' How was this consistent with justice, reason or legality? Gardner's comments on the way evidence was given at the trial and the payment of jurors also suggest he thought a perversion of justice was concealed within the outwardly lawful Assize trial: 'by what law', Gardner asked, were 'men hired to give evidence to take away people's lives, and the convicted estates to come to the jurors?' This sounds as if the witch pricker's fee included the duty to report his conclusions – his 'evidence' of guilt – to the court or present it by proxy. Possibly other witnesses, including the suspects' original accusers, were also paid for their time or trouble. Gardner also alleges that the goods of the condemned people were used to pay the jurors, Newcastle's Burgesses, instead of being confiscated by the state for public use, as was legally permitted. For him, this was both a miscarriage of justice and misuse of public funds, and it was all part of the corruption of Newcastle's oligarchy. Whether they were trading coal or trying witches, the councillors acted illegally and cruelly.

Part of Ralph Gardner's anger comes from his hatred of the council, but some is honest outrage in the face of injustice and inhumanity. Like the people we met in Essex, Suffolk, Norfolk, Northamptonshire and elsewhere, Newcastle's citizens seemed to him to have forgotten that their neighbours were human beings – and this, Gardner averred, was no longer acceptable. Gardner compared the Newcastle council to the Spanish Inquisition and the murderous Byzantine emperor Andronicus, ending his indictment of their witch trial by calling the councillors 'tyrants' and 'heathens'.[20] It was a watershed moment: an unqualified, outspoken attack on a witchfinder and his employers not just as mistaken, greedy or arrogant, but as anti-Christian murderers. It was a milestone on the road that led to the end of witch hunting. And yet some sixteen people had still lost their lives.

After his success in Newcastle, the unnamed Berwick witchfinder left town and went into Northumberland, where he continued his activities. Some of Gardner's informants subsequently heard that he was paid up to three pounds per condemned witch there. However, Henry Ogle, a magistrate and Member of Parliament, issued a warrant for his arrest with a bond to attend court and answer for his activities. Unfortunately, the witchfinder fled out of Ogle's jurisdiction, back to Scotland. His opponents joked bitterly that, 'had he stayed, he would have made most of the women in the north witches, for money'. Later, he was, Gardner reports, arrested in Scotland and executed for having killed over two hundred and twenty women by his 'villainy'; whether this is true or not, we can't be sure.

Little evidence also remains to tell us about the accused people and their fates, in Newcastle or elsewhere. During their occupation of the town, the Scottish army 'tumbled' the corporation's records, which did not recover their regularity until the mid-1650s.[21] But what does survive is the story of a witch trial begun late in the English witch hunt of the 1640s and influenced as much by events north of the border in Scotland as those south of it. The Newcastle trial was in many ways part of a new series of Scottish witch trials as well as the end of a series of English ones, with a newsbook reporting in early 1650 that 'hundreds of poor people' were now being killed as witches in Scotland and 1652 booklets describing Edinburgh authorities' concerns about the torture inflicted on 'hundreds' of witchcraft suspects by ministers and civil magistrates. These large Scottish trials continued intermittently into the 1660s, after which torture was prohibited.[22] The end of the 1640s witch hunt was not universal, nor was it an overnight victory for reasonable people.

However, their efforts mattered – and made a real difference. Ralph Gardner printed his account of the Newcastle witch trial of 1649 to 1650 alongside a host of other complaints because he saw a single thread running through all of them: the 'unchristian, illegal, oppressive practices' of powerful people. His lawsuit was unsuccessful, disappearing into the chaos of the civil wars and never reaching a court judgment, but he left a powerful condemnation of witch hunting as his legacy. Surely, Gardner argued, the witchfinders – both the professional witch pricker and those who employed and assisted him – had 'transform[ed] the very image of God's power and justice, which they sustain, into the image of God's enemy, Satan?' In the witchfinders' drive to purify their land, good and evil, God and the devil, had changed sides. Eventually it was this belief – that witchfinding was a cruel, deluded enterprise more demonic than the illusory acts of any witch – that brought an end to the witch hunt of the civil wars.[23]

CHAPTER 12

Afterlives

With the trial of the Newcastle witches, the witch hunt story comes full circle, with elements of both repetition and closure. The hunt started with a nameless woman executed summarily by Parliamentary forces just before the Battle of Newbury in Berkshire in 1643, given no proper trial and no opportunity to defend herself. Her trial exemplified the growing violence and legal dysfunction of the civil wars and showed how suspected witches could easily become victims of authoritarianism and military haste. Fear and fanaticism flourished in wartime, and the Newbury woman had come to represent everything that godly people worried about. Around her death grew up a propaganda myth: that Royalists and their associates were working with witches to defeat the forces of God embodied in the Parliamentary army and its puritanical supporters. With this polarised thinking in place, suddenly Britain could be seen to be far fuller of God's enemies than most people had imagined: heretics, Sabbath breakers, healers who were really harmers, swearers, fornicators, barrators, liars, all kinds of people who looked like good Christians but were in fact Satanic agents. In Scotland, where religious division was part of the wider British picture but was also animated by localised hatreds, methods of interrogating such enemies of God were refined, and a witch hunt spread among the most pious and self-righteous reformers.

It also spread far to the south among similar reformist activists who drew on Scottish precedents. In Essex's Stour Valley, the partly random, partly predictable factors that animated the Scottish hunt came together to spark a large-scale witch panic across several villages around the town of Manningtree. What was required? Willing witchfinders who could sway opinion: the prurient reforming Rector John Edes of Lawford; in Manningtree, John Stearne, businesslike busybody, keen to test witches; clergymen's sons Matthew Hopkins and Robert Taylor, anxious to be worthy of their fathers' legacies; and intrigued Presbyterian magistrates Harbottle Grimston and Thomas Bowes. There were willing watchers, too: bereaved parents, radical tradespeople, and a group of ill-informed but stubborn women and men who thought they knew everything about the human body, especially the female body, and could diagnose demonic irregularities. Absences were required to start the witch hunt too: this locality was missing the oversight of established, even-handed authorities – not in themselves perfect, but institutional impediments to extreme action and sudden change. The rector of Mistley-with-Manningtree, Thomas Witham, was gone and so were the usual judges of Assize, so that a radical new groupthink could quickly become established. Under the unregulated pressure applied by these new arbiters of so-called godliness, people like Rebecca West and Bess Clarke could not resist confessing the fantasies offered to them, adding their own fears and dreams. Some suspects were also subjected to outright torture of a newly effective kind, related to the Scottish model. And so a template for detecting witches emerged.

As Hopkins and Stearne rode north over the Stour to spread

the new model of witch hunting into their birth county of Suffolk, churchwardens, overseers and political administrators were drawn into the persecution in places like Framlingham, acting against those they suspected of insufficient purity. In a revolt that struck both against established churchmen like Richard Golty and poor dependents on parish charity, the number of people accused began to multiply. While most of the hunt's victims were female, because women were thought weaker and more prone to Satan's temptation, seemingly untouchable men like the vicar of Brandeston, John Lowes, were also accused and executed as witches. John had made too many enemies in his community to withstand an assault on his character and style of religion, and was grouped by his accusers with the devilish Royalists whom they believed had infected the state church. As news of the witch hunters' successes spread and acceptance grew that witches were a major problem across the whole land, communities in Suffolk and Norfolk began inviting Hopkins and Stearne – together or separately – to their towns and villages. Official bodies like Great Yarmouth's council responded to the concerns of their more pious members and were soon using their witch trial to advance their preferred religious agenda. Astutely, Presbyterian clergymen John Brinsley and Thomas Whitfield outflanked Congregationalists and traditionalists, people like the witch defender Thomas Cheshire, forcing godly people to accept their authority and act together against witches, their supposedly shared enemy.

Hopkins's role in the hunt eventually faltered: he was questioned at Norwich and elsewhere, accused of witchfinding for financial gain, and then he fell ill. But for a time he and his co-witchfinder John Stearne moved on through the fenland counties into the English Midlands. Stearne concluded his branch of the witch hunt in 1647. Yet even after he ceased activity and returned home to Suffolk, witchcraft suspects continued to be questioned across

Britain, by godly magistrates like John Tregeagle and William Dawson. Some accused people, like Ann Jefferies, were lucky and escaped conviction. Ann's steadfast refusal to accept the identity of 'witch' helped her defence, but even as the eighteenth century dawned, the shadow of the witch hunt left her reluctant to share her story. In Newcastle upon Tyne, a mass witch hunt could still gather momentum years after Hopkins and Stearne had retired into ignominy. This hunt was influenced by the Scottish model of witchfinding by pricking and by the continuing Scottish belief that witches were roaming the land in large numbers. The doubts of men like Lieutenant-Colonel Paul Hobson and Ralph Gardner were a hugely important breakthrough, helping to move Britain towards the resolution of the witch-hunt era. But they were not enough to stop the spread of a second wave of witch hunting in the north, and that would rumble on from place to place in Scotland through the next decade. However, there was more room for scepticism about witchfinding after 1650, particularly in England, and there the era of mass witch trials drew shudderingly to a close. Yet it was another thirty years before the last English 'witch' was executed, and in Scotland, that happened as late as 1727.

Some of the victims of the witch hunt of the 1640s that we've met seem at first to be unlikely witches: churchwardens like Henry Maggs, clergymen like John Lowes, articulate, sometimes educated, men who were financially secure and apparently pious churchgoers. As far as we can tell, they came under suspicion because, although they looked outwardly respectable, they were thought in reality to be heretical, hypocritical or otherwise a problem for their community: part of the wicked conspiracy of enemies that included Royalists, misbelievers and sinners of all kinds. Most of those accused were more stereotypical suspects, disadvantaged and nonconforming people on the outside of established power structures: magical practitioners like Margaret Thomsone or Mark Pryme; mystics like Ann Jefferies; cash-strapped women like Elizabeth Goodwin, Mary Edwards or Elizabeth Bradwell who fell out with traders, wealthy donors or employers; bullied fantasists like Rebecca West; elderly beggars like John Chirrey; unmarried mothers like Bess Clarke, who was also physically disabled; unpopular neighbours like Nazareth Fassett. But for some, the reasons why they fell under suspicion remain unclear. What did accusers dislike about Margaret Brown, Katherine Coultor or Margery Chimney? Why exactly were John Winwick, Barbara Wilkinson or Helen Clark singled out by their communities when they appear no different to hundreds of others in character or situation? We just don't know.

The accused people's variety, their individuality and their ordinariness, all make the witch hunt of the 1640s even more horrifying. They were people like us – all of us. True, most suspects were women, which makes the history of witchcraft particularly important in the history of misogyny. In some English and Scottish trials, all of the accused were female, while in others, ten, twenty or twenty-five per cent were male – and in a few places more men than women were accused. But the enormous preponderance of women among accused witches was not an accident. As in most witch hunts, women were imagined as a secretive, rebellious enemy within a male-dominated society, and few had the education, resources or capabilities that could save them from suspicion. But male suspects were equally victims of prejudice and malice: those judged too poor, too assertive, too odd or simply in the wrong company at the wrong time. An accusation could plausibly be made against almost anyone and the outcome was a lottery. Whether or not a suspect was convicted and executed could apparently depend on a chance encounter, the composition and mood of a panel of judges or jurors, political, mercantile or military developments, or the presence of a single witness. Pleasingly, the instability of the situation at last impacted on the witch hunters themselves, eroding trust in the expertise they claimed to possess and leaving them exposed. This partial defeat of witch hunting was important: although witch trials would continue into later decades, the carnage of the 1640s became a historical reference point for those who wanted them to end. People who held back fanatics, spoke out to help individual suspects on trial or later held to account those who had victimised them, all played a part in that ending. They showed that resistance to injustice was both possible and worthwhile.

While an overall pattern emerges, a shaky but noticeable narrative arc from the start to the end of a mass witch hunt, each witch trial was an event in its own right. Each had a unique outcome, drawing on localised community fears and prejudices and claiming unique, irreplaceable victims. Of course, the civil wars, and especially the sectarian divisions of the 1640s, framed and shaped the great British witch hunt. But different villages and towns responded differently to suspicions and the interventionist activities of witchfinders, and it's clear how much we can still learn by finding out about those individual circumstances. Many witch trials of the hunt remain almost completely unexplored, and it's still possible to discover in archives far more about the life stories of many key participants: accused people, their accusers, those who pulled together coalitions of witch hunters or resisted them. These are histories worthy of further research by experts on particular localities, and I hope this book will inspire them. So much remains to be found, even in the communities whose stories are, partially, told here, but also well beyond.

However much detail is missing, and may remain missing thanks to the loss of records, the histories of witch hunts are also worth memorialising. This book finishes its story with a return to Scotland, one of the places that has seen the most determined attempts to remember the victims of witch hunting and apply the lessons of the peak witch-trial era to the modern day. The well-known Witches of Scotland campaign with its long-running podcast, as well as campaigns and exhibitions by other groups such as Remembering the Accused Witches of Scotland and The Creative Coven, were part of efforts that secured an apology to those accused of witchcraft from Scotland's then First Minister, Nicola Sturgeon, in 2022. Acknowledging that Britain's historic witch hunt was an 'injustice on a colossal scale, driven at least in part, by misogyny in its most literal sense – hatred of women', Sturgeon said that 'today, on International Women's Day, as First Minister on behalf of the Scottish Government, I am choosing to acknowledge that egregious historic injustice and extend a formal, posthumous apology to all those accused, convicted, vilified or executed'. Alongside her apology, there was also an unsuccessful but noteworthy attempt by Member of the Scottish Parliament (MSP) Natalie Don to introduce legislation that would allow a formal pardon of people convicted of witchcraft in Scottish history.[1]

In other places, too, the accused witches of the 1640s are remembered. Manningtree has its blue plaque, remembering some of the Stour Valley residents killed in 1645. There is also a blue plaque fixed to St Nicholas's churchyard gate by the Great Yarmouth Local History and Archaeological Society, commemorating the deaths of seven accused witches in 1584 and 1645 and their burial. In Suffolk, Brandeston remembers its vicar John Lowes on a slate slab in his church. It reads:

> In memory of the Rev'd John Lowes, Vicar of Brandeston 1596–1645. Hanged aged 80 for witchcraft on the evidence of Matthew Hopkins, self-appointed Witchfinder General, at Bury St Edmunds, 27th August 1645. Protesting his innocence, he read his own funeral service to ensure a Christian burial.

The plaque concludes with an optimistic statement: 'May no such blind and bloody superstition and madness ever get head again within this land'. The words are adapted from a phrase in the Bury St Edmunds clergyman Francis Hutchinson's *An Historical Essay Concerning Witchcraft* (1718), a longer extract from which was also copied into Brandeston's parish register sometime in the eighteenth century, summing up the Suffolk community's rejection of its age of witch hunting. The Brandeston plaque was dedicated by the Archdeacon of Suffolk in 2004.[2]

At Chelmsford, where the Essex suspects were tried, the route taken by condemned people from the Assize court to the gallows is marked by street art commemorating their last journey. The images, by Shelley Ings, depict the women in contrasting ways: going about their ordinary lives in happy, natural settings among pets and garden flowers, and then falling victim to the Witchfinder General, their hands tied and their pets transformed into sinister familiars. An information board has also been placed in the town's park, near the gallows site, alongside a memorial tree. With text by the local historian John Worland, it tells readers about witch hunting in sixteenth- and seventeenth-century Essex and remembers those executed, totalling over one hundred across the two centuries. 'In hope of an end to persecution and intolerance. Never forgotten,' it concludes soberly. With Headgate Theatre company, Worland also made *Witchfinder* in 2007, a film telling the story of the 1645 Essex trial. Today an Essex Witch Museum has been founded online to raise funds for a physical site where similar stories can be shared, and a television series, *Witches of Essex*, presented by Professor Alice Roberts and the Essex-born reality TV celebrity Rylan Clark, was broadcast in 2025.[3]

In Bury St Edmunds, site of many of the Suffolk executions, is a museum collection telling the story of witch hunting. It's housed in Moyse's Hall, the medieval merchant's house which over eight centuries has been a Jewish home, pub, witch prison, reformatory for 'fallen' women, fire station and postal delivery hub. At the centre of the exhibit, a TV screen plays a cartoon history of the trials. It shows an elderly man being pricked by John Stearne. If he bleeds, then he is innocent, the cartoon explains, but if he doesn't, he'll be judged a witch. While Stearne wasn't a career pricker like the Newcastle witchfinder, he did sometimes search for insensible marks in this way. The dismay and confusion on the cartoon suspect's face is a moving sight. He doesn't bleed and is summarily hanged. Alongside the screen are two 'witch bottles', stoneware jars once filled with items like pins and urine and buried or boiled to cure witch-inflicted disease. There's a selection of other protective charms and three dried and twisted feline bodies of the kind often known as 'mummified cats'. These poor creatures were walled up, apparently to rid houses magically of pests and possibly to keep out witches. The exhibition also features a gibbet cage, in which the bodies of hanged criminals were displayed as they rotted after their execution, and another iron device labelled 'please do not touch the scold's bridle'. It's a cage that could be fitted over a woman's head once she'd been judged a slanderous nag. The exhibit is an important, if depressing, testament to human cruelty.

Some of the accused witches of the 1640s are commemorated in more cheering ways. There is a Witches of Scotland tartan. The website Runes n Roses celebrates the life of Great Yarmouth's Elizabeth Bradwell, including showcasing an embroidery made of beads, salvaged fabric, shells and sea glass. It incorporates the image of a blackbird, referring to her supposed bird familiar. This project feeds into the We Are Witch Quilt project, commemorating accused witches across East Anglia, which includes an image of Margery Chimney of Framlingham. Similarly, the online East

Anglian Museum of Witchcraft has created an interactive map featuring witch trial histories and folklore, a patchwork of stories. Further south, London artist Susan Pui San Lok created the 2019 exhibition 'A Coven A Grove A Stand' to remember the Essex witch hunt of 1645, with an installation featuring embroidery and soundscapes and encouraging visitors to write and speak the names of those convicted. In 2022, the East Anglian foundation Cohere Arts, which specialises in arts access for people living with ill health and disability, staged a musical theatre performance based on the same events, called *Witchfinder*. At the Cromwell Museum, Huntingdon, the Sealed Knot re-enactment group staged a dramatised version of the 1646 witch trial in 2021, and this was recreated in 2025. Ann Jefferies is remembered at the Bodmin Jail museum, in storytelling performances, podcasts and with a Spotify playlist themed on witches and fairies.[4]

The 1650 Newcastle witch trial is still rightly described as 'little known', largely due to the loss of all documentation from the court that judged the accused people and the difficulties historians face in tracing their names among the city's large seventeenth-century population. There's clearly still more to discover in the town's records, but additional cultural factors may have impeded such archival searching in the past. 'Historically, there's been an element of embarrassment about it [the witch trial],' suggests David Silk, Learning Manager at Newcastle Castle. Cultural historian Katie Liddane explains why: the city saw itself as a progressive industrial powerhouse for much of its history, prompting most of its Victorian and twentieth-century writers to keep silent about anything considered superstitious or backward-looking. Now that deindustrialisation is changing the city's self-image, she argues, the witch trial can be rediscovered. A memorial to the convicted people was unveiled in 2025 on the 375th anniversary of the executions, and there is growing interest in their story, including a local television report that was screened on the 374th anniversary and a dedicated podcast discussing aspects of their trial. The story of the 'Newcastle witches' feels ready to become a widely recognised part of the city's history, not least because it showcased the possibility of resistance to witchfinders.[5] As in many places around the world, the accused witches of the seventeenth century are being rediscovered as a striking example of historical injustice: a group of diverse, disempowered people, accused of crimes they could not possibly have committed and killed by their neighbours' self-righteous prejudice. In this version of history, witch trials are a warning against modern fanaticism in politics or religion, against misogyny and other types of hatred, and against the suspension of established legal rights in favour of cruel persecution.

But what of our witchfinders? Because of their status – male, literate, wealthy – the witchfinders who brought about all this misery have historically been more famous than their victims, most of whom did not have lives after their trials and were quickly consigned to the past. I do not wish to give them more page-time than they have already had, but their stories are entwined with those of their victims, and so, in brief:

Matthew Hopkins

Matthew Hopkins is the most notorious witchfinder, partly thanks to his image appearing on the title page of his 1647 book *The Discovery of Witches*: most likely it's not a portrait, but it is a memorably sinister representation. The book was his last word on witchcraft – or, it turns out, any other subject. Hopkins may already have been sick when he accused Anne and Rebecca West, Bess Clarke and their friends of witchcraft. Perhaps he even thought they had bewitched him, although he brought no formal charge against them for such an attack, or not one that has survived. Either way, he died in 1647, still in his mid-twenties. The cause was likely the same illness that might have killed his brother John Hopkins at a similar age a few years before: tuberculosis, known in the seventeenth century as 'consumption'. Certainly this is what John Stearne says Hopkins died from. The disease spread across families, typically killing its sufferers between the ages of fifteen and thirty-five. While his youthful death was tragic, his removal from public life had the positive consequence of helping to halt the East Anglian witch hunt. By 1646, some significant voices – John Gaule's and then those of anonymous critics at Norwich Assizes – were already raised against him. He seems to have died angry. While in his book he admitted charging up to twenty shillings per town he visited to hunt witches, he added that for a few malefactors that was 'cheap enough' – in other words, it was good value for money. It is an ugly statement, capturing the tone of the publication: a peevish ten-page snarl, devoid of empathy or humility. Even Hopkins's self-mythologising as 'the Discoverer' and 'Witchfinder General' in his book looks needy and arrogant, though it ensured him centuries of bogeyman fame.

After his death in early August 1647, he was buried on the 12th at Mistley, at his stepfather Thomas Witham's old church. Someone – probably Matthew Hopkins's stepbrother, Thomas's son John Witham, who was about to be appointed rector there – took the trouble to record his funeral in the parish register, during a time when no one else was bothering to record baptisms, marriages or burials across Mistley-with-Manningtree parish. In the register, Matthew is described as the 'son of Mr James Hopkins minister of Wenham'.[6] That was correct, but minimal and a little coy. By 1647, the Withams must have known what many of their neighbours thought: that a terrible injustice had been done to hundreds of people by Matthew Hopkins. John Witham was not keen to document his family's relationship to the witchfinder who had slaughtered his father's parishioners after Thomas Witham's removal to London. He needn't have worried. After Hopkins's death, people forgot the Witham-Hopkins connection anyway, until it was rediscovered in the early twenty-first century.

Perhaps because he disappeared so suddenly from public visibility, inaccurate rumours circulated that Hopkins had himself been hanged as a witch, often reported with glee by his many detractors.[7] Even those most closely associated with him, people who thought his campaign well intentioned, brushed his name out of history. His fellow witchfinder Stearne mentioned Hopkins's death only briefly in his *A Confirmation and Discovery of Witchcraft* in 1648 and gave no further details of his life. 'Master Hopkins dead', he wrote, and with those three words Hopkins was gone.

John Stearne

John Stearne remained unrepentant long after the execution of his and Hopkins's last victims, choosing to defend Hopkins's methods after his collaborator's death. His book *A Confirmation and Discovery of Witchcraft* was indeed a 'confirmation' that he and Hopkins were right, despite its title page bearing a biblical quotation that might have prompted doubts in better men:

> Thou shalt therefore inquire, and make search, and ask diligently whether it be truth, and the thing certain.

Unmoved and consistent, Stearne was convinced his enquiries had indeed proven 'the thing certain', which was that 'there are witches', and the people he'd condemned were all deservedly killed. He was still comfortable stating that he'd been 'an agent in finding out or discovering ... about two hundred in number, in Essex, Suffolk, Northamptonshire, Huntingdonshire, Bedfordshire, Norfolk, Cambridgeshire and the Isle of Ely in the County of Cambridge, besides other places, justly and deservedly executed'. That tally of the hanged excluded, of course, all those accused but acquitted, those convicted and imprisoned, those condemned but reprieved, and all the suspects who had fled or died in prison, broken and wretched, their lives in tatters. Stearne brazenly told readers who thought 'that there are no witches, but that there are many poor, silly, ignorant people hanged wrongfully', that their views were incorrect. Even more wrong was any suspicion that people like himself, who had 'been instruments in finding or discovering those [witches] of late made known, have done it for their own private ends, for gain, and such like'. That was just fake news, far from the pure motives that had sent the witchfinders on their spree. Stubbornly, Stearne continued to believe that witches existed in large numbers across eastern England and elsewhere, that they 'worship devils, they invocate them, crave help of them, work by them and do them homage'. Therefore, they ought to be hunted down and removed from society by all necessary means.

Indeed, so self-righteous was he that by 1648 Stearne was complaining in his book that he hadn't been paid by some of the places whose inhabitants he had killed, and that he faced lawsuits from other dissatisfied customers of his witchfinding activities. In Colchester, powerful unnamed citizens had gone so far as to have him declared an outlaw, he whinged. These people may have been the grieving relatives of those executed for witchcraft, or suspects who had survived and wanted to prove Stearne had defamed them. No records of these particular lawsuits have, so far, been discovered, but let's hope they cost him sleepless nights.

Further legal troubles followed in 1651 when he had to petition a government committee for help to defend himself against a charge of stealing. This charge – a felony indictment, in theory punishable by death – had been made because he had accused a neighbour, George Crouch, of Sabbath-breaking in 1651 when he saw him working with his horse on a Sunday. Furious, George then 'molested and indicted' Stearne with a counter-claim alleging some sort of theft. Stearne told the Parliamentary committee members that he had less than five pounds in ready money, which was either untrue or indicated a spectacular fall into poverty – indeed, later in his life he worked as a scrivener, a lowly administrator and writer of formal documents, and he may have been doing that in 1651. Accordingly, he was given state help to employ a counsel for his defence and presumably was not convicted. He returned to his former home at Lawshall in Suffolk but kept up a property at Manningtree, and in 1657 he was bound over to keep the peace, suggesting he was still being a nuisance to his neighbours. Stearne died at Lawshall in January 1670.[8]

Harbottle Grimston, Thomas Bowes, John Edes

Sir Harbottle Grimston, already in his seventies when he questioned Hopkins and Stearne's Manningtree suspects in 1645, died three years later. Sir Thomas Bowes whiled away the next thirty years in a prolific series of disputes relating to his properties in London, Essex and Suffolk and from time to time continued to commit witchcraft suspects for trial in his role as a Justice of the Peace; he died in 1676. Rector John Edes, whose role in starting the witch hunt in 1645 in Lawford and spreading it to Manningtree has often been underestimated, died in 1658. His grandson John emigrated to America, settling in the Carolinas and then moving north to Cambridge and Marblehead, Massachusetts, where at the end of his life he would have heard news of the Salem witch trials taking place close by.

Miles Corbet

Compared to the later years of most of these men, those of the Great Yarmouth Justice Miles Corbet were shockingly turbulent. He advanced in the legal profession, took on administrative roles for the Parliamentarian government across eastern England and Ireland, continued to be active in Great Yarmouth's Congregational church and served as an elder at a London church.

At the time of the witch trial in 1645, he was a Member of Parliament for Great Yarmouth, and he remained in that role until 1653. In this capacity, Miles was appointed to the court that tried the former King Charles I for treason against his people. When the king was convicted and sentenced to be beheaded in 1649, Miles signed the death warrant. That made him a regicide, a king-killer, in the eyes of the Royalist party. When they returned to government in 1660, Miles therefore fled to the Netherlands, ignoring a call to surrender himself and face the consequences of his actions. There he was arrested, shipped back to Britain, tried in 1662 and hanged for the treason of the king's 'murder'. His ghost is still said to haunt his Irish castle.

Back in Great Yarmouth, his fellow witch hunters John Brinsley and Thomas Whitfield were dismissed from their ministry at St Nicholas. Mark Pryme's defender, Thomas Cheshire, though, seems to have disappeared into obscurity.[9]

John Tregeagle

Ann Jefferies's antagonist, the Cornish magistrate John Tregeagle, was by the nineteenth century being portrayed in much the same way that Miles Corbet and Matthew Hopkins were caricatured by their opponents during their lifetimes: as a brutal villain. Perhaps he was more of a witch hunter than surviving records now suggest to us, but whatever the case, he was locally unpopular. He appears as an archetype in folklore and fiction: the wicked steward who would return from hell itself to check a rent book (as he actually does in one of the ghost stories about him).

In life, he certainly enthusiastically chased debts owed to him, as a lawsuit of the early 1650s shows. Here, arguments rage about the 'trouble and expense' Tregeagle was enduring to recover arrears from the Carter family, who, in 'great distress for want of money' due to John Carter's death while serving the Parliamentary army, had mortgaged their land to Tregeagle in 1645. Tregeagle argued he'd followed the letter of the law, but some witnesses, including a Parliamentary soldier who'd been a prisoner of war in Bodmin, slyly pointed out that while the Carters had suffered for their beliefs, Tregeagle had flourished under regimes on both sides of the civil wars. Very little of his wealth had been seized (or so his enemies said) and two witnesses thought he'd been on surprisingly friendly terms with Royalists. After his death in 1655, wild tales proliferated that Tregeagle was a serial wife-murderer and social climber who'd made a pact with the devil. So, like Hopkins, this witchfinder was transformed by folklore into a witch. Tregeagle's ghost is still said to haunt Bodmin Moor, forced into impossible tasks such as emptying a pool using only a seashell, and pursued by demons and the hounds of hell. These stories, gathered by Victorian folklorists, are eagerly retold in tourist publications, film, theatre and even opera.[10]

Ralph Gardner

Ralph Gardner also has a substantial place in the history of his locality, although, despite his role as a defender of accused witches, his reputation has often been surprisingly poor. This is no doubt in part because he was a thorn in the side of Newcastle's corporation for many years, even if he was unable to win his lawsuit against them – and as the victors, they determined how he was remembered. The eighteenth-century Newcastle historian and councillor Henry Bourne described him as 'a bitter enemy' to the town, while the anonymous biographer of another councillor called him 'malicious' and spread a rumour that Gardner had been hanged for currency forgery, which was untrue.[11]

Gardner continued to attack the corporation for years after the witch trial, in the face of violent intimidation. By the 1650s, he was running a brewery in North Shields, which – according to Newcastle's monopolists – was supposed to be regulated by their Bakers and Brewers Guild. However, the guild would not recognise his right to trade and continually harassed him. In 1652, he was arrested for illegal brewing and a supposed debt of nine hundred pounds and imprisoned for several months. He protested that his jailers kept him in 'locks and chains', in an unheated cell with no privy, would 'scarce let any of his friends come to him' and – the taunt of a proud brewer – gave him beer tasting 'like horse piss'. In 1653, he escaped by tunnelling through the wall and climbing thirty-six feet down a rope, but was pursued by corporation officers who shot at him and his wife Catherine as they fled.

This assault seems to have forced Gardner to leave his home. So, later in 1653, he went to London. There he sought redress against the corporation as well as enrolling in legal training so that he could best argue his own case. He petitioned the government – causing the Newcastle corporation a flutter of panic and costing them large sums in travel expenses and legal fees as they prepared to defend themselves against his accusations – and joined one of the Inns of Court. He also put his case forward in print, and his long, angry book *England's Grievance Discovered* was published in 1655. Gardner's case dragged on for months without outcome, and although it's clear he continued to be active in both North

Shields and London throughout the 1650s and 1660s, he disappears from history. The story that he'd been hanged in the 1660s was discovered to relate to another man with a similar name and seems to have become attached to him as – even centuries later – Newcastle's historians sought to rebut his claims against the city's seventeenth-century leaders. However, the people of North Shields value their pugnacious forebear and have fought back against the misrepresentation of his career and life. They dedicated a memorial to him in 1882, with an inscription reading 'a faithful son of Father Tyne', and a school was named after him in 1935. Today he is remembered as something of a local hero in North Shields.[12]

Paul Hobson

Lieutenant-Colonel Paul Hobson is better known for his military and religious exploits than his role in the Newcastle witch trial. Like Ralph Gardner, he had a colourful life after the trial ended. Hobson continued to serve in Parliament's army until the early 1650s, but his dissenting intervention in the witch trial seems to have indicated increasing uncertainty about his career. As England and Scotland warred over the future of their shared governance, Hobson began to urge English troops to focus on the similarities between themselves and their Scottish enemies rather than on sectarian or political differences. Tolerance and fellowship had been important themes in his preaching for a decade, and he – surely like many other Britons of the mid-seventeenth century – must have wondered if continuing ideological conflict was worth the misery and loss it entailed. Particularly traumatically, Hobson was put in charge of Scottish prisoners of war, men who had been marched a hundred miles down the east coast from Dunbar to Durham, just south of Newcastle. During the march, some 1,600 of the prisoners died, and even more succumbed when they were imprisoned at Durham Cathedral, partly due to starvation. After that, Hobson left the army and devoted himself to founding Baptist churches and arguing matters of doctrine. By 1659, he was calling for the return of the monarchy, and when that occurred in 1660, he founded a utopian community near Durham, as well as continuing evangelical efforts in London and Rotterdam.

In 1663, however, Hobson surprisingly took part in a conspiracy to oust the king whose restoration he'd supported. Apparently, he thought the new regime too Catholic and insufficiently tolerant of new religious sects like his own. He was imprisoned in the Tower of London, narrowly escaping execution. Some of his former associates thought this clemency suspicious: had Hobson been an agent provocateur? Curiously, he was granted an audience with King Charles II in 1664, at which the two men spoke about Charles I and their 'good thoughts of the old King', and Hobson was then released in 1665. He soon became involved in another controversy, accused of adultery with two female worshippers in London. This passionate, conflicted man died in 1666, leaving a confusing legacy – a thriving Baptist church that would spread around the world, many pleas for Christian compassion, suspicions of espionage and sexual misconduct, and a witch pricking with a lucky survivor. Hobson also left mystical verses that summed up his search for truth and freedom of judgement:

Patience with balm my soul supplies
I live above control,
In prison though my body lies,
They can't enslave my soul.
My free converse with Christ is sweet,
Which brings in choice supply,
That they which now my body keep
Know no such liberty.[13]

Nevertheless, one early twentieth-century biographer described him as dying in an 'odour of unsanctity' because of the adultery accusations, and in 2022 the hosts of The Newcastle Witches podcast were equally unimpressed by his rationale for rescuing that particular suspect. Hobson picked this woman for the pricker to re-examine because she was 'personable' or pretty, prompting the reflection: 'so she can't be a witch because he has a crush on her? Oh my goodness . . .'[14]

That comment is a helpful reminder of just how different the motivation prompting even the most benign actions of those who defended seventeenth-century witches was from today's expectations. Sometimes we can't know why they asked questions, raised doubts or obstructed legal processes, and even when we do know, we may not find their choices sound or their rebuttals of witchfinding groupthink convincing. Some, like John Gaule, demonstrably held more or less the same views as the witchfinders, objecting only to their methods. But every now and again the defenders' effect is demonstrable, as when Thomas Cheshire spoke up for Mark Pryme at his trial and Mark was acquitted. It's important to remember that sometimes such a brave intervention was dangerous or fatal for the defender, as when Isobel Ewart was summoned before her kirk session for protesting against the treatment of Mid Calder witchcraft suspects or when John Lowes's protection of Ann Amison led, together with other factors, to his own accusation and eventual execution as a witch. But without such interventions, as well as the accused people's refusal to confess, witch trials would not have diminished in number and may never have ultimately ceased. The fact that any of those accused during the witch hunt of the 1640s had physical, earthly afterlives – as opposed to spiritual or memorial ones – is due in part to the interventions of these defenders. They deserve to be remembered alongside the 'witches' they helped to save.

Perhaps, too, Paul Hobson's imperfect struggles with the problems of his time help us to understand better the witch hunters of the 1640s, especially those drawn into the hunt by reforming idealism or family tragedy. How many of them must have agonised over the choices they had to make! How, they must have wondered, could they best decide the right course of action? In theory, prayer would have helped those debating whether or not to make an accusation, or questioning how to handle an investigation process, as would the consultation of friends, ministers and educated neighbours. Yet once conversations about witches started – with God or fellow humans – events gathered their own momentum. Accusers, magistrates, juries and judges were swept along, and all of them must have fretted to some degree, questioning everything they thought they knew about their world.

Which kinds of authority mattered as the civil wars ripped apart established truths? Which societal rules were still relevant? Should they trust sermons, criminal law codes, royal or Parliamentary edicts, theological textbooks, rumours and gossip, their own common sense? Did their duty lie in eliminating evil from their communities, and if so, how? Were they being cruel to be kind, or just cruel? In 1621, a jury exemplified their problems. While debating a London witch trial verdict, the foreman turned in panic to the judge, asking, 'what to do in a matter of such great import, [so that] life – they deemed – might be conserved?' The judge had little to say to the jurors: 'do it as God shall put in your hearts', he replied. After a search found what appeared to be demonic marks on the suspect, the jury convicted her and she was hanged. If the jury believed that witches existed, and the law stated that this was the case, what else could they do? And if that was the outcome in 1621, at a comparatively stable moment in British history, what must the same dilemma have felt like in 1645 or 1650?[15] Which of us hasn't felt similar anxieties about truth, belief, justice, law, right and wrong, as – like these people of the seventeenth century – we negotiate a time of polarisation, fake news, corruption, unreason and anger? We have little to be smug about as we look back on the lives caught up in the witch hunt of Britain's civil wars.

~

Witch hunts flourish in troubled times. Today, we are experiencing an apparently worldwide slippage into division and extremism, not unlike that of mid-seventeenth-century Britain. The violence caused by politicised emotion, the growth of conspiracy theory and the spread of unlikely untruths is at times recognisable from the civil wars of the seventeenth century – only an echo, rather than a repeat, of that brutal age, but a worrying one nonetheless. In the seventeenth century, violence ignited with troubling ease from sparks of anger and fear, from name-calling and stereotyping that took hold and spread in the early 1640s until people were swept up in hatreds they could not control and war broke out. That historical example highlights a depressing human truth: in times of hardship, people love to create villains, to find a fantasy of enmity, and it suits power-hungry groups to manipulate such enmities for their own gain. If the ordinary conflicts generated by political opinion, economic uncertainty or personal misunderstanding aren't enough, they'll invent a culture war to fight – and within that, a witch hunt can readily take hold.

In this way, the echoes of the witch trials of the 1640s resound today, worldwide. People are still being accused literally of witchcraft, and the metaphorical term 'witch hunt' is widely used in politics – most famously in the United States, whose current President is fond of the phrase. This echo down the corridor of history is not an accident.

During and after the civil wars, many people like those in this story emigrated to the Americas, taking with them the notion of the witch hunt. Often they were witch-believers. Settlers came from all over Britain, but there was an especially strong link between the communities of the witch hunt and the colonies on the North American east coast. Matthew Hopkins's brother Thomas apparently followed the instruction in their father James's will and went to live among 'our friends in New England', as James called them. Many others like him, and like John Edes's grandson, set out for the New World full of hope from the Suffolk towns of Ipswich, Haverhill and Sudbury, from Wethersfield, Billericay, Braintree, Danbury and Colchester in Essex; from King's Lynn, Great Yarmouth and Attleborough in Norfolk. They called their New England settlements the same names as their hometowns – Ipswich, Billerica, Braintree, Attleboro, Haverhill, Sudbury and Lynn in Massachusetts; Wethersfield, Colchester and Danbury in Connecticut; Yarmouth in Maine; Colchester and Sudbury (again) in Vermont. That meant people from the towns at the centre of the English witch hunt became the founders of new communities on the other side of the Atlantic. Many took their magical beliefs and, more importantly, their magical intolerances with them.

One group of this kind emigrated from Framlingham, Suffolk, in 1634. Nicholas Danforth the elder took his family to Massachusetts, where they founded the town of Framingham, named – more or less – after his birthplace. This Nicholas died in 1638. Meanwhile, his namesake back in England helped to raise forces to defend the town and the Parliamentary cause, mustering men in September 1643 and volunteering to fight himself: remember how he injured his head during drill exercises and had to be patched up at the expense of parish funds? In 1645, he watched and perhaps participated as at least fourteen women from his town were accused of witchcraft, then tried and some of them executed at Bury St Edmunds along with dozens of others, even a vicar from the neighbouring village of Brandeston.

Did Framlingham's Nicholas write to his cousins in Massachusetts, telling them about the trial? Did both Nicholas Danforths, in Britain and America, believe similar things about witches? Whatever the case, the American Nicholas Danforth's son Thomas would find himself presiding over the trials of the accused witches of Salem, Massachusetts, in 1692. He is the judge portrayed by Arthur Miller in his famous play *The Crucible*, a 1950s parable about hatreds and lies that is referenced today every time a group is perceived as being scapegoated or a politician shouts 'witch hunt!'

In real life, Thomas Danforth did not serve on the initial panel of judges at the Salem trials, but he was on the bench of the Superior Court of Judicature that decided verdicts in the later cases. In all the cases that Thomas judged, the witchcraft suspects were acquitted, freed or reprieved from execution. At least some of the lessons of the great British witch hunt had been learned – but by no means all, or twenty people would not have been killed during the infamous Salem trials. Witchcraft accusations continued in North America well into the eighteenth century.

The lessons from the dark years of witchfinding are as much needed today as they were in the seventeenth century: look around you and you will see who might be today's Anne Wests, Nazareth Fassetts, Matthew Bowmers and, indeed, Marion Gibsons.[16] It is important that we remember and reinstate the names of the accused witches of history, reflecting on the legacy of their stories, the injustice of their persecution and the mistakes made by witchfinders, other accusers and judicial systems. If we forget these people from our witch-hunting past, we'll face a witch-hunting future.

Acknowledgements

This book couldn't have been written without the resources, expertise and help of many different organisations and people. Most important are record offices, archives, libraries and university collections. These institutions and their experts make history in all its forms: researching and writing non-fiction and fiction, film and TV production, performance, art, publishing, podcasting, heritage conservation and marketing, museum curation, family, company and house histories, and much else. Visit them, use their archives, donate to support them! In particular, I would like to thank the British Library, National Archives, Essex Record Office, Norfolk Record Office, Suffolk Archives (both The Hold, Ipswich and the former Bury St Edmunds branch), Kresen Kernow, Northamptonshire Archives, Huntingdonshire Archives, Northumberland Archives, Tyne and Wear Archives and Museums, Scotland's People and National Records of Scotland, Cambridge University Library, Pembroke College Library, Cambridge, Shropshire Archives, Newbury Library, West Berkshire Museum, the East Anglian Film and Television Archive, The Box Archives and Local Studies, Plymouth, Smith College Special Collections, Northampton MA, and the University of Exeter Library and Special Collections. Much of the East Anglian and Midlands research for the book was funded by a grant awarded by the Leverhulme Trust, titled 'England's Mass Witch Hunt'. Thanks to the Trust for their generous faith in the project. Other work drew on support from the University of Exeter, for which I'm also very grateful.

Also vitally important in writing this book were the individual people who've helped and encouraged me so much, contributing ideas and research resources, taking me to interesting places, finding and granting access to obscure documents, cheering me on, sparking new thoughts during incisive chats and interviews and reading chapters. Top of the list are Tabitha Stanmore, whose collegiality and expert postdoctoral work on 'England's Mass Witch Hunt' has been invaluable; Neil Wiffen, whose excitement about Essex history is an inspiration, and his wife, Sarah Honour, Neil's colleagues at Essex Record Office – Martin Astell, Diane Taylor, Vanda Jeffrey, Kate O'Neill, Catherine Norris, Edd Harris, Robert Lee and everyone else at ERO; Philip Cunningham of Manningtree Museum and Local History Group for his kind welcome and tour; Susan Gillanders, Mairi Harkness and the Calder Witch Hunt Project who helped me with Scottish records; Lizzy Ennion-Smith at Pembroke College, Cambridge; Emily Shepperson, Judith Berry, Jane Ingle and Emily Tillett at Suffolk Archives; Victoria Draper, Vaughan Griggs, Alison Barnard, Jenny Watts, Claire Bolster and all at Norfolk Record Office; Zoe Walter and Rebecca Cross at Tyne and Wear Archives and Museums; Paul Ternent and Sarah Littlefear at Northumberland Archives; Rachel Barrett at London Archives; the staff of the Tolhouse Gaol Museum, Great Yarmouth and Moyse's Hall Museum, Bury St Edmunds and the kind people who gave me information at the many parish churches I visited; and Francis Young, Julian Goodare, David Silk, Katie Liddane, Laina West, Danny Buck, the Last Tuesday Society, Far From the Madding Crowd Books at Linlithgow, Catherine Rider, Jennifer Farrell,

Icy Sedgwick, Tim Ward, Debora Moretti, Maureen Cubitt, Annie Garthwaite, A. D. Bergin, Julie Peters, Jan Machielsen, Holly Bamford, Kirsty Wark, Ann Draisey, Taylor Aucoin, Mikki Brock, Damien Gaucher, Alex Wright, Janina Ramirez, Candia McKormack, John Woolf, Becky Pott, Daniella Gonzalez, Rita Voltmer, Simon Coxall, Paul Armfield and Medina Books, Jonathan Barry, Toppings Edinburgh, Christina Oakley Harrington and Treadwell's Books, Suzannah Lipscomb, Jo Esra, Emily Cockayne, Joel Halcomb, Sarah Jack and Josh Hutchinson, Maria Caruana Galizia and Caitlin Bramwell, Margaret Meyer, Emma Wardall, Julia and Paul Wakelam, Michael Leach, The Falmouth Bookseller, Ivybridge Books, Liz Baalham, Miranda Melcher, Tracey Borman, Malcolm Gaskill, Sian Eleri, Syd Moore, Claire Mitchell KC and Zoe Venditozzi, Witches of Scotland, Rebecca Beattie, Eastgate Books, Mark and Tracey Norman, Richard Pugh, Cassidy Cash, Laura Kounine, We Are Witch Quilt, Elizabeth Sankey, everyone at DASH Pictures, Lucy Stein, AK Blakemore, Ellie Cawthorne, Charlotte Hodgman, Megan Jones, Serena Constance, Jen and the team at Plymouth Waterstones, Flo Reynolds, Joe Crawford, Paul Olding and Mindhouse, Cathy Rentzenbrink, Emily Selove, Viktor Wynd, Jessie Childs, Ben Nathan, Laura Bettney, Nele Dehnenkamp, Naomi Russell, Ceri Houlbrook, Owen Davies, Shelley Ings, Harvey Osborne and website wizard Jess Cook.

This book will contain errors, such is its breadth and detail, but those are my responsibility alone and the people who have helped me have prevented several. The book wouldn't exist at all without my fabulous agents, Joanna Swainson at Hardman and Swainson and Sarah Levitt at Aevitas Creative Management, Hana Murrell, Lucy Malone, Caroline Hardman, the exceptionally kind and friendly team at Simon & Schuster – my first editor Fran Jessop, who so thoughtfully welcomed me and supported my work throughout her time at S&S, my second editor Kat Ailes, whose enthusiasm and eye for detail has been invaluable, the lovely publicity team Jess Barrett, Rebecca McCarthy, Gen Barrett, Richard Hawton and everyone who helped organise events and promotions. Sophia Akhtar, Assallah Tahir, Maudisa King and copyeditor Victoria Denne; and Sally Howe at Scribner, whose acute editorial ideas pushed me in new directions, and the smart publicity team Sophie Guimaraes, Abigail Novak, Eleanor Crowley, Madison Than and all; the booksellers, tweeters, posters, academic colleagues and readers who have taken time to be interested in my work, let me know about and suggest new interpretations, material and stories. Finally, thanks to our neighbours and their dogs, and especially Harry Bennett and our little dogs Storm and Friday.

This book is for Cecil L'Estrange Ewen, with gratitude for his pioneering research on witch trials – I wish I could have met him.

Notes

Introduction. The Rediscovery of Witches

1. Norfolk Record Office (NRO) PD 436/1, NAS 1/1/2/150, 151, 152, MC 1862/2–3 863x1, MC 1862/4 862x9; Maureen P. Cubitt, *Hempnall: A Treasure Trove of History* (Wellington: Halsgrove, 2008), 35, 38–9, 40–42, 152–4 and email 9/3/25; Peter Elmer, 'East Anglia and the Hopkins Trials 1645–1647: a County Guide', at https://practitioners.exeter.ac.uk/wp-content/uploads/2014/11/Eastanglianwitchtrialappendix2.pdf.

1. The Troubles of Seventeenth-Century Britain: Religion, War, Witchcraft

1. Suffolk Archives (SA) B105/2/1.
2. Essex Record Office (ERO) D/P 343/1/1, D/P 347/1/1; Northumberland Archives (Northumb A) EP 86/1.
3. Stephen Porter, *The Blast of War: Destruction in the English Civil Wars* (Stroud: The History Press, 2011), 41–5.
4. For the best account, see Diarmaid MacCulloch, *The Reformation* (London: Penguin, 2003).
5. SA B105/2/1; Paul Hobson, *The Fallacy of Infants' Baptism Discovered* (London, 1645), and, contradictorily, John Brinsley, *The Doctrine and Practice of Paedobaptism Asserted and Vindicated* (London, 1645).
6. *The Woeful and Lamentable Waste and Spoil Done by a Sudden Fire in S. Edmonds-bury* (London, 1608).
7. There are many good civil war histories, most recently Michael Braddick, *God's Fury, England's Fire* (London: Penguin, 2009), Diane Purkiss, *The English Civil War* (London: HarperPress, 2006)

and Jonathan Healey, *The Blood in Winter* (London: Bloomsbury, 2025).
8. SA B105/2/1.
9. NRO PD 436/1.

2. Murder on the Battlefield

1. *A most certain, strange and true discovery of a witch, being taken by some of the Parliament forces, as she was standing on a small plank board and sailing on it over the river of Newbury* (London, 1643).
2. Michael McNair-Wilson, *Battle for a Kingdom* (Reading: Deirdre McNair-Wilson, 1993), 36–7, 45–6, 48–50; Malcolm Wanklyn, *Decisive Battles of the English Civil Wars* (Barnsley: Pen & Sword, 2006), 66–7; Joan A. Dils, 'Epidemics, Mortality and the Civil War in Berkshire 1642–6' in R. C. Richardson, *The English Civil Wars* (Stroud: Sutton, 1997), 149; Robert Morris, *The First Battle of Newbury* (Bristol: Stuart, 1993), 7–11, 17; H. C. B. Rogers, *Battles and Generals of the Civil Wars* (London: Seeley, Service & Co, 1968), 103.
3. *Mercurius Civicus*, 18 (21–28 September 1643), 140; Anne Somerset, *Unnatural Murder* (London: Weidenfeld & Nicolson, 1997). Although neither Anne nor Frances was formally charged with witchcraft, magical practices were alleged and the judge's summing-up referred to Anne as a witch.
4. *Mercurius Civicus*, 140; Diane Purkiss, 'Desire and its Deformities: Fantasies of Witchcraft in the English Civil War', *Journal of Medieval and Early Modern Studies*, 27:1 (1997), discusses the Newbury 'witch' and cases of civil war violence against suspected witches, as does Sheilagh O'Brien, 'A "Divellish" Woman Discovered: The Witch of Newbury, 1643', *Cerae*, 2 (2015), https://ceraejournal.com/volume-2-2015/; Cecil L'Estrange Ewen, *Witchcraft and Demonianism* (1933; London: Frederick Muller, 1970), 251–4; B. H. Cunningham (ed.), *Records of the County of Wilts* (Devizes: G. Simson, 1932), 154. See also Joad Raymond (ed.), *Making the News* (Moreton-in-Marsh: Windrush, 1993), 131, 137–8, *The Moderate Intelligencer*, 27 (28 August–4 September 1645), *Mercurius Rusticus*, XV (October 1643).
5. *Signs and Wonders from Heaven* (London, 1645), 4; T. B., *Observations upon Prince Rupert's White Dog Called Boy* (London, 1642), *A Dialogue, or Rather a Parley Between Prince Rupert's Dog ... and Tobie's Dog* (London, 1643), *The Parliament's Unspotted Bitch* (London, 1643) and *A Dog's Elegy* (London, 1644);

Mark Stoyle, *The Black Legend of Prince Rupert's Dog* (Liverpool: Liverpool University Press, 2011), 37–8, 45–9, 57–62, 64, 98, 108–9.

6. See Purkiss, 'Desire', O'Brien, Malcolm Gaskill, *Witchfinders* (London: John Murray, 2005), 147–8, Stoyle, 117–27, and Roy Booth, 'The Witch at Newbury 1643', at *Early Modern Whale*, https://roy25booth.blogspot.com/2011/09/witch-at-newbury-1643.html (2011), which adds other newsbook and letter accounts for the story's authenticity.
7. The original is British Library (BL) Wing M2870, shelfmark E.69 [9]; Patrick Nother, 'The Mystery of the Woodehouse Journal Forgery – Criminal Deception or Victorian Parlour Game', *Camden History Review*, 26 (2002), 15–19. On Waugh, see also National Archives (NA) C14/463/W49, C15/607/C58 and J. W. de Longueville Giffard (ed.), *Reports of Cases Adjudged in the High Court of Chancery*, Vol. II (London, 1861), 201–9.
8. Ephesians 6:11–17.
9. Hugh Latimer, 'Sermon on Ephesians VI. 10–20' from *Sermons*, ed. H. C. Beeching (New York: E. P. Dutton, 1906) at Project Canterbury: http://anglicanhistory.org/reformation/latimer/sermons/ephesians.html.
10. NRO PD 28/1, ANW 2/74; North A EP 86/1.

3. Torture in the Church

1. This chapter was inspired by the team at the Calder Witch Hunt Project, whose website contains carefully researched stories of the 'Calder witches': https://www.calderwitchhunt.co.uk/.
2. Hardy Bertram McCall, *The History and Antiquities of the Parish of Mid-Calder* (Edinburgh, 1894), 12–18, 25, 46, 70–72; https://www.calderwitchhunt.co.uk/history/kirks-calder.
3. Julian Goodare, 'Introduction' in Goodare (ed.), *The Scottish Witch-Hunt in Context* (Manchester: Manchester University Press, 2002), 4–5; Joyce Miller, 'Devices and Directions: Folk Healing Aspects of Witchcraft Practice in Seventeenth-Century Scotland' in Goodare (ed.), *Scottish Witch-Hunt*, 91–5; Owen Davies, 'A Comparative Perspective on Scottish Cunning-Folk and Charmers' in Julian Goodare, Lauren Martin and Joyce Miller (eds), *Witchcraft and Belief in Early Modern Scotland* (Basingstoke: Palgrave, 2008), 186–7, 189, 192.
4. Scotland's People (SP) CH2/266/1, Mid Calder marriages 694:13; McCall, 31–32; https://www.calderwitchhunt.co.uk/women/agnes-bishope; https://www.calderwitchhunt.co.uk/witch-hunters.

5. SP CH2/266/1; McCall, 28.
6. SP CH2/266/1; https://www.calderwitchhunt.co.uk/women/other-women.
7. SP CH2/266/1, CH2/242/3; Goodare, 'Witch-Hunting and the Scottish State' in Goodare (ed.), *Scottish Witch-Hunt*, 125–9; Brian Levack, *Witch-Hunting in Scotland* (London: Routledge, 2008), 4–5.
8. Levack, 7–9.
9. The process of trial is confusing and records offer conflicting evidence – in particular about whether the trial was or was not authorised by the Privy Council and when Agnes was punished for her 'crime'. There is no evidence that her investigation and trial was authorised, though records are incomplete. But later complaints and conflict between kirk and council (below) suggest procedural irregularity was widespread.
10. SP CH2/266/1, CH2/242/3; McCall, 33; https://www.calderwitchhunt.co.uk/women/jonet-bruce.
11. Again, the process is unclear as described. Thanks to Julian Goodare for his painstaking review of the evidence of trial, guarding and outcome.
12. SP CH2/266/1, 17 November 1644; https://www.calderwitchhunt.co.uk/women/margaret-thomsone.
13. SP CH2/266/1, 17 November; Miller, 102; McCall, 32–33; it's possible the belt was either rope or leather, but the record is hard to read; Nicola Whyte, 'The Afterlife of Barrows: Prehistoric Monuments in the Norfolk Landscape', *Landscape History*, 25:1 (2003), 5–16, and 'An Archaeology of Natural Places', *Huntington Library Quarterly*, 76:4 (2013), 499–517; similar magic was imagined as far back as the 1570s, e.g. Robert Pitcairn, *Criminal Trials in Scotland*, Vol. 1:1 (Edinburgh, 1833), 191–201.
14. SP CH2/716/5: it is also possible this is a different Margaret Thompsone.
15. United Nations, *Convention against Torture and Other Cruel, Inhuman or Degrading Treatment or Punishment* (1984), https://www.ohchr.org/en/instruments-mechanisms/instruments/convention-against-torture-and-other-cruel-inhuman-or-degrading.
16. P. Hume Brown (ed.), *The Register of the Privy Council of Scotland*, Series 2, Vol. VIII (Edinburgh, 1908), 37, 108–9; https://www.calderwitchhunt.co.uk/women/margaret-thomsone; https://www.calderwitchhunt.co.uk/history/kirks-calder.
17. SP CH2/242/3.
18. McCall, 31–32; SP CH2/266/1; https://www.calderwitchhunt.co.uk/

women/other-women; Scotland had its own currency until the eighteenth century. Values are difficult to calculate exactly because of multiple conversions and historic revaluations, but the Scottish mark or merk was worth thirteen Scottish shillings and fourpence. However, a Scottish shilling was equivalent to a contemporary English penny.

19. A Scottish pound was worth twenty contemporary English pence; https://www.calderwitchhunt.co.uk/women/helen-stewart; SP CH2/234/1.
20. SP CH2/266/1; McCall, 178–83; https://www.calderwitchhunt.co.uk/women/margaret-thomsone; https://www.calderwitchhunt.co.uk/women/jonet-bruce; https://www.calderwitchhunt.co.uk/blog/making-money-witches-part-one-isobel-ewart-and-calder-witch-hunt.
21. McCall, 28–9; *Register of the Privy Council*, 37, 108–9, 117–18, 119–20, 137–8; SP, CH2/242/3.
22. https://www.calderwitchhunt.co.uk/women/margaret-thomsone; https://www.calderwitchhunt.co.uk/women/other-women.
23. SP Mid Calder marriages 694: 48 and 50, CH2/467/1; The Survey of Scottish Witchcraft at https://witches.hca.ed.ac.uk/home/.

4. The Greatest Enemy

1. ERO D/P 347/1/1, 2 November 1632, 18 January 1635; H. F., *A True and Exact Relation of the Several Informations, Examinations and Confessions of the Late Witches* (London, 1645), 2; Gaskill, 40; Ewen, *Demonianism*, 254, points out that Anne is referred to as 'the elder' in previous court records, so there was also a younger Anne West; John is mentioned in *The Full Trials, Examination and Condemnation of Four Notorious Witches* (London, 1590), which inexplicably cites the events in Worcester, blames Anne's daughter Rebecca West for John's murder and states that she was convicted of it – at least some of which is untrue (Ewen, 255). Another account of the Wests and others is *A True Relation of the Arraignment of Thirty Witches* (London, 1645), which includes additional, sometimes inaccurate, detail – for example, placing them in Colchester.
2. NA ASSI35 83/9, 84/2. H. F., 11–13; Gaskill, 36–40.
3. H. F., 12, 5, 2; ERO A14693 Box 1, T/P 51/3, DP 347/1/1; C. L'Estrange Ewen, *Witch Hunting and Witch Trials* (London: Kegan Paul, Trench, Trubner, 1929), 220, 224; Gaskill, 37–8. Previously some historians have thought George Francis came from Rivenhall, but see H. F., 12, ERO D/ACA 35, DP 347/1/1 (29 May 1643),

Peter Elmer, 'East Anglia and the Hopkins Trials 1645–1647' at https://practitioners.exeter.ac.uk/wp-content/uploads/2014/11/Eastanglianwitchtrialappendix2.pdf 27 – Rebecca West lived in Rivenhall, George Francis and Anne West in Lawford; *The Division of the County of Essex into Several Classis* (London, 1648) – a classis is a Presbyterian group of governing ministers and elders in a district.

4. ERO D/DU 250/1, D/DC 14/32, A14693 Box 1.
5. ERO A14693 Box 1, D/P/347/1/1; Gaskill, 40; when she was Thomasine Dereham aged twenty-six, 13 December, Joseph Lemuel Chester and George J. Armytage (eds), *Allegations for Marriage Licenses Issued by the Bishop of London* (Vol. 2; London, 1897), 47; Elmer, 'East Anglia'; NA PROB 11/280/6 (miscatalogued as Edee).
6. H. F., 11; thanks to Philip Cunningham for guiding me around Lawford and Manningtree; Tom Judson, *St Mary's Church, Lawford* (Harwich: Entrac, 2007), 17; ERO D/ACA 35; Gaskill, 40.
7. H. F., 1; 'Witch Finder's Step Sister'; ERO D/DA T212; Gaskill, 40, 58–60; John Stearne, *A Confirmation and Discovery of Witch-Craft* (London, 1648), 38–9; *The Full Trials* pamphlet suggests Rebecca might have been questioned as early as 4 March about the death of John Hart, and that Thomas Hart and John Edes might have given a statement about her then as well as later, but that is uncertain since this account contains major errors.
8. H. F., 12–13; Gaskill, 40–42, 60. Gaskill suggests Rebecca West's testimony of 21 March was incorrectly dated in H. F.'s pamphlet, but it is not likely Rebecca would return from Colchester to give further evidence to the magistrates at Manningtree on 21 April – his redating of her statement – so the pamphlet's date of 21 March is accepted.
9. H. F., 11–12; Gaskill, 58–9; *The Division ... into Several Classis*, ERO T/P 51/3.
10. Frances Timbers, 'Witches' Sect or Prayer Meeting? Matthew Hopkins Revisited', *Women's History Review*, 17:1 (2008), 21–37; H. F., 12, 17, 20–21; Stearne, 39; ERO D/DCA 35; 1 Samuel 15:23.
11. H. F., 'The Preface', 1.
12. ERO D/DHw T55, T/P 64/21; Gaskill, 60; Charles Partridge, 'The Angier Family', *The East Anglian* (January 1908), 198–201.

5. Fatal Changes

1. ERO D/DU 40/17, 40/18, 40/19; Gaskill, 294.
2. ERO D/DU 161/441; Walter Bridges, *A Catechism for Communicants* (London, 1645).
3. ERO D/DHw T120, D/DA T218, D/P 343/1/1, D/DA T218, D/

DA T223, D/DHw Q1, D/DHw M72; W.E.A.A., 'Angier, John', *Dictionary of National Biography*, Vol. I, eds Leslie Stephen and Sidney Lee (London, 1917), 417; Gaskill, 41.

4. ERO D/P 343/1/1, D/DA T212, D/P 173/1/1; Gaskill, 38, 41; Stearne, 14–15; Ronald Holmes, *Witchcraft in British History* (London: Frederick Muller, 1974), 134; the elder Jane was only twelve and in 1653 the minimum marriage age for girls was raised to fourteen, see Loretta A. Dolan, 'Child Marriage in Sixteenth-Century Northern England: The Emotional Undertones in the Legal Narratives', *Limina*, 20:3 (2015), 3 (1–12); H. F., 11, 16. NA ASSI 35/62/1-35/86/1 (6 March 1620–17 July 1645), E 179/328; Marion Gibson, *Witchcraft: A History in Thirteen Trials* (London/New York: Simon & Schuster/Scribner, 2023), 84–105.
5. ERO D/P 343/1/1, D/DCm T99/14, D/DHw T120, D/DA T212, T/P 51/3 quoting 8 James I 4/9; A. H. and R. J. Horlock, *Mistleyman's Log* (Hove: Fisher Nautical Press, 1977), 2, 20.
6. ERO D/P 343/1/1, D/DA T212, T218, D/ACW 14/282, D/DA T223, D/DHw Q1, T/P 51/3, D/DHw M72; Gaskill, 34, 41; NA HL/PO/JO/10/1/245; Janet Cooper and C. R. Elrington (eds), *A History of the County of Essex: Volume 9, the Borough of Colchester* (London: 1994), 19–26, 121–32; Gaskill, 9–27; Timbers, 'Witches' Sect' valuably reconstructed much of the Witham-Edwards family; Elmer 'East Anglia'; Helen Barrell, 'Mistley and the Witchfinder' (2015) and 'The Witchfinder General' (2017) at https://essexandsuffolksurnames.co.uk/mistley-and-the-witchfinder/ and https://www.freeukgenealogy.org.uk/news/2017/10/25/halloween-special-guest-post/; Philip Cunningham, 'The Witch Finder's Step Sister' at www.manningtree-museum.org.uk.
7. ERO D/DA T223, T/P 51/3, D/P/343/1/1, D/DHw T120; H. F., 7–8; Gaskill, 37; Stearne, 53 – he describes 'many' of the Hopkins family as suffering from 'consumption'.
8. Matthew was not mentioned in a bequest made to his family in 1619, although his older brothers James, Thomas and John were, suggesting he was born after this date; SA IC/AA1/55/173; Gaskill, 11–16.
9. NRO 1633/233; NA PROB 11 358 114–115; ERO D/P 26/1/2, D/DA T212; Gaskill, 20–21; Matthew Hopkins, *The Discovery of Witches* (London, 1645), 2, 4, 6; H. F., 11–13; Stearne, 322.
10. H. F., 1–6; Hopkins, 2–3; Stearne, 14–15; Gaskill, 41, 49–52.
11. ERO D/P 343/1/1, D/DCm T99, D/DHw T59, D/DHw M73; Gaskill, 48–9; Stearne, 17–18; Hopkins, 3, 5; H. F., 2–3.
12. ERO D/DHw T59, D/P 173/1/1, D/DCm T99/14. John's wife was

Agnes Cawston – they also lived at Lawshall, Suffolk, where they had other children; Gaskill, 38, 41, 275–6, 293; Stearne, 14–15, 18–19.

13. Stearne, 'To the Reader', 13–15; H. F., 2–3, 13; Peter Elmer, *Witchcraft, Witch Hunting and Politics in Early Modern England* (Oxford: Oxford University Press, 2016), 28; Hopkins, 5.
14. H. F., 2; Stearne, 15; Thomas Ady, *A Candle in the Dark* (London, 1655), 65.
15. ERO D/P 343/1/1, D/DHw M58, D/P 173/1/ 1, T/P 51/3; H. F., 3, 6–7; Stearne, 14–15, 28–9, 43–7; Thomas Taylor was buried at Bradfield on 7 August 1617 and had a daughter, Marie, born 1608, buried 1610. Jane's name, Alderson, is sometimes spelt Alderton; ERO Q/SR 378/44 refers to Robert's son; *The Division … into Several Classis.*
16. H. F., 8–9; ERO D/DHw T120, D/DQs 4, D/DA T221; NA ASSI 35/86/1.
17. H. F., 8–9; Ewen, *Witch Hunting*, 227–8; ERO D/P 343/1/1. Sara had children with her husband Thomas, who died in 1634: Dorothy (1619, died 1620), Marie (1621), Jeremy and Sara (1625, Jeremy died 1626), Richard (born and died 1628); the witnesses against her were Henry Woolvett, Eliza Potter (probably Elizabeth, wife of Jeffery Potter), 'widow' Winterflood (probably Mary, who had an illegitimate child, John, who died in 1634) and 'widow' Applegate, perhaps a relative of Joseph, father of Bess Clarke's daughter (see Gibson, *Witchcraft*)?
18. H. F., 13–15; Gibson, *Witchcraft*, 100–102; NA ASSI 35/86/1.
19. NA ASSI 35/86/1; Gaskill, 123–7; Ewen, *Witch Hunting*, 221–31.
20. ERO D/Hw M72, D/DHw M29: more can definitely be found with continued archival searching.
21. NA ASSI 35/86/1; Elmer, 'East Anglia'; Stearne, 11; Ewen, *Witch Hunting*, 221–31, *Demonianism*, 259–62; Gaskill, 198, 203; in 1655, Thomas Ady (101) reported there had been fourteen executions at Chelmsford, so with the four at Manningtree (below), that makes eighteen. Numbers are ambiguous because of record loss as well as recorders' frequent lack of care.

6. The Framlingham Witches

1. John Ridgard, *Medieval Framlingham* (Woodbridge: Boydell Press/ Suffolk Records Society, 1985), 5–7, 13; Gaskill, 108–9.
2. SA FC101/E2/26, B105/2/1; Pembroke College, Cambridge (Pemb C) court book 4; Gaskill, 108–9; Elmer, 'East Anglia'; Cotton Mather, *Magnalia Christ Americana*, quoted in John Booth, *Nicholas*

Danforth and his Neighbours (Framingham, MA: Framingham Historical and Natural History Society, 1935), 7 – although Mather overestimates Nicholas's social standing; Booth, 21, 30, 33–4.

3. SA FC101/G11/2/1-30, E2/25, G5/3 and 4, E2/19, B105/2/1.
4. SA FC101/E2/26; Helen Pitcher, *The Church of Saint Michael Framlingham* (Norwich: Jarrold, 2005), 1.
5. SA B105/2/1, FC101/E2/26; Pemb C L10, court roll N2, court book 1635–1652; Gaskill, 14–16; Elmer, 'East Anglia'. The Framlingham records show there was confusion about who was to inherit after James's death, since the family did not live locally.
6. BL Add. MS. 27402, see also Ewen, *Witch Hunting*, for a transcript; Ewen, *Witch Hunting*, 304; SA FC101/E2/26; Booth, 49.
7. SA FC101/G7/1/1 and 2, E2/26, E2/21, FC 101 D/3/1; Booth, 49; BL Add. MS. 27402; Ewen, *Witch Hunting*, 305; Gaskill, 111; Marion Allen (ed.), *Wills of the Archdeaconry of Suffolk, 1620–1624* (Woodbridge: Boydell, 1989), 47–8; Pemb C L13, court book 4.
8. BL Add. MS. 27402; Ewen, *Witch Hunting* 306–7; SA FC101/G7/1/1, E2/17, 18–23, G11/2/1–30, E2/26, D/3/1; Booth, 26; Pemb C L14, L15, court book 4; Elmer, 'East Anglia'.
9. SA FC101/E2/26, G7/1/1, 2, E2/26, E2/18–23, 25–26, G4/1/2, G11/2/1, D/3/1. The Driver families might be conflated, but in the accounts one appears as 'Driver' or 'Driver's wife', another as 'Robert Driver'. In one entry, 'Robt' has been omitted and inserted in superscript, showing the name was an important distinction (FC101/E2/23); Booth, 48–50; Marion E. Allen (ed.), *Wills of the Archdeaconry of Suffolk 1625–1626* (Woodbridge: Boydell, 1994), 34; Pemb C. court book 4, N1; BL Add. MS. 27402; Ewen, *Witch Hunting*, 303–4, 306; Gaskill, 112–13.
10. SA FC101/G7/1/1, 2, E2/26, D/3/1. There are several Ann Palmers, but this seems to be the same poor, widowed woman; Booth, 49; Pemb C L12–13, court book 4, N1; Gaskill, 109; Elmer, 'East Anglia'; BL Add. MS. 27402; Ewen, *Witch Hunting*, 305.
11. There are many Smiths; SA FC101/G7/1/1, 2, FC101/G11/2/1–30, G4/1/2, G5/4/2, E2/17, E2/21, E2/26, D/3/1; Allen, ed., *Wills … 1620–1624*, 438–9, 166–7; Pemb C L12, 13, N1, court book 4; NA PROB 11/291/702; BL Add. MS. 27402; Ewen, *Witch Hunting*, 304.
12. SA FC101/G7/1/1, 2, G11/2/1–30, E2/26, D/3/1, G11/2/1–30; Pemb C L13, L14; BL Add. MS. 27402; Ewen, *Witch Hunting*, 304–5; Booth, 53; Allen (ed.), *Wills … 1620–1624*, 47–8.
13. BL Add. MS. 27402; Ewen, *Witch Hunting*, 306; SA FC101/G7/1/1, FC101/E2/26, FC101/E2/18, FC101/E2/22, D/3/1; Booth, 51; Elmer, 'East Anglia'.

14. SA FC101/G7/1/1, G11/2/1–30, E2/24, D/3/1; Booth, 49–50; Allen (ed.), *Wills … 1625–1626*, 9–10; Gaskill, 110–11; Elmer, 'East Anglia'; Pemb C L10, 12, 13 and 14; BL Add. MS. 27402; Ewen, *Witch Hunting*, 307.
15. SA FC101/G7/1/2, D/3/1; another 'Edwards wife' and Widow Nevell are also listed; Elmer, 'East Anglia'.
16. *A True Relation*, 5; Stearne, 25; SA FC101/G7/1/2.

7. The World Turned Upside Down

1. Cecil L'Estrange Ewen, *The Trials of John Lowes* (London: printed for the author, 1937), 1; SA FC105 D/1/1; Patrick Collinson, John Craig and Brett Usher, *Conferences and Combination Lectures in the Elizabethan Church: Dedham and Bury St Edmunds 1582–1590* (Woodbridge: Boydell Press/Church of England Record Society, 2003), cii–cv; *A Magazine of Scandal* (London, 1642), A3v; Gaskill, 138–9.
2. SA HA10/50/18/4.3 (3); Pemb C L10, L12; Ewen, *Demonianism*, 291; Elmer, 'East Anglia'.
3. SA FC105/D/1/1; Robert Warner, *All Saints' Church, Brandeston, Suffolk*, rev. ed (Brandeston, printed for the author, 2004), 3; Gaskill, 139–40; Ewen, *Lowes*, 4; NRO DN/DEP 33–36a and 'Intoxicants and Early Modernity' database, https://www.dhi.ac.uk/intoxicants and Suffolk Archives HA10/50/18/5/1 (4); *Magazine of Scandal*, A3–A3v. The church court records I've been able to examine don't show unusually high levels of presentments from Brandeston, but parishioners perceived their vicar was keen to report them and there may be further evidence across the forty-plus years of his tenure that I have not seen.
4. SA FC105/D/1/1, HA10/50/18/6.2 (3); NA STAC 8/200/27; Stearne, 23; Ewen, *Lowes*, 2–4; Gaskill, 139–40.
5. Ewen, *Lowes*, 4–5; NA STAC 8/200/27; SA FC105/D/1/1, HA10/50/18/6.2 (3); Alison Rowlands, 'The Witch-Cleric Stereotype in a Seventeenth-Century German Lutheran Context', *German History*, 38:1 (2020), 1–23; *Magazine of Scandal*, A4.
6. Ewen, *Lowes*, 5; SA FC105/D/1/1, HA10/50/18/6.2 (3), HA10/50/18/5.1 (4); see also NA C2/JasI/P19/23, C2/JasI/B14/69 (Pope).
7. Ewen, *Lowes*, 5–6; *Magazine of Scandal*, A2–3; Gaskill, 138; Alan Everitt, *Suffolk and the Great Rebellion 1640–1660* (Ipswich: Suffolk Records Society, 1960), 23–5, 63–5; SA FC105/D1/1.
8. BL Add. MS. 27402; Ewen, *Witch Hunting*, 300–301; *A True Relation*, 3; Elmer, 'East Anglia'; Ady, 101–2.

9. SA B105/2/1 – both petitions were retrospective, submitted in autumn; Mary D. Lobel, 'The Gaol of Bury St Edmunds', *Proceedings of the Suffolk Institute of Archaeology*, 21:3 (1933), 203 (203–7); 'Moyses Hall', http://www.historicengland.org.uk (1974); Stearne, 14; from other sources, Ewen, *Demonianism*, 281, totals the witchcraft suspects at 124 known people, plus other unknown persons; Gaskill, 145, 156, 178, suggests 150.
10. Edmund Calamy, *God's Free Mercy to England Presented as a Precious and Powerful Motive to Humiliation* (London, 1642), 2; Samuel Fairclough, *The Prisoners' Praises for their Deliverance from the Long Imprisonment at Colchester* (London, 1650), 38–9, and *Hagioi Axioi or the Saints' Worthiness and the World's Worthlessness* (London 1653), 29; Francis Hutchinson, *An Historical Essay Concerning Witchcraft* (1718; London, 1720), 85–6; Gordon Blackwood, *Tudor and Stuart Suffolk* (Lancaster: Carnegie, 2001), 134–5; Stearne, 54; Gaskill, 150; Samuel Clarke, *The Lives of Sundry Eminent Persons* (London, 1683), 172.
11. Edmund Gillingwater, *An Historical and Descriptive Account of St Edmund's Bury* (Bury St Edmunds, 1804), 168, 236; David Gill, 'Monitoring at St Margaret's House, Bury St Edmunds BSE 440' (Bury St Edmunds: Suffolk County Council, 2013), 2; Bidwells, 'A Character Assessment of the Shire Hall Complex, Bury St Edmunds' (Bury St Edmunds: West Suffolk Council, 2008), 20; SA B105/2/1; Gaskill, 150–9; Hutchinson, 89.
12. *A True Relation*, 3; Stearne, 24–5; Ewen, *Demonianism*, 291–2; Hutchinson, 89.
13. Stearne, 11, 14, 23–5; Ady, 101; Gaskill, 166; Everitt, 73; Andrew Sneddon, *Witchcraft and Whigs: The Life of Bishop Francis Hutchinson (1660–1739)* (Manchester: Manchester University Press, 2008), 100.

8. The Devil and the Deep Blue Sea

1. NRO Y/S 1/2.
2. A. W. Ecclestone (ed.), *Henry Manship's Great Yarmouth* (Great Yarmouth: printed for the author, 1971), 26, 40–45, 72; NRO WLP/20/4/23-28; NRO MC 3372/2; Paul B. Patterson, *The Great Wall of Yarmouth*, Vol. II (Great Yarmouth: Printed Word, 2018), 28–9, 62, 70, 100–101, 106.
3. NRO Y/C 27/2, Y/S 1/2, ANW 6/8; Danny Buck, 'Presbyterianism, Urban Politics and Division: The 1645 Great Yarmouth Witch Hunt in Context' (thesis, UEA, 2021), 45–6, 54–5; Gaskill, 168–70.

4. Colin Tooke, *The Rows and the Old Town of Great Yarmouth* (Great Yarmouth: Blackwell, 2007), 1, 43, 48; Ecclestone (ed.), 53–4, 68; Thomas Nashe, *Lenten Stuff Containing the Description and First Procreation and Increase of the Town of Great Yarmouth*, ed. Charles Hindley (London, 1871), 9, 26, 113; NRO MS 12876; Nazareth was a Christian name in at least one other Norfolk reformist family, the Pitchers, see James Stevenson Cushing, *The Genealogy of the Cushing Family* (Montreal: Perrault, 1905), 21.
5. Buck, 158–63; Gaskill, 168–9.
6. NRO PD 28/1 and 2, Y/S 1/2, Y/C 29/1, Y/C 39/8, Y/C 19/7; Buck, 97; Elmer, 'East Anglia'; John Taylor (pseudonym Anthony Roily), *A Brief Relation of the Gleanings of the Idiotisms and Absurdities of Miles Corbet* (London, 1646), 7. Some writers have suggested Mark's surname might be Prince, but it is spelt Pryme in multiple sources and see Ralph E. Prime, *The Descendants of James Prime* (New York, 1895).
7. NRO PD 28/1 and 2, MC 268/187; Buck, 212–13; Abigail died in 1636, Bridget's name is sometimes mistakenly given as Grace because of issues of legibility.
8. NRO PD 28/1 records Daniel's mother as 'Margaret' Fossett, but there are no other John and Margaret Fossetts and the way that 'Margaret' and 'Nazareth' were written makes it hard to tell them apart; William's mother is recorded as 'Alice Fawcett' but at his burial he was called Fassett; NRO Y/D 28/2–27, Y/L 10/3, Y/L 7/8–10; *A Calendar of the Freemen of Great Yarmouth* (Norwich: Norfolk and Norwich Archaeological Society, Goose and Son, 1910), 69; Tooke, 12, 15, 23, 40; Patterson, 165.
9. NRO PD 28/1 and 2, Y/S 1/2, Y/C 19/7; *Calendar*, 60. 'Spinster' could mean a woman of unknown marital status (rather like 'Ms'), but it could also mean an unmarried woman; James Lambert and Lucy Holmes married on 27 April 1636; Elmer, 'East Anglia'.
10. Matthew Hale, *A Collection of Modern Relations of Matter of Fact Concerning Witches and Witchcraft* (London, 1693), 46–8; Stearne, 53; Gaskill, 170–72; NRO Y/S 1/2, PD 28/1 and 2, Y/C 29/3; Lesley A. O'Connell Edwards, 'The Hand Knitting "Industry" of Norwich in the Later Sixteenth Century' (dissertation, University of Oxford, 2019), 11, 40, and 'The Production and Trade of Hand-Knitted Wool Stockings in Elizabethan and Early Jacobean England (c.1580–1617)', *Textile History*, 53:2 (2024), 131–5.
11. Buck, 75–93; NRO PD 28/1 and 2, ANW 6/8; Elmer, 'East Anglia'; Richard Cust, 'Anti-Puritanism and Urban Politics: Charles I and Great Yarmouth', *The Historical Journal*, 35:1 (1992), 3–5, 8–9,

18–22; Brinsley had married Elizabeth Owner, daughter of Edward, Great Yarmouth shipping magnate and churchwarden, on 19 June 1627, so was a popular local choice to return to office: she died in 1630; the Owners attended Brinsley's out-of-town church services and were presented at the Archdeaconry Court for it.

12. NRO FC 31/83, PD 28/1 and 2; Buck, 102–24, 147–57; Elmer, 'East Anglia'.
13. John Brinsley, *A Breviate of Saving Knowledge* (London, 1643), 6, *Church Reformation* (London, 1643); see also the more conciliatory *The Healing of Israel's Breaches* (London, 1642); Thomas Whitfield, *A Refutation of the Loose Opinions and Licentious Tenets Wherewith Those Lay-Preachers Which Wander Up and Down the Kingdom Labour to Seduce the Simple People* (London, 1646).
14. NRO PD 28/1 and 2, Y/S 1/2; Elmer, 'East Anglia'; Ewen, *Demonianism*, 281. Mark Pryme's client John Sparke was also charged with consulting Mark, in itself a magical crime, though rarely prosecuted. The choice to charge him suggests local commitment to stamping out magical activity, especially Mark's. John Sparke was, however, acquitted alongside Mark.
15. NRO Y/S 1/2; Buck, 195, 204–5.
16. Taylor, *Brief Relation*, 6–8.
17. Bernard Capp, *The World of John Taylor, the Water Poet* (Oxford: Oxford University Press, 1994); Elmer, 'East Anglia'; John Taylor, *Persecutio Undecima* (London, 1648), 17; Buck, 87–9, 92–3, 140–41, 218; Cust, 18; Thomas Cheshire, *A True Copy of that Sermon which was Preached at St Pauls the Tenth Day of October Last* (London, 1641), 11–12, *A Sermon Preached at St Peter's Westminster on St Peter's Day* (London, 1642), 23; *Brasenose College Register 1509–1909* (Blackwell: Oxford, 1909), 130; Joseph Foster, *Alumni Oxoniensis* Vol. I (Oxford, 1891), 267; Gaskill, 181; 'Great Yarmouth's Early Modern Astrology' (2021), https://norfolkrecordofficeblog.org/2021/11/06/great-yarmouths-early-modern-astrology/.
18. It was thought Joan Lacey was reprieved permanently (e.g. Ewen, *Demonianism*, 280; Elmer, 'East Anglia'), but in October 2025 Laina West discovered a second copy of the parish register showing she was executed and buried with the other women. Thanks to Laina for sharing this discovery and for her help with the parish and sessions records. NRO Y/S 1/2, microfilm 69:17, Y/C 39/2, PD 28/1/2 – Elizabeth Dudgeon's surname is also spelled Bugden and Elizabeth Bradwell appears as Bardwell; Tooke, 39; Mary Vervy was prosecuted again in 1647 but acquitted, Elmer, *Witchcraft*,

133, and 'East Anglia'; Elmer and Gaskill (172–3, 181) believe the 1645 trial was held in December, with the September session being a committal hearing, but the September record of executions shows this is incorrect; however, there was a committal hearing before the trial and the trial date is incorrectly recorded as December in the sessions book.

19. Hopkins, 1–10; Gaskill, 234–5.
20. John Gaule, *Select Cases of Conscience Touching Witches and Witchcrafts* (London, 1646), 7, 76, 78–9, 183–5, 192, preface; Ady, 163–4.

9. Give Me Your Poor

1. *The Most Strange and Admirable Discovery of the Witches of Warboys* (London, 1593); *The Witches of Northamptonshire* (London, 1612), Dv; Marion Gibson, *Early Modern Witches* (London: Routledge, 2000), 170–71; Elmer, *Witchcraft*, 60; Gaskill, 201; Northamptonshire Archives (Northants A) NPL.1246-7 – the Pickerings held land in Molesworth too, Huntingdonshire Archives (Hunts A) KAH.30.8, Acc 1956/46, Dorset History Centre D/WLC/T273; William Ryland Dent Adkins (ed.), *Victoria History of the County of Northampton*, Vol. III (1930; London: Dawson, 1970), 144.
2. Stearne's spelling, Winnick, is presumably how the name was pronounced, but it is spelt Winwick in the Molesworth parish register, below. John was probably surnamed Winwick after the village of that name.
3. NA PROB 11/125/34 and PROB 11/161/738; Andrew Daunton-Fear and Neil Busby, *St James Thrapston Parish Church* (Thrapston: Thrapston Heritage, 2021), 38; Northants A 325P/1 and 2, M (B) X873, 874; *Thrapston: An Overview of its History: Part One* (Thrapston: Thrapston Heritage, n.d.), 5, 11; John Davenport, *The Witches of Huntingdon* (London, 1646), 3; Elmer, 'East Anglia'; Adkins, 141.
4. Hunts A C 3/9/3; Bernard (sometimes spelt Barnard) was also a judge. Nicholas Pedley married Bernard's daughter Lucy, and was – like his father-in-law – Recorder of Huntingdon and later an MP; John Venn and J. A. Venn, *Alumni Cantabrigiensis*, Vol. I (Cambridge: Cambridge University Press, 1922), 91; E. R. Edwards, 'Pedley, Nicholas (1615–85)', *History of Parliament Online*, ed. B. D. Henning (Woodbridge: Boydell & Brewer, 1983), https://www.historyofparliamentonline.org/volume/1660-1690/member/

pedley-nicholas-1615-85; Elmer, 'East Anglia'; NA PROB 11/ 320/365.

5. Davenport, 3–4; Stearne, 11, 21; Elmer, 'East Anglia'; Gaskill, 210–11; Ewen, *Demonianism*, 310.
6. Jane Whittle and Li Jiang, 'Gender, Wages and Agricultural Day Labour in England c.1480–1680', *Agricultural History Review*, 72:2 (2015), 177, 181–2; Mary Humphries, 'Thrapston's Markets and Fairs' (2015), https://www.thrapstonheritage.org.uk/content/topics/businesses/high-street-feature-pages-businesses/thrapstons-markets-and-fairs.
7. Jeremy Lake, *Northamptonshire Vales* (London: Historic England, 2020); Hunts A, KHP54.1.1.1 and *Molesworth St Peter, Huntingdonshire* register transcript by Jean Bent (Huntingdonshire Family History Society, 1999).
8. Davenport, 3–4; Elmer, 'East Anglia'; Hunts A KCON 3/9/5, 6, 7, 8 and 9; Walter C. Metcalfe, *The Visitations of Northamptonshire* (London, 1887), 134.
9. Northants A RO 325P/1 and 2; Daunton-Fear and Busby, 12–13, 17, 29; Venn and Venn, Vol. III, 158; Hunts A, KHP54.1.1.1 and *Molesworth St Peter*; Gaskill, 201; Adkins, 141.
10. Rob Hardy and Zoie Horecny, 'Washington Family' (2025), https://www.mountvernon.org/library/digitalhistory/digital-encyclopedia/article/ancestry, and Albert Welles, *The Pedigree and History of the Washington Family* (New York, 1879), 12, 86, 88–114; Elmer, 'East Anglia'.
11. Stearne, 34–5; Welles, 88–9; Northants A RO 325P/1 and 2; Elmer, 'East Anglia'; Gaskill, 202.
12. Stearne, 35; Krista Kesselring, 'Early Modern Coroners' Inquests into Deaths in Custody' (2017), https://legalhistorymiscellany.com/2017/07/09/deaths-in-custody/#:~:text=Looking%20at%20some%20of%20these,January%206%20and%20February%2022; Ewen, *Demoniansim*, 306–7.
13. On the Keyston Wallis family, see Huntingdonshire Archives KAH/15/1/18, 22; Stearne, 13, 17, 20–21; Peter Higginbotham, 'County and Borough Gaol, Huntingdon, Huntingdonshire' (n.d.), https://www.theprison.org.uk/HuntingdonCTG/; Gaskill, 205–9, 211–12.
14. Stearne, 20–21; Davenport, 1–2, 5–14; John McKinnie, 'Huntingdon Hangings' (n.d.), https://stives100yearsago.blogspot.com/2024/01/executions-at-mill-common-huntingdon.
15. Bernard Christian Steiner (ed.), *Proceedings of the Provincial Court 1658–1662* (Baltimore: Maryland Historical Society, 1922), 327–9; Maureen Rush Burgess, 'The Cup of Ruin and Desolation:

Seventeenth-Century Witchcraft in the Chesapeake' (thesis, University of Hawaii, 2004), 97–106; Francis Neal Parke, *Witchcraft in Maryland* (Baltimore: Maryland Historical Society, 1937), 6–7.

10. Fairyland

1. Mark Stoyle, *A Murderous Midsummer* (New Haven: Yale University Press, 2022), especially 45–9, 81–9; folkloric creatures often adorn church bench-ends in Cornwall and Devon, for example at Zennor and Altarnun, Cornwall.
2. Moses Pitt, *An Account of One Ann Jefferies* (London, 1696), 1–2; S. R. Young (ed.), *Ann Jefferies and the Fairies*, 2nd ed. (n.p.: Pwca Books and Pamphlets, 2023), 66–8, 20–21; NA PROB 11/440/280; Michael Harris, 'Pitt, Moses, bap.1639, d.1697', *ODNB* (2004), https://www.oxforddnb.com/display/10.1093/ref:odnb/9780198614128.001.0001/odnb-9780198614128-e-22331?rskey=PpwkQK&result=1; Ewen, *Demonianism*, 305–6.
3. Pitt, 10; in the 1930s, Barbara Spooner suggested Ann was in fact Elizabeth Jefferies or Jeffery, baptised 13 February 1625, but this is improbable – over eighteen months before the date given by Moses and the wrong name. Elizabeth's father's name was also misread as Thomas (by the clergyman who assisted Spooner), but is actually Henry – see Barbara Spooner, 'Cornish Parish Records', *Western Morning News* (14 July 1931), 3, in Young (ed.), 78, and Kresen Kernow (KK) P219/1/1, 398.2094237 RBO; Young (ed.), 27.
4. Pitt, 11, 14; Young (ed.), 27–9, 31, 34, 37. Moses' account of Ann's illness – peaking in April 1646 when Florence Pitt died – suggests it probably began in later 1645; P. A. S. Pool, *The Death of Cornish* (Penzance: Pool, 1975), 6–10; Jacqueline Pearson, '"Then She Asked It, What Were Its Sisters' Names?": Reading Between the Lines in Seventeenth Century Pamphlets of the Supernatural', *The Seventeenth Century*, 28:1 (2013), 65–6, comments sensitively on her status.
5. Pitt, 11–12; Young (ed.), 27–30, 78; Moses was christened – as Moyses, a common spelling of the time – in March 1629, the hard-to-read date possibly being the 11th or 12th.
6. Pitt, 11, 13–14; Florence was buried on 16 April 1646.
7. Pitt, 12–14; Young (ed.), 30–31; Pearson, 65.
8. On the history of fairies, see Diane Purkiss, *Troublesome Things* (London: Allen Lane, 2000) and Ronald Hutton, 'The Making of the Early Modern British Fairy Tradition', *Historical Journal*, 57:4 (2014), 1135–57; on seventeenth-century fairies, Peter Marshall, 'Ann Jeffries and the Fairies: Folk Belief and the War on Scepticism

in Later Stuart England' in Angela McShane and Garthine Walker (eds), *The Extraordinary and the Everyday in Early Modern England* (Basingstoke: Palgrave Macmillan, 2010), 127–41; Pitt, 10–11, 15–16; Young (ed.), 32–3.

9. KK BK/466 – at Nether or Lower Suffenton; Pitt, 16–18; Pearson, 65.
10. Pitt, 18; Young (ed.), 35–36.
11. Pitt, 16–18; Young (ed.), 34–35.
12. Anne Duffin, 'Robartes, John, First Earl of Radnor', *ODNB* (2004), https://www.oxforddnb.com/display/10.1093/ref:odnb/9780198614128.001.0001/odnb-9780198614128-e-23707?rskey=ouOrfg&result=5; NA PROB 11/251/287; Pitt, 18–20. Tregeagle may not have been one of Ann's first questioners, but he was certainly involved in later action against her and, as a local Justice of the Peace, it seems likely he was an initiator of the investigation.
13. Pitt, 19–20; Young (ed.), 37–38.
14. Pitt, 20–21; Young (ed.), 38.
15. Pitt, 20–22; Young (ed.), 23, 39; John Maclean, *Parochial and Family History, Parish and Borough of Bodmin* (London and Bodmin, 1870), 137.
16. Bodleian Library, Clarendon MS 29/2443, 2478 and 2466 in Young (ed.), 16–17; Marshall, 133–5.
17. J. S. Cockburn (ed.), *Western Circuit Assize Orders 1629–1648* (London: Royal Historical Society, 1976), 257; Stuart Handley, 'Rolle, Henry', *ODNB* (2008), https://www.oxforddnb.com/display/10.1093/ref:odnb/9780198614128.001.0001/odnb-9780198614128-e-24021?rskey=uciQP8&result=3. Rolle became Lord Chief Justice in 1648. He also treated another prophet/heretic and his follower with politic leniency: Humphry Ellis, *Pseudochristus* (London, 1649), 50–52.
18. Young (ed.), 22–3, 44. Will went on to be receiver (treasurer) and mayor of Plymouth in 1655 and 1677 – R. N. Worth, *Calendar of Plymouth Municipal Records* (Plymouth, 1893), 24, 167; The Box, Plymouth 1/720/125, 1/23, 1/28, 81/H1/244, 37/1, 1232/65, 79, 78, 90–91. In 1931, Barbara Spooner identified a St Mabyn marriage record (20 January 1665) as 'Ann Jefferies', but this is of Elizabeth Jeffrey and William Werrin, not Warden. This couple had three children, the last born in 1681 when Ann Jefferies was in her mid-fifties. Elizabeth Werrin, who died in 1713, cannot be Ann. Warden is a common surname in north Cornwall, but no surviving, legible record found so far is of William Warden or Ann Jefferies Warden.

19. Pitt, 7–9; Young (ed.), 22–3; Lower also had property in St Breward, Lanreath, London and Middlesex (NA C6/222/34, C10/180/117, C10/187/56, C10/219/48, C10/162/125, C10/123/105, C10/113/150, C10/154/132, C8/410/27, E134/24 and 25, Chas2/Hil18, C10/79/110, C8/441/5 and others, The Box, Plymouth 74/672/2), so William could have lived elsewhere. Slanning's lands were almost all in Devon (The Box, 70/166, 167, 122, 123, 124, 231, 372/17/4/16, NA C8/583/42, C8/352/220) but he did own property at Budock, Cornwall, too (NA C8/531/56).
20. Young (ed.), 24–25; she would have heard of other witch trials – e.g. the newsbook *Mercurius Politicus*, 181 (24 November–2 December 1653), reported fifteen women were accused of witchcraft in west Cornwall in 1653 (Raymond [ed.], 152). Eight were sent for trial at Launceston but further details are now unknown.

11. Borderland

1. Peter D. Wright, 'Water Trades on the Lower River Tyne in the Seventeenth and Eighteenth Centuries' (thesis, Newcastle University, 2011), 17, 49.
2. Roger Howell, *Monopoly on the Tyne 1650–58: Papers Relating to Ralph Gardner* (Newcastle: Society of Antiquaries of Newcastle upon Tyne, 1978), 1; Ralph Gardner, *England's Grievance Discovered in Relation to the Coal Trade* (1655; North Shields, 1849), anonymous introduction, iv; Northumb A EP 9/1: Devereux Gardner and Joan Watson married at All Saints, Newcastle, on 3 December 1618 and had a son, Robert, baptised there on 18 May 1624; Tynemouth parish register, https://www.familysearch.org/en/search/record/results?count=20&q.batchNumber=P000191&q.surname=Gardiner&f.collectionId=5.
3. Henry Bourne, *The History of Newcastle upon Tyne* (Newcastle, 1736), 230–38; Rogers, 115–16, 193.
4. Peter D. Wright, 'The Ballast Trade: An Economic Driver in Seventeenth- and Eighteenth-Century Newcastle Upon Tyne', *Northern History*, 57:1 (101–19), 102–5, 108; Wright, thesis, 5–6, 24–6, 28–30, 33, 52, 55; William Gray, *Chorographia or a Survey of Newcastle* (Newcastle, 1649, 1660), ed. Andrew Reid (Newcastle, 1884), 84–6; Gardner, 111–17, 121–3, 126, 128, 131–2, 134–5, 147–8, 151, 154.
5. Tyne and Wear Archives (TWA) Acc. 1074/36, Vol. I., MD.NC/FN/1/1/17; Gardner, 168–9; Peter Rushton, 'Crazes and Quarrels: The Character of Witchcraft in the North East of England 1649–1680',

Bulletin of the Durham County Local History Society, 31 (1983), 7–9; Bulstrode Whitelocke, *Memorials of the English Affairs* (London, 1732), 424, 434; Ewen, *Demonianism*, 138.

6. Roger Howell, *Newcastle upon Tyne and the Puritan Revolution* (Oxford: Clarendon, 1967), 71, 173–5, 226, 229, 232; Robert Jenison, *Newcastle's Call to her Neighbour and Sister Towns and Cities* (London, 1636), A5v, 39, 68, 267, *The Cities' Safety* (London, 1630), 5, 103–29, *The Faithful Depository of Sound Doctrine and Ancient Truths* (London, 1649), 1–3, *The Return of the Sword* (London, 1648); Mary Moore, *Wonderful News from the North* (London, 1650), 15; Elmer, *Witchcraft*, 142–3; Rushton, 11, 18; Ewen, *Demonianism*, 317–19; Diane Purkiss, 'Invasions: Prophecy and Bewitchment in the Case of Margaret Muschamp', *Tulsa Studies in Women's Literature*, 17:2 (1998), 235–53; Madeleine Hope Dodds (ed.), *Extracts from the Newcastle upon Tyne Council Minute Book 1639–1656* (Newcastle: Northumberland Press, 1920), 37–8, 47–8, 56–7, 66–7, 72–3, 228; Joseph Foster (ed.), *Alumni Oxoniensis*, Vol. III (London, 1891), 382.
7. TWA MD.NC/FN/1/1/17, DX 657/1; Gardner, 168–9; Eleanor Loumsdale (also spelt Lomdell and Lambdell) later testified in support of Gardner's lawsuit against Newcastle, TWA MD.NC/D/4/5/22; Huntergroome is also spelt Huntergrome.
8. Richard L. Greaves, 'Paul Hobson', *ODNB* (2008), https://doi.org/10.1093/ref:odnb/37554; William Thomas Whitley, 'Colonel Paul Hobson', *Baptist Quarterly*, 9:5 (1939), 307–10; Elmer, 'East Anglia'; Paul Hobson, *Fallacy*, 3; Northumb A EP 86/1, EP 9/2; TWA Acc. 1074/36, Vol. I; Elmer, *Witchcraft*, 143.
9. Northumb A EP 86/1; TWA MD.NC/FN/1/1/17, QS/NC/1/1; Bowmer is sometimes spelt Bulmer or Boulmer in later sources, and there were families of these names, but Matthew appears as Bowmer in contemporary court records; Rushton, 8–9.
10. Bourne, 123; Gray, 63–68; 'Historic England Research Records: Bessie Surtees House', https://www.heritagegateway.org.uk/Gateway/Results_Single.aspx?uid=955102&resourceID=19191; TWA BC.NC/1/1 and 1/2, DX 217/1, DX 331/1, BC.RV/1/1.
11. Gardner, 168.
12. Gardner, 169; Howell, 248; Rushton, 9–10; Paul Hobson, *Practical Divinity* (London, 1646), 19–23, 57, and *A Garden Enclosed and Wisdom Justified* (London, 1647), 'To the Impartial Reader', *A Treatise Containing Three Things* (London, 1653), 103, 125–8.
13. Gardner, 169.
14. Jo Bath, *Dancing with the Devil and Other True Tales of Northern*

Witchcraft (Newcastle: Newcastle Libraries and Information Service and Tyne Bridge Publishing, 2002), 36–8, and 'The Treatment of Potential Witches in North-East England c.1649–1680' in John Newton and Jo Bath (eds), *Witchcraft and the Act of 1604* (Leiden and Boston: Brill, 2008), 136, 140; Greaves; Ewen, *Witch Hunting*, 62–3.

15. TWA QS/NC/1/1; Rushton, 9. As Howell shows, the puritanical Dawsons dominated Newcastle's council, with William's relatives Henry and George serving in key offices and as mayor in succeeding years, but witchfinding was happening simultaneously at Durham and Berwick (and possibly in Cumberland), so the Dawsons were not leading a unique hunt.
16. Northumb A EP 9/3, 2 and 1, EP 13/1. An Elizabeth Man was buried there in March 1653, and bell man Thomas Huntergroome in April 1650; Gardner, 170; see also Moore, 24–8: Jane Martin was accused of witchcraft along with her sister Margaret White and Dorothy Swinnow, both of Chatton, but although these other women were indicted in April 1650 at Alnwick, Northumberland, neither could be found to be arrested.
17. TWA QS.NC/1/1; an Isabel Brown (or perhaps two women of that name) appears four times as mother to 'bastard' children in All Saints parish with four different fathers: EP 9/3. Gardner reports an Elizabeth Brown being executed, which may be a mistake for Isabel, or another woman; Rushton, 10.
18. Wright, 105; Gray, 36, 61, 94; Bourne, 125; Gardner, 170; David Silk in The Newcastle Witches podcast, 9 February 2023; in October 1650, an Ann Bowmer requested twenty shillings from the council to apprentice herself in London – was she a relative of the recently executed Matthew? Her petition was granted: TWA MD.NC/FN/1/1/17.
19. TWA MD.NC/FN/1/1/17; Silk in The Newcastle Witches podcast, 9 February 2023; Northumb A EP 13/1, EP 9/1; as at Great Yarmouth, executed people were buried in Newcastle's parish graveyards – this went beyond 'witches', e.g., EP 73/2 St John's parish register (six men executed at the castle, 1606), EP 86/1 St Nicholas's register (an executed deserter and thief, 1649); Rushton, 9.
20. Gardner, 106–10, 117, 119, 120, 141, 159, 165, 170–71.
21. Gardner, 107, 117, 161, 170; *House of Commons Journal*, 7:2 (London, 1802), 2 July 1659, https://www.british-history.ac.uk/commons-jrnl/vol7/pp700-702#h3-s4; Gray, 76.
22. Paula Hughes, 'Witch-Hunting in Scotland 1649–1650' in Julian Goodare (ed.), *Scottish Witches and Witch-Hunters* (Basingstoke: Palgrave Macmillan, 2013), 85–102.

23. *Several Proceedings in Parliament*, 15 (4–11 January 1650), *Mercurius Politicus*, 126 (28 October–4 November 1652) and 127 (4–11 November 1652), Raymond (ed.), 154, 309–11; Brian Levack, 'The Decline and End of Scottish Witch Hunting' in Goodare (ed.), *Scottish Witch-Hunt*, 175; Gardner, 181–96, 216–26; TWA MD.NC/D/4/5/1-33.

12. Afterlives

1. Nicola Sturgeon, 'International Women's Day 22: First Minister's Statement' (8 March 2022), https://www.gov.scot/publications/international-womens-day-2022-first-ministers-statement-8-march-2022/; Natalie Don-Innes, 'Proposed Witchcraft Convictions (Pardons) (Scotland) Bill' (22 June 2022), https://www.parliament.scot/bills-and-laws/proposals-for-bills/proposed-the-witchcraft-convictions-pardons-scotland-bill.
2. 'Tragic Priest to be Commemorated', *East Anglian Daily Times* (26 May 2004). Lowes's exact age is not known, but Hutchinson and others described him as appearing to be around eighty.
3. Shelley Ings' work can be seen here: @shelleyings, Instagram; John Worland (@JohnWorland, fadetoblacktv.co.uk, YouTube) and others designed the information board; https://essexwitchmuseum.co.uk/; John Worland and Kerry King (dir.), *Witchfinder*, Headgate Theatre/Fade to Black Television, 2007; https://www.history.co.uk/shows/witches-of-essex.
4. Quilting: https://www.runesnroses.com/news/2021/9/28/witchery-tricks-the-murder-of-elizabeth-bradwell-great-yarmouth-1645; https://www.instagram.com/wearewitchquilt/; East Anglian Museum, https://www.museumofwitchcraft.co.uk/mission-and-vision; Cohere Arts, https://coherearts.org/home/witchfinder/; Julian Makey, 'Museum Recreates a Time When Huntingdon Experienced Witch Trials' (2021), https://www.huntspost.co.uk/news/22955860.museum-recreates-time-huntingdon-experienced-witch-trials/; Cromwell Museum, 'Past Events: The Trial of the Huntingdonshire Witches', https://www.cromwellmuseum.org/events/the-trial-of-the-huntingdonshire-witches; Bodmin Jail, https://www.bodminjail.org/bodmin-jail-its-inmates/bodmin-jail-blog/the-case-of-anne-jeffries-where-law-folklore-meet/; Keith Wallis, The Piskie Trap podcast (29 November 2024), https://shows.acast.com/the-piskie-trap/episodes/ann-jefferies-the-fairies.
5. Emily Reader, 'Newcastle Witch Trials: A Little Known History and One of the Largest Mass Hangings in Nation's Past', with

David Silk, Katie Liddane and Ruth Connelly, ITV News, Tyne Tees, 22 August 2024; Katie Liddane, 'Bewitching the North East: The History and Heritage of Witch Persecution in Newcastle and Northumberland 1642–1675' (thesis, Northumbria University, 2023); The Newcastle Witches podcast with Caitlin Bramwell and Maria Caruana Galizia (2022–23), https://candleandbell.com/newcastle-witches-podcast; 'Newcastle Witch Trials with Dr Katie Liddane' with Sarah Jack, Josh Hutchinson and Katie Liddane, The Thing About Witch Hunts podcast (2024), https://witchhuntshow.com/2024/03/12/newcastle-witch-trials-with-dr-katie-liddane/; see also brief earlier accounts: Claire Nally, 'The Last Witch Hunter' (2015), https://northumbria.ac.uk/about-us/news-events/news/2015/11/comment-the-last-witch-hunter-why-modern-visions-of-witches-dont-conjure-up-reality/, and Douglas Smith, 'The Anatomy of a Witch Hunt', *North Magazine*, 33 (1974), TWA L/PA 207.

6. Hopkins, 3, 10; ERO D/DRc B10, D/P 343/1/1; Gaule, A3–A4; Stearne, 60–61.
7. By the Canadian scholar Frances Timbers and the genealogist and Essex/Suffolk historian Helen Barrell; Stearne, A2v, 53.
8. Stearne, A2–A3, 11, 58; NA SP 24/10; Gaskill, 275–6, 332; Elmer, 'East Anglia'; SA B105/2/3, 2/4, FL 600/4/1; Ewen, *Demonianism*, 261.
9. John and John Bernard Burke, *A Genealogical and Heraldic History of the Extinct and Dormant Baronetcies of England* (London, 1838), 229; NA C 3/468/93, 468/139, C 5/149/31, C 6/46/20, C 7/68/49, 88/115, 110/7, 464/52, 87/96, 49/47, 424/11, C 8/139/7, 139/19, 139/114, 139/153, 197/75, 330/8, 325/109, 93/6, 122/19, 426/56, C 10/185/15, 57/294, 126/234, 180/122, 157/36, TS 21/940, SA 1754/3/13; Helen Barrell, 'The Travails of Matchmaking: William Cardinall and Sir Thomas Bowes', https://essexandsuffolksurnames.co.uk/history/the-cardinall-family/charles-cardinall-of-great-bromley/the-travails-of-matchmaking-william-cardinall-and-sir-thomas-bowes/; Gaskill, 274; Larkin T. Tufts and Edward C. Booth, 'Tufts Genealogy – Earlier Generations', *New England Historical and Genealogical Register*, 51 (1897), 1; William Richard Cutter, *New England Families* (New York: Lewis, 1913), 400; NA PROB 11/280/6; Chris Kyle, 'Corbet, Miles', *The History of Parliament*, ed. Andrew Thrush and John P. Ferris (Cambridge: Cambridge University Press, 2010); https://historyofparliamentonline.org/volume/1604-1629/member/corbet-miles-1595-1662; Sarah Barber, 'Corbet, Miles', and Howard Nenner, 'Regicides', *ODNB* (Oxford: Oxford University Press, 2004), https://www.oxforddnb.

com/display/10.1093/ref:odnb/9780198614128.001.0001/odnb-9780198614128-e-6290 and https://www.oxforddnb.com/display/10.1093/ref:odnb/9780198614128.001.0001/odnb-9780198614128-e-70599#odnb-9780198614128-e-70599; 'The Story of Malahide Castle's Irish Ghosts', *Authentic Vacations* (n.d.), https://www.authenticvacations.com/the-five-ghosts-of-malahide-castle/.

10. NA C22/771/44 and 45; Robert Hunt, *Popular Romances of the West of England* (London, 1865), 133–51; William Bottrell, *Traditions and Hearthside Stories of West Cornwall*, Series 2, Vol. II (Penzance, 1873), 224–6; Odd Planet Studios, *The Legend of Jan Tregeagle* (in production), https://oddplanetstudios.co.uk/the-legend-of-jan-tregeagle/; Colin Wilson and Phil Beer, *Jan Tregeagle*, performed by Oddfolk, vinyl, 1974; 'Legend of Jan Tregeagle' (n.d.), https://www.cornwalls.co.uk/myths-legends/jan-tregeagle.htm.
11. Bourne, 11; John Brand, *The History and Antiquities of the Town and County of Newcastle upon Tyne* (London, 1789), 4.
12. Howell (ed.), 17–18, 83, 110, 118–22; Luan Hanratty, 'The Ralph Gardner Memorial on Chirton Green in North Shields is to be Restored!' (April 2025), https://www.penbal.uk/2025/05/02/ralph-gardner-obelisk-to-be-restored/; Yorkshire Film Archive/North East Film Archive, 'Opening of Ralph Gardner High School', https://www.yfanefa.com/record/22677. Ralph and Catherine's children included John (born 1650), George (born 1651), Ralph (born 1652) and Ann (born 1655): https://www.familysearch.org/en/search/record/results?count=20&q.batchNumber=P000191&q.surname=Gardiner&f.collectionId=5.
13. Greaves; Stephen Kent, 'Paul Hobson: "The Odour of Unsanctity?"', *Baptist Quarterly*, 53 (2022), 128–39; Paul Hobson, *Innocency, Though Under a Cloud* (London, 1664), 137; 'To Althea, From Prison' by Richard Lovelace (1642) is a model for this verse.
14. The Newcastle Witches podcast, 30 June 2022.
15. Henry Goodcole, *The Wonderful Discovery of Elizabeth Sawyer, a Witch* (London, 1621), B2v.
16. SA FC101/E2/26; John Joseph May, *Danforth Genealogy* (Boston: Pope, 1902), 1, 3–4; Allen (ed.), *Wills . . . 1620–1624*, 131–2; for example, 'Migrant Groups Decry "Witch Hunt" As Greece Tightens Grip', France 24 (21 November 2022), https://www.bbc.co.uk/news/live/c7842lojnvet or 'Trump Calls Epstein Controversy a "Witch Hunt"', BBC (22 July 2025), https://www.bbc.co.uk/news/live/c7842lojnvet.

Index